Centralized Processing
for Academic Libraries

The Final Report (Phase III, Jan. 1 – June 30, 1969)
of the Colorado Academic Libraries Book Processing Center:
The First Six Months of Operation

by
Richard M. Dougherty
and
Joan M. Maier

The Scarecrow Press, Inc.
Metuchen, N.J.   1971

Table of Contents

List of Figures within the Text

vii

In October, 1966 the National Science Foundation awarded the Colorado Council of Librarians a two-part grant to investigate the feasibility of cooperative centralized processing to serve Colorado academic institutions. The first studies were primarily feasibility and design efforts. In August, 1968 N.S.F. awarded a grant to fund partially an experiment to test the findings of the Phase I-II report. That experiment is the subject of this report.

Although this report deals primarily with cooperative acquisitions and processing, we believe it also contributes to a better understanding of cooperative programs. The experiment was designed to monitor operations throughout the acquisition/cataloging cycle. Performance and cost measurements were made on most internal and external aspects of the system. Monitoring also extended into the participating libraries where a product acceptance study was conducted.[1] A secondary objective of the project was to observe the relationships which formed between the participants and the central agency, such as the interface of systems and the human interaction of participants and the Center. All unpublished documents generated during the project are cited by document number (1), and are listed at the end of the report. The documents themselves are available at the Center.

Although we could have larded the presentation with the usual bromides about cooperation, we have tried to document the experiences as they occurred, the good with the bad. Many of our difficulties can be traced to the fact that CALBPC

and the participants have been under a microscope for over four years.

The authors, however, believe that the experience has been well worth the effort because this cooperative project has succeeded. In the spring of 1970 the Legislature of Colorado, at the request of the Colorado Council of Librarians, strongly supported by the Colorado Commission on Higher Education, appropriated $100,000 to the Center. Fifty thousand dollars are to be used to encourage expanded participation in the Center by providing subsidies for a one-year period. The remaining portion will be spent in support of development activities. The appropriation by the Legislature, in our view, is recognition of the progress that the Council of Librarians has achieved.

ACKNOWLEDGEMENTS

Many people have given of their time, effort, and ideas to the CALBPC project over the past four years. If we have forgotten to acknowledge any of those who have contributed, we hope they will forgive us.

First, we are appreciative of the support and cooperation of the directors and staffs of the participating libraries. The directors are: Le Moyne W. Anderson (Colorado State University), Daniel A. Seager (Colorado State College), William Weigand (Adams State College), Virginia L. Wilcox (Colorado School of Mines), Charlene Alexis (Metropolitan State College), and Ralph E. Ellsworth (University of Colorado).

We also valued the suggestions of Vivian Brockman (Community College of Denver), Arleen Ahern (Temple Buell College), Leo York (Western State College), Richard Gobble (Fort Lewis College), Joseph Sprug (Loretto Heights College), Agnes Meyers (Loretto Heights College), Delaine

---

1. In some cases, such as the product acceptance study, the names of the schools have been coded to avoid unwarranted comparisons. The coding system was altered several times, i.e. school number one in one figure might be school number six in the next figure.

Barnes (Colorado Alpine College), and Ellen Heacock (Colorado Mountain College). These libraries joined the Center on July 1, 1969 as full participating members.

Individuals who bore the major brunt throughout the experiment were the CALBPC supervisors who, with characteristic resourcefulness, make the Center work. These include: Eugene Petriwsky, Assistant Director for Technical Services; Abigail Dahl-Hansen, Order Librarian; Harriet Rebuldela, Bibliographic Searching; Paul Sheldon, Catalog Maintenance and Preservation; and Violet Wagener and Joe Hewitt, who have served as coordinators following the experiment.

The authors and the Council of Librarians are indebted to Dr. Frank B. Abbott, Executive Director of the Colorado Commission on Higher Education. Dr. Abbott has been sympathetic with the aims of the Processing Center and has often provided sage advice on how the Center could strengthen its viability as a state agency.

The authors would also like to thank those individuals who served in various capacities with the actual project. These include Beth Scott, Bruce Hensley, Charlotta Hensley, Karla Jones, Carolyn Phillips, Carlos Maestas, Shirley Talcott, Shirley Fullen, Barbara Franz, Mohamad Saka, Judith McIntosh, and Laura Vansen as data collectors; Elaine Fowler, Esther Sparn, Glenda De Santis, Carole Dougherty, and Vi Nielsen as typists and revisors.

The principal investigators and the Colorado Council of Librarians wish to thank the National Science Foundation for their support of the experimental project under Grant GN-779, Renewal of GN-588. Without the Foundation's support, this study could not have been conducted.

Richard M. Dougherty, Principal Investigator
Joan M. Maier, Project Director and Coordinator
of the Center, Phase III.

Chapter I

INTRODUCTION

This is the final report of the Colorado Academic Libraries Book Processing Center (CALBPC) project. The CALBPC project was begun in 1965 by nine academic libraries in Colorado in an effort to establish a centralized acquisition and processing center.[1] The report of Phase I-II, completed in June 1968, dealt primarily with a general feasibility study, the design of the central system, costs of acquiring and processing in nine libraries and a number of related concerns such as accounting, the congruence of approval plans and user attitudes toward library services. On February 1, 1969, six of the original nine libraries began an experiment to test the validity of the Phase I-II findings.[2] This report focuses on the experimental operations which were concluded officially on September 30, 1969. Whereas the Phase I-II study dealt with the theory and principles upon which a system might be based, we are presently concerned with the pragmatics of book processing, the obstacles encountered, and the solutions achieved.

For those of us who participated in the experiment, the experience was an exciting one. Emotions often ran the gamut from elation to trauma. The crucial aspect of cooperative programs, one of which is centralized processing, hinges more on the dedication, competencies and willingness of individuals than on the technical aspects of systems or computer hardware. The authors hope our recounting will transmit some of the drama as well as the quantitative data on cost and performance.

The reader must keep in mind that the CALBPC project investigated one approach to centralized acquisition and book processing. It was not our intention to identify the best approach, only to explore the advantages and disadvantages of one approach. As a matter of fact, the findings of this project suggest that a variety of services is necessary if a centralized operation is to operate at optimum effectiveness.

Preliminary Activities

Following completion of the Phase I-II study, attention turned first to the practical problem of obtaining permission for the user librarians to deposit money with the Center. This was necessary if the user libraries were to submit orders directly to the Center, thus avoiding the cumbersome procedure of working through local business offices. A proposal which explained the need for a centralized accounting system was submitted to the Colorado Commission on Higher Education and the Comptroller General of the State in the fall of 1968. (5, 103) In December, 1968, permission was received from the Comptroller General to use the deposit system. This cleared the way for operations to begin.

It was also recognized early that additional financial support would be necessary in order to effect an orderly transition from localized to centralized processing. The Phase I-II study had projected a savings of $159,000 at a total volume level of 160,000 volumes.[3] But these projected savings were expressed in the form of unit cost savings. The budgets of the participating libraries would not immediately be affected unless resources could be reallocated from the local libraries to the central operation. In order to achieve a reallocation of resources, the user libraries would have to transfer staff members from technical services to public services, refrain from filling vacancies as they occurred on their staff and transfer such funds to the central agency, or actually transfer staff members to work at the central agency. It did not seem realistic to expect any of these alternatives to occur immediately; consequently, the savings accrued to the State of Colorado would be in the form of cost avoidance savings accumulated over an appreciable period of time. In the meantime, some mechanism had to be found to promote a gradual reallocation of resources.

At the same time, the full potential for centralized processing had to be sold to State authorities. In an effort to accomplish this goal, a document was prepared for the Colorado Commission on Higher Education outlining the savings that could accrue to eight libraries over a ten-year period if seventy-five percent of their books were processed by CALBPC. (9) If fully utilized, the Center could save the State 4.4 million dollars; but the report cautioned that at present none of the libraries had been allocated funds for book processing and that time would be required to achieve a resource allocation.

Also, during the fall of 1969 the Governor of Colorado appointed a Citizen's Committee, composed of leading industrialist and professional people, to explore ways in which state government could streamline its operations. The Committee interviewed officials of CALBPC and reviewed the findings of the Phase I-II study. Subsequently they recommended that CALBPC be continued and that special funds be appropriated to support a continuing developmental activity. By developmental activity, the Committee was referring to an expanded use of computer technology. [4]

The processing specifications received close attention prior to the experiment's beginning. The Council of Academic Librarians agreed to cataloging, classification, and processing specifications in November, 1967. [5] But as the time for actual operations grew near, it became apparent that there were omissions and some ambiguities in the previously agreed upon specifications; consequently, meetings were held through the fall of 1968. [6] At the first meeting, the specifications were expanded to include procedures for reporting titles processed to the National Union Catalog and to the Rocky Mountain Bibliographical Center. It was also decided that monographic series classed together by

the Library of Congress would not be accepted by the Center. It was also agreed that volume designations such as a volume or number in foreign languages would be printed on spine labels in the vernacular. (26)

The Council convened a month later to consider the question of the format of call numbers; that is, whether double Cutters would be included on the same line, and whether or not the Center would add location symbols at the time of processing or leave this task to local libraries. The classification of fiction also came under review. It was easy for the group to agree on the principle that there should be strict adherence to Library of Congress practice for fiction; but experience showed that this simple principle is not one that the librarians are willing to follow. (27) Each library is committed to its own practice and no two libraries are alike; that is, some use abbreviated systems, others employ PZ3, while a few classify according to the LC suggested literature number, i.e. PR, PS, and PZ. (27) The evolution and refinement of the processing specifications continued throughout and beyond the experimental period.

The Technical Services Division of the University of Colorado had already gained experience in handling processing of external libraries. For several months, CU had been responsible for ordering, cataloging, and processing materials for its two off-campus centers. Consequently, the library was reasonably well prepared to take on the processing of additional libraries; or at least as well prepared as might have been expected. Only two major operational changes were implemented prior to the experiment. The first was the rearrangement of its order/in-process file and LC depository card file from arrangement by main entry to a title arrangement. All concerned were convinced that the Center could better utilize nonprofessional personnel and student assistants if the files were arranged by title. These convictions were based on the experience of staff members who had worked with bibliographical data since the implementation of the Anglo-American code. The second change was to add the capability for matching catalog card sets and books prior to distribution to participants. (84) (The card/book matching routine proved to be a serious operational stumbling block.)

Objectives of the Experiment and Post-Experiment Activities

The remaining portions of this report document the six-month experiment and the first few months of normal operations. The overall objective of the Phase III experiment was to test the validity of the Phase I-II study findings. The specific objectives of the experiment were: 1) to calculate processing costs; 2) to measure lag-times from the time an order left a participating library until the book was delivered; (3) to investigate consumer acceptance of products provided in relation to pre-agreed upon processing specifications; 4) to observe the problems of interface between the Center and its users (from the point of view of administration, public relations, and operating procedures); and 5) to determine the congruence of approval plans presently used at two institutions.

The experiment was scheduled for completion on July 1, 1969; but due to a variety of circumstances, the processing on the last Phase III books was not completed until December and data tabulation not completed until March 1970. The reasons for the delays will be brought out in the ensuing discussions, but the reader should keep in mind that actual operations commenced on a small scale before the experimental operations had been concluded. Thirteen libraries had joined the Center by October 1, 1969, at which time they began officially sending orders. The libraries included eight state-supported schools, four private institutions, and one junior college. Although none of the Phase III libraries used the Center to a great extent during 1969, the experience gave them an opportunity to see at first hand what they could expect from centralized processing. As we cautioned earlier, 1969 was to be a year of ups and downs, successes and failures.

Notes

1. Lawrence E. Leonard, Joan M. Maier, and Richard M. Dougherty, Centralized Book Processing (Metuchen, New Jersey: Scarecrow Press, 1969) p. 401.

2. The participating institutions were: Adams State College, Colorado School of Mines, University of Northern Colorado (formerly Colorado State College), Colorado State University, Metropolitan State College, and the University of Colorado.

3. Leonard, ibid., p. 142.

4. Colorado Committee on Government and Economy, Department of Higher Education, 1969, p. 39.

5. Leonard, ibid., p. 145-7.

6. A Technical Advisory Board composed of one technical services supervisor from each member library also met during the period from October 1968 to September 1969 to review details on the specifications so that the Council would have sufficient information to vote on changes.

Chapter II

PERFORMANCE DURING THE EXPERIMENT

Overview of Production

With the funds available, CALBPC proposed to process 24,000 volumes for the participating libraries. The average cost per volume was estimated to be $2.50 or $60,000 for the projected workload. Thirty-six thousand dollars from the National Science Foundation and $24,000 from local contributions were budgeted to support processing activities. (115, 116) Since funds were limited, a quota was assigned to each participant. The quotas were based on the size of the 1967/68 book budgets. The volume allotments were as follows: Colorado State University, 10,000; Colorado State College, 8,000; Metropolitan State College, 3,000; Adams State College, 2,000; and Colorado School of Mines, 1,000. (117)

By the time the experiment actually got under way, most participants found they could not take full advantage of their quotas because most of their book budgets had already been committed. Consequently, it was decided that each library could supplement its quota by sending to the Center books from its uncataloged arrearage. The Center agreed to accept forty-eight hundred items from arrearages in lieu of purchase requests. (117) In fact, the libraries shipped only 2,651 titles from arrearages to the Center. (See Figure A2.1)

Overall CALBPC processed 88,973 volumes during 1969. (See Figures A2.2 and A2.3) Of this total 12,600 volumes were shipped to the participating libraries. (117) The remaining 76,373 were added to the collection of the University of Colorado. Eleven thousand three hundred forty-eight volumes had been both ordered and cataloged by CALBPC; 1,212 volumes were titles from cataloging arrearages. (119) At the close of the experiment, approximately 1,400 volumes had not yet been shipped. (118)

Although we are getting ahead of ourselves, the prospects for 1969-70 were encouraging. Twelve libraries, in addition to the University of Colorado, agreed to sample the services of the Center. Although the projected workload of 20,481 volumes was not numerically impressive, it was a beginning. (84) The project team was indeed gratified that twelve libraries were willint to participate amidst a period of rapid, sometimes hectic change. To be frank, there were still many knotty problems yet to be resolved.

We were somewhat disappointed that most of the libraries could not divert a larger percentage of their book budget to centralized processing. But since the State does not allocate funds specifically to support book processing, the levels of commitment were actually reasonable. Another influencing factor was some librarians were and still are somewhat skeptical of centralized processing. They are reluctant to do business with a centralized operation. We believe that time and performance will overcome this skepticism and reluctance.

The Phase I-II study data showed that about half of the titles ordered by the Libraries were domestic current imprints. Ninety-three percent of the titles ordered during 1966-67 were English language imprints, the remaining seven percent foreign language materials.[1] In the Phase I-II study, a current imprint was defined as any title published in 1965 or later. Earlier titles were classified as retrospective. In this study, a current imprint is defined as a title published in 1966 or later.

The participants, however, did not conform to the predicted ordering patterns. Instead they used the Center to obtain the more difficult materials including foreign language materials. Only 16.8 percent of the orders received from CSU were

14

for current imprints. Whereas, based on the data collected in the Phase I-II study, 30 percent of the orders from CSU should have been for current imprints. Furthermore, in the first study, foreign language materials comprised only 12 percent of CSU's orders; but almost 49 percent of the orders submitted to the Center by CSU were for foreign language materials. (See Figures A2.4-A2.6)

In contrast, almost 65 percent of the orders received from Metropolitan State College were for current imprints; whereas this category comprised only 40 percent of MSC's orders in the Phase I-II study. (See Figures A2.4-A2.6)

Overall, 21 percent of the titles ordered were foreign language materials. An analysis of orders placed between January and June, 1969 revealed that less than 10 percent of the orders were for 1969 imprints, and 57 percent were for titles published between 1965 and 1968. The remaining 34 percent were materials published prior to 1965.[2] (73)

At the conclusion of the experiment, the 2,659 orders still outstanding were analyzed. The study showed that over 90 percent of the domestic titles ordered had been placed with jobbers; only five percent were ordered direct from publishers. (See Figure A2.7) Ten percent of the outstanding orders had been placed by the University of Colorado for items to be advertised in the out-of-print market.

Claims were sent for less than 10 percent of the orders. Most claims were issued in response to a specific request for a badly needed item. Finally, on the basis of publishers' reports, items were occasionally assigned to new vendors. The complete analysis of items not received is shown in Figure A2.7.

Participants were directed to order imprint titles only. The analysis shown in Figure A2.7 indicates that the participants successfully ferreted out o.p. titles. Most of the o.p. materials ordered were placed by the University of Colorado, and these were known to be o.p. at the time the order was placed.

In summary, the analysis of titles not received suggests that claiming was not so effective as had been hoped. Even books published recently may not be supplied by vendors; therefore, careful consideration must be given in choosing sources of supply if one is to achieve optimum performance. Obviously, the Center should have placed more orders with publishers rather than relying so heavily on jobbers.

Evaluation of Sources of Supply

Two advantages of centralized processing hypothesized in the conclusions of the Phase I-II study were increased discounts and better jobber performance.[3] These advantages, it was assumed, could be realized from the consolidation of orders. Prior to the experiment, CALBPC entered into negotiations with two local book jobbers in an effort to forge closer relations. In short, we tried to convince them to increase their inventories of new titles. With expanded inventories, we reasoned that the time-lag from the submission of an order to its receipt at the Center could be reduced from the fifty-eight days observed in the Phase I-II study.[4] We also contacted three jobbers about their interest in increasing discount rates if CALBPC would agree to concentrate its orders with them. Two vendors did not respond. The third expressed keen interest in further discussions. Eventually two different discount schedules were evolved. Discount schedule one applied to materials ordered by the University of Colorado for multiple copies of titles destined for its college library and its two off-campus center libraries. The discount schedule one rates were: trade books, 37 percent; science and technology, 12 percent (when the discount received by the jobber from the publisher was 16 percent or better), other titles were priced net. Discount schedule one was to apply also to new titles ordered by the participating libraries. The alternate discount schedule was to apply to materials published prior to 1969. This discount schedule allowed: 33 percent for trade books, 12 percent for science and technology (when the discount received from the publisher was 15 percent or greater), other items were priced net (13, 17, 19).

Based on the above agreements, we believed there was just cause for optimism. It appeared reasonable to anticipate vendor performance would not only be improved, but that the participants by using CALBPC would increase the purchasing power of their book budgets. Considering the following analysis, the reader will learn that we were premature in our judgment and somewhat naive.

Discounts -- The agreement on discounts proved to be a complete flop. After three months, the CALBPC staff reported that the 37 percent discount had not been received for any title, and the 33 percent discount had been granted to very few titles. (16) Complaints were lodged with a representative of the vendor. At the ensuing discussions, the company representative confessed that it was not economically feasible for his firm to continue discount schedule one. He cited as justification the fact that the Center was not ordering the proper mix of titles; that is, most orders were for science and technology titles rather than for trade books which carried higher discount rates. The representative proposed a substitute discount schedule of 34 percent for trade books and a sliding scale of from zero to 25 percent for science and technology and short discount titles. (60) But by this time, the Center was so disenchanted with this particular vendor that his offer was purely academic since the Center had already begun to direct its business to other vendors. It is not our intention to castigate one jobber. In his defense, we should point out that CALBPC did not order either as many different titles or as many multiple copies as had been anticipated, so that the incentives for granting special discount concessions were diminished.

Two studies of discount rates received from five jobbers were also conducted. The first study covered the period immediately prior to the beginning of the experiment; the second study reflects discounts received during the first half of fiscal

1969/70. The results are shown in Figures A2.8-A2.9. A comparison between the two periods is shown in Figure A2.10. It is undeniably obvious that CALBPC had no impact on discounts. The discounts of some jobbers increased slightly, while others decreased. It was interesting to learn that while the five jobbers employed distinctly different discount schedules, the weighted averages were very similar, with the exception of Engineering Book Service which offers a more favorable discount schedule.

The above results should be interpreted with some caution. It is indeed possible that the books ordered from Engineering Book Service might have included a disproportionate share of long discounted titles, although it was the Center's intention to provide each jobber with a comparable mix.

Vendor Delivery Performance Analysis -- An analysis of delivery time-lags was performed for all vendors from which fifty or more items were ordered. The institution/fund/transaction number (IFT) stamped on each purchase request form (PR) was used to indicate the date of order. (See Figure A3.1). The date on which an invoice was cleared for payment by the Center was used to show receipt. The data were based on the records accumulated as by-products of the computer-based accounting system.

This methodology was not error-free. First, an order sometimes was not mailed until a day or two after the IFT was assigned. So too, as much as two weeks occasionally elapsed between receipt of a book and clearance of the invoice for payment. In other words, the lag-time could be overstated by as much as two to three weeks. Moreover, a peak work load which occurred during May, June and July caused some book to remain unpacked for up to one month. (See Figure 5.2) During each period, several thousand books arrived at the Center almost at once. The quantities represented much more than the system could absorb in so short a period. In order to insure that this system perturbation had not seriously skewed the data, a follow-up lag-time study covering an extended time period was conducted.

Another source of error was the method of recording monographic series received on standing order. Since the IFT number is assigned after a title is received, the time interval from order to receipt appears to be very short. The numbers circled in Figures A2.11 and A2.12 represent items probably received on standing order. The over-all effect of this error is to understate the actual time lags. We must also point out that the University of Colorado receives books on approval from dealers 3, 6, and 12, and these titles were included in the study; therefore, the performance for CU is considerably better than for the other libraries for which all titles were ordered on a title-by-title basis. Note the contrast in performance of dealer 6 for CSU and for Adams State College.

The over-all performance of vendors was disappointing--a classic example of understatement. (See Figures A2.11-A2.12) For the University of Colorado, the weighted average for all vendors studied was forty-five days; but this included 15,000 items received from dealer 6, the bulk of which were received on approval. Excluding this dealer, the CU average jumps to seventy-seven days, which falls into the range of the other participating libraries.

The results of the follow-up study were similar to those of the initial study.[5] The performance of some vendors improved while others declined. The over-all performance was about the same except for Metropolitan State College where a noticeable decline was discovered from 92 days to 129 days. The performance of some jobbers appears to have deteriorated during the latter months of the year. In such cases, the titles received represent the dregs of titles ordered during the earlier stages of the experiment. For one reason or another, the Center discontinued ordering from these firms before the end of the experiment. However, these time lags do provide a realistic picture of how long it can take to acquire an item thought to be in print at the time of order.

Interpretation of Results -- What conclusions can we draw from our experiences? Overall, we were far from satisfied. However, much of the blame can be laid at our own door. When our vendors promised too much, we were too eager to hear, too gullible. We should have known better for several reasons. Why did we assume a jobber could absorb a peak load of activity any more easily than could CALBPC; yet we flooded some jobbers with a large volume of orders within a short time span? If we knew that publishers took forty to seventy days to fill orders, what reason was there to suppose that a jobber ordering the same title from the same publisher would receive appreciably better service? Several jobbers, in fact, have reported a gradual deterioration in the service they receive from publishers. Unless one jobber can demonstrate an ability to handle a specified volume of orders, a library or a CALBPC may anticipate better over-all performance by distributing its work among several qualified jobbers. Although all jobbers will experience peak load activities, spreading among several jobbers lessens the impact when the performance of one jobber suddenly declines.

CALBPC must pay closer attention to the publication date of titles to be ordered. Some jobbers may have decreased the size of their inventories because of the high cost of borrowing money. This may not be true in all cases, but a library will likely receive better service by ordering older materials direct from publishers.

The failure of CALBPC to negotiate more favorable discount rates, plus the similarity in the over-all discount rates received from vendors, suggests the need for a thorough review of purchasing policies. The discounts received from three selected publishers shown in Figure A2.13 are, on the average, higher than those received from the five jobbers. (Of course, these data are not truly comparable since we do not know what discounts the jobbers would have offered for the same titles.) There can be little doubt that ordering direct from some publishers is an attractive alternative. A continued inability of CALBPC to achieve more favorable discounts could prompt state purchasing officials to revive the ugly specter of bidding. In such a case, jobbers, publishers, librarians, and users would all lose. It is entirely possible that larger volume levels will effect a more favorable discount schedule.

Finally, we believe the long delays experienced in acquiring materials from jobbers affects the type of automated system that the Center might wish to develop. Much has been said about the value of interactive on-line systems; but if one must wait three months before a title enters the system, the value of on-line query, in our view, is greatly diminished. From a user's point of view, to be told in a few seconds that a book he ordered three months ago has not yet arrived will not satisfy his need for the book. In short, we believe vendor performance will bear on the selection of a system configuration to support book acquisition and processing.

Vendor/CALBPC Programs and Relations

We have already painted a pretty bleak picture; but in the long run we are convinced that far-sighted jobbers and centers such as CALBPC can reap a rich harvest of benefits through mutual cooperation. Many jobbers are already providing libraries with preprinted order cards. These cards (or multiforms) are included with materials received on approval plans, or they are distributed in lieu of books for titles that fall outside a library's approval plan profile. Throughout the experiment, the Center encountered considerable difficulties in using dealer-prepared multiforms. Often a user library had to discard the dealer's form and prepare a second form which was compatible with the CALBPC system. There is no reason why this is necessary since the data printed on all forms are essentially identical. If jobbers could agree on a standard form, a great deal of typing and inspection time would be eliminated. Jobbers themselves would be well served if all firms supplying forms were to standardize the location of data elements on their forms.

The concept of coordinated ordering is anathema to many academic librarians. The experience gained during this project suggests that some forms of coordinated ordering would prove highly

beneficial. First, there is the matter of delivery times. Reexamine the performance of dealer 6 in Figure A2.13 against the performance of other jobbers. A large percentage of the books received at the University of Colorado were shipped on approval. Assuming new books are shipped to customers shortly after publication, a processing center could reasonably expect to receive new books faster.

However, an approval plan does not guarantee that books received on approval will be the ones participants are interested in purchasing. On this point, the Colorado project produced sufficient data to formulate several tentative observations. First, the data collected in the Phase I-II study showed a probability of from .70 to .81 that a book purchased by any one of the participating libraries would also be acquired by the University of Colorado.[6] Second, 12 percent of the 1966 English language imprints had been acquired by more than four libraries at the time the Phase I-II data were tabulated. But the duplication is understated since, even three years later, seven percent of the items ordered were for 1966 imprints. These statistics suggest a commonalty or a common collection core among the libraries. (73) Although there might be exceptions to this generalization, library service would have been improved if 1966 imprints acquired in 1969 had been in the library shortly after their date of publication.

Vendors and librarians must work to develop the mechanisms for small scale approval plans which focus on the core of common titles. If vendors could identify titles basic to all liberal arts schools, then inventories could be organized to anticipate accurately titles likely to be selected centrally, or the vendor himself might automatically supply all basic titles. Obviously, close coordination and a great deal of confidence among participants and vendors would be a prerequisite. As an alternative to vendor selection, the participants could appoint a specialist or a group of specialists to designate the core selections. In either case, the participants would benefit from faster delivery; and it does not seem unreasonable to expect dealer concessions on discounts.

In the Colorado experiment, coordinated ordering has been broached from time to time. The concept, however, has been neither pushed nor accepted. It is hoped that coordinated ordering will be reconsidered within the foreseeable future. The project team believes that a study should be conducted among the participants to determine exactly what title overlap now exists for titles purchased in 1966. Such a study will identify the characteristics and scope of the core collection.

Processing Lag-Time Study

The objectives of the processing lag-time study were to calculate the effectiveness of each CALBPC system component in order to detect system shortcomings and blockages, and to calculate the turn-around time each member library received during the experimental period.

Processing slips for all monographic materials conforming to specifications which passed through the Center between January and December, 1969 were collected. These slips were purged from the on-order file after books had been shipped to member libraries. The data sheets (see Figure A2.14) were constructed so that one systematic sample could be used as the basis for not only the lag-time study but also the investigation of ordering patterns (see Figures A2.4-A2.6) and the product acceptance study. Sample I was drawn in August so that the product acceptance study could be conducted in September. The second sample was drawn after the end of the experiment.

Originally we planned to record lag-time data for eighteen different control points. (See Figure A2.15 for a summary of all eighteen checkpoints.) Consequently, the size of the original sample reflected this intention. But as the study progressed, it became evident that only eight dates had been consistently recorded. (See Figure A2.16) These were:

1. Date Purchase Request (PR received and date IFT number assigned.
2. Date IFT number assigned and date book received from vendor.

3. Date book received and date cataloging completed.
4. Date book received and date shelf list filed.
5. Date received and date book SILO'd (book card/pocket/label set).
6. Date book received from vendor and date book received at local library.
7. LC copy availability at the time PR received.
8. LC copy availability at the time book received from vendor.

The initial sample size drawn for Sample I was 1,999 and for Sample II was 1,812. This sample was sufficiently large to study 31 characteristics of the data. But since only eight dates had been recorded, the usable sample size was reduced to 1,153 slips for Sample I and 1,038 slips for Sample II; consequently, the sample size requirement was recalculated. Fortunately, the samples already drawn were large enough to insure 95 percent confidence interval in a study of eight characteristics. The sample size calculation is shown below.

Sample I

Calculation of Sample Size

$$N = 11000 \quad N_p = \frac{11000}{13} = 846 \quad 0 = .50 \text{ (worst possible case)}$$

$$.05 = \frac{0\,(1-0)}{N} \times \frac{N_p - N}{N_p - 1} \qquad .05 = 95\% \text{ confidence level}$$

$$.05 = \frac{(.50)(.50)}{N} \times \frac{846 - N}{845} \qquad 11 = \text{maximum number of categories of data collected in any given table}$$

$$.0025 = \frac{.25}{N} \times \frac{846 = N}{845}$$

$$.0025 = \frac{211.5 - .25N}{845\,N}$$

$$2.1125\,N = 211.5 - .25\,N$$

$$2.3625\,N = 211.5$$

$$N = 89$$

$$11\,N = 979$$

Performance, from the participating libraries' point of view, is best measured from the date a PR was received at the Center until the processed book arrived at the local library.

Figure 2.1

COMPARISON OF PROCESSING LAG TIMES OBSERVED

IN THE PHASE I-II[7] AND PHASE III STUDIES

Library	Order request received to Order Placed		Order Placed to Book received		Book Received to Book Cataloged		Total Processing days		Phase III to Phase I-II ($\pm$)
	I-II	III	I-II	III	I-II	III	I-II	III	
Colorado University	23	27	79	40	12	105	123	115	+ 8
Colorado State University	12	27	80	85	188	56	280	184	+96
Colorado State College	57	25	56	86	91	61	205	178	+28
Adams State College	24	29	52	90	73	50	148	190	-42
Colorado School of Mines	62	34	43	78	22	34	126	153	-27
Metropolitan State College *	-	36	-	104	227	39	227	198	+29

* Formerly used services of commercial processor

Unfortunately, the date of arrival of titles at local libraries could be obtained only for a small percentage of the samples. As a result, alternative check points were used. These included: 1) the date a book was released from cataloging; 2) the date the shelf list was filed; and 3) the date the book/card/pocket/label sets were printed. An overall mean lag-time for each alternative was calculated, then the means of the two samples were combined to yield one overall average.

Interpretation of Results -- The Center's performance was surprisingly good considering the problems which had been encountered. The total processing cycle ranged from a low of 115 days for the University of Colorado to a high of 198 for Metropolitan State College. (See Figure A2.17) At four schools the Center's performance during the experiment represented an improvement over the performance observed during the Phase I-II study. For two of the libraries, the processing cycle was extended--in one case by 42 days, in the other by 27 days. (See Figure 2.1) The improvement at the University of Colorado was due almost entirely to a shortened vendor lag-time.

Two significant contributants were beyond control of the Center, vendor time lags and LC card copy availability. As can be seen from Figure 2.1, performance of vendors has declined significantly since 1967 for three of the institutions. And at the University of Colorado, the significant improvement was due to the use of approval plans, which again underscores a major benefit of vendor approval plans.

Many books, upon receipt from vendors, had to be held in a Holding Unit until Library of Congress cataloging copy became available. Figure 2.2 summarizes the availability of cataloging copy both at the time when PR's were received at CALBPC and when books were received from vendors. The average availability at the time of receipt of PR's was eight percent, and 38 percent at the time a book was received. This is not an impressive performance when one realizes that cataloging copy was available for 57.5 percent of

all books processed by CALBPC, and that copy was available for 66 percent of the books processed for Adams State College and 75 percent for Metropolitan State College. (See Figure A2.19)

The consensus of the CALBPC administrators is that the Center performed much better than they had expected. Moreover, they believe turn around times have improved considerably since regular operations commenced. One library recently reported a three- to four-month turn around time for some items. It is evident that the performance has improved in other libraries as well.

The improvement can be attributed to a number of factors. Procedures which proved balky during the experiment have now been debugged; new procedures such as the Advanced Card Production system (which is discussed later) has lessened peak load activity; the discontinuance of the card/book matching subsystem has eliminated a serious bottleneck; and more judicious selection of vendors has shortened vendor waiting time. Periodic reviews of cycle time performance will be conducted on a routine basis.

Sources of Cataloging Copy

The availability of LC depository cards does not reflect the total picture of catalog copy availability. Cataloging copy is also obtained from other sources, such as a Xerox enlargement from the National Union Catalog or a locally typed master card. In order to gain an understanding of how often a cataloger is provided with some form of catalog copy, the lag-time data were analyzed to determine the frequency and source of cataloging copy.

CALBPC cataloging copy is obtained from the following sources: 1) Library of Congress depository cards; 2) Xerox enlargement from the National Union Catalog; 3) Polaroid enlargement from the National Union Catalog; 4) typed entry from the National Union Catalog; 5) typed entry from the University of Colorado catalog; and 6) a reproduced card from the University of Colorado catalog. The results of this study are

Figure 2.2

AVAILABILITY OF LIBRARY OF CONGRESS
CATALOGING COPY

	Sample Size		% LC Copy Available When PR Form Received		% LC Copy Available When Book Rec. From Vendor	
	Sample I	Sample II	Sample I	Sample II	Sample I	Sample II
University of Colorado	936	682	18	19	38	45
Colorado State University	36	102	3	5	33	47
Colorado State College	84	117	10	2	37	37
Adams State College	22	51	5	10	36	38
Metropolitan State College	55	51	2	0	33	36
Colorado School of Mines	15	35	7	23	27	53
Totals	1148	1038	7.5	9.8	34.0	42.6

shown in Figure A2.18.

It was surprising to learn that some form of cataloging copy was provided for 90 percent of the books processed. As might have been expected, the major source was Library of Congress depository cards. The Xerox enlargement procedure was used extensively during the late stages of the experiment because many retrospective titles from local cataloging arrearages were processed.

Readers should not infer from the data that cataloging copy was available for 90 percent of the books cataloged, only that some form of cataloging copy was available 90 percent of the time. Included in the 90 percent are cooperative cataloging and copy for different editions. A different edition might involve only a minor difference in imprints, or an edition written in an entirely different language. Some different editions were processed through mass cataloging and others turned over to an original cataloger. The analysis also includes added copies, added editions, etc. The breakdown of books cataloged originally and those handled through mass cataloging are analyzed in detail in the following section.

Analysis of Materials Cataloged

The CALBPC administration was particularly concerned about the proportion of materials which would require original cataloging, since this affected both costs and staffing patterns. Equally important were the language and subjects of the books to be cataloged. While it is easier to catalog new, U.S. imprints, one important advantage of the Center is that subject specialists and foreign language capabilities can be concentrated, neither of which any one participating library can hope to match. But which languages and what subjects?

When the Center agreed to process titles from each library's cataloging arrearage in lieu of purchasing new titles, there was some apprehension among the Center's staff. No one knew for certain what type of books would be diverted to the Center. We only suspected they would be dusty, old and in foreign languages, and from a cataloger's point of view, nasty to handle. These fears were not entirely unfounded.

An analysis of the titles cataloged was performed to profile the distribution of subjects among the LC classifications, the proportion of mass to original cataloging, and the frequency and distribution of foreign language materials. All catalog cards, before being sent to the National Union Catalog beginning February 1969 through January 1970, were photocopied. A total of 42,348 card images were collected.

A sample size was calculated based upon 37 categories of data or degrees of specificity. The calculations were:[8]

$$Np u = 42328 \qquad Np = \frac{42328}{37} = 1144$$

$$.05 = 95\% \text{ confidence level}$$
$$0 = .50 \text{ (worst possible case)}$$
$$.05 = \frac{0(1-0)}{N} \quad x \quad \frac{Np - N}{Np - 1}$$
$$.05 = \frac{(.50)(.50)}{N} \quad x \quad \frac{114 - N}{114 - 1}$$
$$.0025 = \frac{.25}{N} \quad x \quad \frac{1144 - N}{1143}$$
$$.0025 = \frac{286 - .25N}{1143N}$$
$$2.86N + .25N = 286$$
$$3.11N = 286$$
$$N = 92$$
$$37N = 3404$$

Every twelfth card was pulled from the universe and tabulated, thus the sample size totalled 3,529 cards. The data collector tabulated as "mass cataloging" any card with an LC call number. Cards with no LC call number were tabulated as "original cataloging." (See Figure A2.19) The ratio of mass to original cataloging held constant at two to one for all schools except Colorado State University and the University of Colorado. For Colorado State University original cataloging exceeded mass cataloging slightly, 50.6 percent to 49.4 percent, whereas 44 percent of the titles acquired by the University of Colorado required original cataloging.

This heavy volume of original cataloging caused deep concern because the Center was staffed to handle primarily English language imprints. In this instance, the data from the Phase I-II study had proven misleading. The earlier study had predicted an acquisition rate of only seven percent foreign language imprints, not an inflow of 25 percent. (See Figures A2.4-A2.6)

The experiment was somewhat atypical because of the large number of German language imprints submitted by Colorado State University. The majority of these materials required original cataloging. This is borne out by the data in Figure A2.20 which shows that 45 percent of the titles submitted by CSU were written in one of the Western European languages. Overall, the language analysis revealed that 75 percent of the materials cataloged were in English, 19 percent in one of the Western European languages, and the remaining five percent in one of the Eastern European or Oriental languages.[9]

Catalogers at the Center possessed the subject competencies to handle efficiently almost all materials submitted for processing. The only exception was some specialized agricultural monographs submitted by Colorado State University. Here was one instance where the user possessed more expertise than the central agency.

The distribution of materials cataloged according to the Library of Congress classification schedules are summarized in Figures A2.21-A2.27. Figure A2.21 summarizes the proportion of original cataloging to mass cataloging under each subject classification. Figures A2.22-A2.24 are categorized by language according to the classification schedules, and Figures A2.25-A2.27 summarize the subject distribution for each institution.

An almost infinite variety of inferences can be drawn from the data in these figures. To embark on a detailed analysis in this report would be belaboring the obvious and would serve no real purpose. As CALBPC grows, it will no longer be dominated by the host institution. Consequently, the present mix of titles ordered and cataloged will gradually change. However, it would be wise if the Center periodically monitored production characteristics such as language, type of materials cataloged, and proportion of mass to original cataloging in order to identify trend shifts.

Customer Acceptance of Products

One major objective of the experiment was to investigate whether or not the participating libraries were accepting the products produced at the Center. As mentioned earlier, a great deal of time was spent refining the processing specifications, but there was still no assurance that the products were acceptable to users. Or, stated in other terms, did the participants really adhere to the agreed upon specifications? There is no need to dwell on the obvious, but if participants of a processing center (or any other cooperative activity) do not accept the products of the central agency, then the advantages of centralization are largely diminished. Whereas a governmental agency could dictate staffing patterns to insure conformity to standards, the Colorado project was and still is a voluntary undertaking.

A random sample of 2,424 titles was selected from books processed before the end of August. This sample was in fact the original Sample I used to record processing lag-time data. Thirty-seven percent of the sample represented items processed for participating libraries, the remainder were for the University of Colorado. Because of time limitations, 447 items were selected from the 900 titles processed for participants. The project team traveled to each library to conduct a follow-up study. We wanted to learn the degree of product acceptance and to isolate problem areas. The product acceptance study was divided into three parts. First, the intellectual aspects of cataloging and classification; that is, the choice of main entry, classification, subject headings, etc. Second, the physical or mechanical processing of books. And third, the handling of catalog cards and shelf list cards.

Interpretation of Results -- The participants accepted the cataloging and classification data for 97 percent of the products. (See Figure 2.3) The range of acceptance of the classification number was 97.2 percent to 100 percent. The modifications observed usually involved the PZ classification. The acceptance of Cuttering ranged between 96 percent and 100 percent. Overall, the most frequently identified change in the call number was the addition of location information such as a branch library designation or the addition of the word "REF." The acceptance of cataloging, specifically the choice and form of main entry, ranged between 99 percent and 100 percent. Subject headings were altered by only two libraries and, even then, only three percent of the headings were changed. The frequency of alteration to secondary entries was observed to be greater, but this was due almost entirely to one library which systematically added a title card to all sets for which a title card was not prepared by the Center. This library maintains a divided catalog. A few changes were noted in the descriptive cataloging such as noting the inclusion of a bibliography. (See Figure 2.3)

The investigators were delighted with the results. The willingness of the libraries to accept the intellectual aspects of bibliographic data supplied by the Center reinforces the viability of centralized processing. Even though uniformity and standardization did not extend either to the mechanical processing activities or to the handling of catalog cards, these are mechanical rather than intellectual considerations.

The analysis of mechanical processing procedures used to prepare books received from the Center for the shelves revealed considerable diversity among the libraries. (Chapter V analyzes these procedures.) However, no one system was rated vastly superior to any of the others. In summary, the libraries did not alter the location of the book pockets. The only pockets removed were in books which were not to circulate. One library discarded the book card because it is not used in its circulation system. Spine labels supplied by the Center were removed only when the label was damaged or loosened. Most libraries modified the truncated title printed on the book card and book pocket. Acceptance of the truncated data ranged from a low of 16.7 percent to a high of 95.8 percent.

The lack of guidelines for keypunching truncated titles proved to be one of the major weaknesses of the Center's system. Subsequently, guidelines were prepared in response to the observed widespread customer rejection. Plastic jackets were generally not used. One library pastes publishers' blurbs from dust jackets inside the front cover. Property markings stamped in each book ranged from three to six. Two libraries formerly transcribed source information on the flyleaf of each book, but this practice was discontinued at both libraries midway through the experiment. Finally, two libraries use accession numbers. One stamps the book in five locations, the other stamps the book in three locations. (See Figure 2.4)

A great deal of variation was observed in the procedures used to handle catalog card and shelf list cards. (See Figure 2.5) One library maintains an extremely elaborate control system of checking-in and verifying each catalog card set. Included as in examination of all subject headings, the typing of an additional card for an official catalog and, for a few categories of books, the typing of a second additional card for a special bibliographical project. This same library also includes complete sourcing information in its shelf list and official catalog. The other libraries do not maintain such complicated control systems. For the most part, they either stamp an accession number or record the date received on the shelf list. One library reproduces an additional card for security purposes and, for certain titles, a second additional card for an off-campus branch. One library rejected all Polaroid copy. This library retyped all sets reproduced by Polaroid. The other libraries, although they objected to Polaroid copy, filed the cards into the catalog as received.

In reviewing the procedures used by the participants to prepare books and catalog cards for use, one cannot help but wonder why the diversity. Do any of the local variations have a substantive impact on library service? If one library has found it possible to accept Polaroid copy, why not

Figure 2.3

PRODUCT ACCEPTANCE:

CATALOGING AND CLASSIFICATION

	No. 1 Sample Size 77		No. 2 Sample Size 36		No. 3 Sample Size 125		No. 4 Sample Size 72		No. 5 Sample Size 137		Range of Acceptance
	Accept %	Modify %	Accept %	Modify %	Accept %	Modify %	Accept %	Modify %	Accept %	Modify %	
CLASSIFICATION:											
Class number	100.0	0.0	97.2	2.8	100.0	0.0	98.6	1.4	100.0	0.0	97.2-100
Book number (Cutter)	100.0	0.0	97.2	2.8	100.0	0.0	98.6	1.4	95.6	4.4	95.6-100
Additions to call number	100.0	0.0	100.0	0.0	100.0	0.0	98.6	1.4	97.8	2.2	97.8-100
Location info. (Ref., etc.)	96.1	3.9	91.6	8.3	99.2	0.8	92.9	7.1	86.2	13.8	86.2-99.2
CATALOGING:											
Main entry	100.0	0.0	100.0	0.0	99.2	0.8	100.0	0.0	100.0	0.0	99.2-100
Subject headings altered	100.0	0.0	100.0	0.0	99.2	0.8	97.2	2.8	100.0	0.0	97.2-100
Subject headings added	100.0	0.0	100.0	0.0	99.2	0.8	95.8	4.2	100.0	0.0	95.8-100
Subject headings decreased	100.0	0.0	100.0	0.0	99.2	0.8	100.0	0.0	99.2	0.8	99.2-100
Added entries altered	100.0	0.0	100.0	0.0	99.2	0.8	90.2	9.8	100.0	0.0	90.2-100
Added entries increased	100.0	0.0	100.0	0.0	99.2	0.8	76.1	23.9	97.7	2.3	76.1-100
Added entries decreased	100.0	0.0	100.0	0.0	99.2	0.8	97.0	3.0	100.0	0.0	97.0-100
Other changes in descriptive cataloging	100.0	0.0	100.0	0.0	100.0	0.0	91.0	9.0	96.3	3.7	91.0-100

Figure 2.4

PRODUCT ALTERATIONS: PHYSICAL PROCESSING

OF BOOKS[a

	No. 1 Sample Size 74		No. 2 Sample Size 36		No. 3 Sample Size 136		No. 4 Sample Size 78		No. 5 Sample Size 135		Range of Acceptance
	Yes %	No %	Yes %	No %	Yes %	No %	Yes %	No %	Yes %	No %	
Book pocket position changed	1.4	98.6	0.0	100.0	0.0	100.0	0.0	100.0	0.0	100.0	98.6-100
Book pocket removed	4.0[b]	96.0	0.0	100	2.2[bd]	97.8	1.3[b]	98.7	4.4[bd]	95.6	95.6-100
Circulation card removed	4.0	96.0	0.0	100.0	2.5	97.5	97.3	2.7	15.4	84.6	2.7-100
Truncated title on book and/or pocket book card changed	13.5	86.5	83.3	16.7	4.2	95.8	6.4	93.6	33.8	61.2	16.7-95.8
Plastic jacket added	0.0	100.0	5.7	94.3	0.0	100.0	0.0	100.0	0.7	99.3	94.3-100
Spine label replaced	0.0	100.0	2.8	97.2	0.7	99.3	2.6	97.3	3.0	97.0	97.0-100
Dust jacket blurb pasted in	30.1	69.9	0.0	100.0	0.0	100.0	0.0	100.0	0.0	100.0	69.9-100
LOCAL PROCEDURES ONLY											
Property Stamps	(3) 98.6	1.4	(6) 94.6	5.4	(3) 100.0	0.0	(4) 100.0	0.0	(5) 100.0	0.0	94.6-100
Sourcing Info	11.0[c]	89.0	5.6[c]	99.4							
Price written on title page	5.4	94.6									
Date slip removed or location changed	1.4	98.6			1.4	98.6					
"Ref." stamped above call no. on fly leaf and spine	2.7	97.3			(3) 100.0	0.0					
Accession nos.	(5) 100	0.0									
Author's name completed on title page e.g. (H.) Smith to (H)enry Smith			39.9	60.1							

Figure 2.4 (Continued)

PRODUCT ALTERATIONS: PHYSICAL PROCESSING OF BOOKS

	No. 1 Sample Size 74		No. 2 Sample Size 36		No. 3 Sample Size 136		No. 4 Sample Size 78		No. 5 Sample Size 135		Range of Acceptance
	Yes %	No %	Yes %	No %	Yes %	No %	Yes %	No %	Yes %	No %	
Date received from CALBPC written inside front cover			55.6	44.4							
Special location symbol added			2.8	97.2							
Date stamped on fly leaf									100	0.0	
"REF." stamped on date due slip											
Add "Folio" to spine label							3.8	96.2	10.0	90.0	
Modify cutter number							2.5	97.5			
Add "copy no." to spine label							2.5	97.5			
Call number added to page following title page							1.2	98.2			

KEY:

no   Product accepted
yes   Alteration found
a.   Alteration due either to local variations in procedure or errors detected in products received.
b.   Reference books
c.   Sourcing recently discontinued
d.   Book pocket replaced
○   **Frequency**

Figure 2.5

PRODUCT ALTERATIONS: INFORMATION ADDED TO
CATALOG CARDS AND SHELF LIST

	No. 1 Sample Size 77 %	No. 2 Sample Size 36 %	No. 3 Sample Size 113 %	No. 4 Sample Size 72 %	No. 5 Sample Size 128 %
Extra card or card set for Branch				60.1	4.6
"C.1-2" types on verso of main entry card	1.3				
"V.1-2" typed on verso of main entry card	2.6				
If continuation card needed for secondary entries, card set increased		5.6		12.6	0.9
Tracings ticked (✓)		63.8			
Additional card typed for official catalog		30.6			
"OFFICIAL CAT" stamped on card		8.3			
Holings card typed		2.8			
Extra card for Chemical abstracts		5.5			
Card set retyped			14.6		
Extra card for security file				13.9	

Figure 2.5 (Continued)

PRODUCT ALTERATIONS: INFORMATION ADDED TO
CATALOG CARDS AND SHELF LIST

Information added to shelf list	No 1 Sample Size 77 %	No. 2 Sample Size 36 %	No. 3 Sample Size 113 %	No. 4 Sample Size 72 %	No. 5 Sample Size 128 %
Acession number	100.00				
"Ref." or other special location stamped above call no.	3.9			0.8	
Tracings added	12.8	39.9			
"OFFICIAL S.L." stamped		77.7			
Source documentation typed		97.7			
Plastic jacket added to denot reference					13.8
Date received				91.5	99.2
Holdings data				1.4	
Extra card for series added entry				2.6	0.8

others? Why does one library find it necessary to use six property markings or accession numbers, and another library three? Why can some libraries operate without an official catalog while others feel the need for this control? Why do some libraries find they need sourcing information recorded in the shelf list while others do not? In the opinion of the researchers, there is no basic need for the observed diversity. Fortunately, this kind of variety does not preclude centralization although, from a taxpayer's point of view, it does add to the operating cost of libraries.

Another aspect of product acceptance is the procedures used by libraries to process products received from a central agency. It was observed that most libraries have structured their procedures to insure that all mistakes will be caught. Frankly, some libraries did not trust the Center; but this was to be expected since the Center was an experiment. However, more than one library went to such an extreme that its inspection routines were tantamount to a second cataloging operation. What is needed is to develop local procedures that dovetail effectively with the central operation. In other words, the points in the procedure where inspections will prove most productive must be identified. The interfacing of procedures is discussed in greater detail in Chapter V.

Errors and their Effect on the System

Participants had been forewarned that errors were inevitable, and to notify the Center when they were discovered to insure that corrective action could be taken.[10] The feedback would also be used to correct malfunctioning systems, improved training, etc. In spite of the warning, the emotional reaction to errors created a serious morale problem at the Center--the error problem was exaggerated far beyond its importance. Project personnel maintained a careful record of all books rejected by participants throughout the experiment. We wanted to learn what kind of mistakes the Center was making and to learn if participants were able to distinguish between errors which were acceptable within the framework of the agreed upon

specifications and those errors which the Center should have corrected. The results of this analysis have no statistical validity because some libraries corrected errors locally without notifying the Center, whereas other libraries conscientiously notified the Center whenever an error was detected. The following results are intended only to provide the reader with a flavoring of the categories of "errors."

As previously mentioned, one library judged Polaroid-produced copy as an error. This same library objected to the stacking of some call numbers. Other libraries accepted these books, even when the stacking varied from the agreed upon specifications. Another library returned books for which the truncated title on the book card and the book pocket were judged unacceptable. Two examples were: "Volunteers for P" changed to "Volunteers for Peace" and "Angkor: Art" changed to "Angkor: Art and Civilization." (71) These and similar difficulties resulted in the return to the Center of tens of dozens of books. Most libraries did not judge the poor keypunching to be serious enough to justify returning books. (75)

The product acceptance study revealed that some libraries, on occasion, modified the cataloging copy by adding information: for example, adding a title card when the Library of Congress did not supply one; or adding a subject heading for the subject of an autobiography when an entry was not supplied by the Library of Congress. These and similar modifications were not judged as errors since the processing specifications stated that Library of Congress cataloging would be observed. (100)

At the beginning of the experiment, the Board of Directors agreed that only obvious errors, if discovered, would be corrected on Library of Congress depository cards. (100) The definition of an "obvious error" is yet to be resolved and this fuzziness, more than once, has created a local imbroglio. On one occasion, the Library of Congress omitted the letter "a" from the subtitle of a book entitled, The Paintings of Nicholas Poussin: A Critical Portrait . . . . The receiving library insisted that the letter "a" be inserted. The center took the position that it had followed Library of Congress specifications; consequently, if the receiving library wished to insert the letter, it should be done locally. This should have ended the discussion, but it did not. The book was eventually returned to the Center for correction. The Center countered by warning that in such a case the library would be charged for the cost of original cataloging. In other words, a book that initially cost $1.85 would now cost an additional $3.95, all for the insertion of the letter "a". The point is not to ridicule or to dwell on this absurdity; but only to caution that when errors such as these are not handled in a dispassionate, objective manner, they can have a debilitating effect on morale. (56)

Two libraries maintained a record of errors detected during local inspection routines. These errors are divided into two categories. The first category includes mistakes which were acceptable within the processing specifications. The second category consists of errors which should have been corrected at the Center. One shipment of thirty-five items included:

Type of Error	Frequency
Call number incorrectly stacked.	12
Abbreviations used in the sub-heading of subject entries.	3
No title card provided	1
No copy number added to call number.	1
No continuation card included.	2
Series was not traced.	1
The word "joint" was omitted from the entry. (It had also been omitted by the Library of Congress.)	2

The second category of errors, those which should have been corrected at the Center, included a series card incorrectly formatted, a missing title card, two cards with an incorrect title transcription, eight with a period or comma omitted from the truncated title printed on the book card and book pocket, and one loose date-due slip. (80)

A second library reported on errors which had been found in a single shipment of 234 items. Forty card sets produced from a Polaroid master were rejected. In each case, a new card set was typed. New card sets were also typed whenever continuation cards were not provided by the Center. The call number format was rejected for 52 items, again a matter of incorrect stacking. In one case, the catalog cards were judged messy; in another, the spine label had pulled loose from the book; for still another the spine label was wrinkled; and finally, one card set and book did not match. (89)

It is interesting to note that more than half of the errors had not violated the processing specifications. Possibly more importantly, none of the errors was caused by disagreements on intellectual judgments, but rather on mechanical and procedural disagreements.

In summary, the most serious aspect of error detection and correction was an occasional inability to maintain an objective prospective. For this reason the Center must strive to ensure that errors of all types and shades are kept at a minimum--hence quality control. On the other hand, users must learn to accept the inevitability of errors, and that perfection is an impractical objective; consequently, CALBPC and its users must formulate parameters for acceptable error levels.

Quality Control

Since October, 1969, after the local modification data had been analyzed, the prevention of errors received a top priority at the Center. The inspections conducted throughout processing are extensive and varied. There are inspections to ensure consistent and acceptable quality of cataloging as well as for the mechanical aspects of book processing, such as card production, labeling, etc.

The revisions performed within the Cataloging Department include the following: 1) all titles completed by new catalogers (this includes both original cataloging and cataloging with the assistance of Library of Congress depository cards, which is performed by library assistants); 2) mass cataloging (LC card copy) for which cross-references are needed; and 3) mass cataloging for which a series authority card is needed. The inspection procedure itself consists of checking and comparing the book, the cataloger's copy slip or LC depository card, and the PR form. The objective of this inspection is to ensure that the call number, title, destination, processing fee, identification flag, and instructions to the typist are all correct. Spot checks are occasionally performed to assure acceptability of descriptive cataloging. (110)

The Cataloging Maintenance and Preservation Department (CaMP) also carries on extensive inspection activities. Revisions are performed following keypunching, matching of spine labels with books, following the labeling procedure, and during the packing operation. The computer-produced labels are verified against the call number recorded on the fly leaf of the book. The title as printed on the title page is compared against the title as recorded on the original PR form. The inspection performed during the packing operation is to ensure that all books listed on the invoice are in fact packed for shipment. (111)

Catalog card sets are revised four times. However, the objective of each check is different. The first revision is to be sure that the information transcribed from the cataloger's copy slip onto the processing instruction sheet is correct. This information includes the number of cards required for the card set; the check also ensures that the destination noted on the instruction sheet matches the destination recorded on the copy slip. The cards are next checked before, during, and after the stamping of the NUC symbols. This task is performed by a Pitney-Bowes tick-o-meter. The quality and completeness of the machine stamping is inspected on a sampling basis.

All typing is 100 percent revised. It is revised for accuracy, neatness, correctness of not only typing but other stamped and/or penciled information. This inspection is based on unit card information and the instructions recorded on the typist's instruction sheet. (110)

Most of the above inspection routines were already in force prior to the initiation of the experiment. However, existing procedures were reviewed carefully in order to keep errors at a minimum. In spite of the safeguards taken, midway through the experiment several specific problems were identified. The following are examples: 1) the title printed on the book card and book pocket did not agree exactly with the title printed on the title page (in order to avoid this difficulty, the cataloger now changes the form of title recorded on the PR to agree with the title page version); 2) misinterpretation of destination symbols (there was not a high incidence of misrouting books, but it occured frequently enough to become an irritant; this was a short run problem which was solved once personnel became accustomed to the multiple locations); 3) incorrect processing charges (a cataloger designated which of three charges a library should be assessed; again, these mistakes were due largely to the newness of the routine); 4) errors made by catalogers in preparing instructions to typists (this type of error can be serious since it results in the wrong number of cards reproduced, the card set sent to the wrong destination, or some other irregularity; these difficulties in part stem from the inconsistent use of symbols to instruct typists. One immediate solution was to develop a procedure manual to establish consistent practice.)

Has the quality control program been effective? Frankly, we cannot document onto yet. The product acceptance study did not reveal a heavy incidence of errors, which suggests that the initial quality control precautions had been reasonably effective. The one exception was the keypunching of the truncated titles, which has already been discussed.

One matter yet to be resolved is the question of level of acceptability. That is, what is an acceptable level of error--one percent, two, three, four or even higher? Pragmatically speaking, two to four percent is probably a reasonable expectation.

On a more abstract level, what is an error? The definition of an error may be rooted in a

person's philosophy toward librarianship. Some librarians place greater importance on the aesthetic
appearance of catalog cards; others are more concerned about the content of a card. One librarian
may disregard a typographical error in the
descriptive portion of a Library of Congress depository card; another will insist that this is an
error and should be corrected. Furthermore,
weights must be attached to errors. Obviously
a transposed digit in the class number is much
more important than the misspelling of the publisher's name. One may prevent a user from
locating the book on the shelf, the other does not.
These are questions that not only must be resolved
in the Colorado processing environment, they must
also be grappled with by others engaged in cooperation.

The inspection program presently in force at
the Center is based on 100 percent inspections. The
CaMP Department believes some inspections can be
performed on a sampling basis. It is proposed,
for example, that the work of a typist need not be
inspected 100 percent to assure acceptable work.
The primary purpose of the inspection is to guard
against sloppy work resulting from carelessness or
poor training.

The pressure of other problems has prevented the implementation of the aforementioned
quality control program based on sampling, but
these types of programs will be initiated in the
near future.

Cost Analysis of the Center

Time observation data, data derived from
the other methodological approaches, and information pertaining to the Center's procedures were
analyzed to yield unit cost figures. Five major
factors were studied to calculate the unit cost
for book processing: labor, supplies, overhead,
transportation (the total distance moved in the
work flow), and binding. The investigator updated
the CALBPC simulated cost analysis completed in
Phase I. There are minor changes in the
methodology for the cost analysis derived in

Phase I-II, and these are pointed out as they are
encountered. The flow process chart of the Center
(Figure 2.6) is an updated version of the one used
in Phase I-II in the development of the mathematical
model.

Unit Labor Cost (L) --

Observed Mean Times (See column a in Figure 2.7)

In order to obtain mean times from
the raw data recorded on the time observation sheets, it was necessary to convert the
readings to decimal times, and key the
steps or blocks of steps to coordinate with
the tasks identified on the Labor Chart.

If an activity was found to be split
into several distinct steps sometimes performed by different people or in combination
with portions of other tasks, it was labeled
with the appropriate function number with a
subscript denoting the sequence of the step.
Next, a mean time was calculated for each
sub-function by summing the observed times
and dividing by the number of items handled
or cycles performed, whichever was appropriate for that particular function.

This information was transferred to
another sheet so that all sub-functions could
be cumulated to yield a total mean time for
each function. (See Figure 2.7) These
mean times were recorded on the labor chart
to be proportioned by frequency.

Simulated Times

By comparing the labor chart with
the flow process chart and the diary studies,
it was possible to identify which remaining
functions could be labeled NA (not applicable),
which could be labeled AF (accomplished by
another function), or which functions needed
raw times. Data from the diary studies of
1967 were used if an adequate number of
entries had been recorded to approximate a
time observation session (noted by a _d_ following the diary time in the labor chart).

Figure 2.6

Book Processing Center Flow Chart

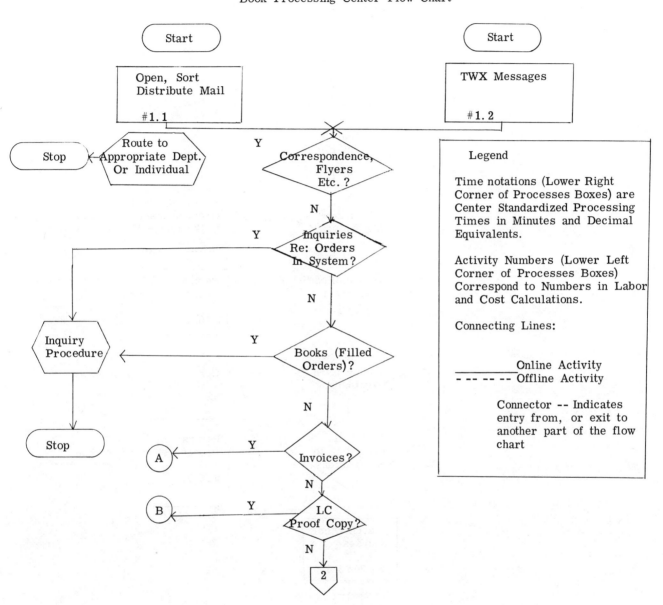

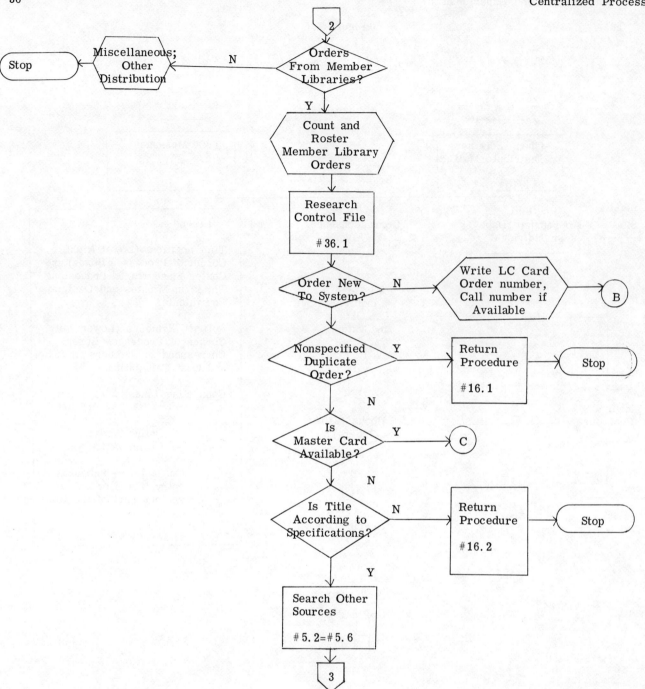

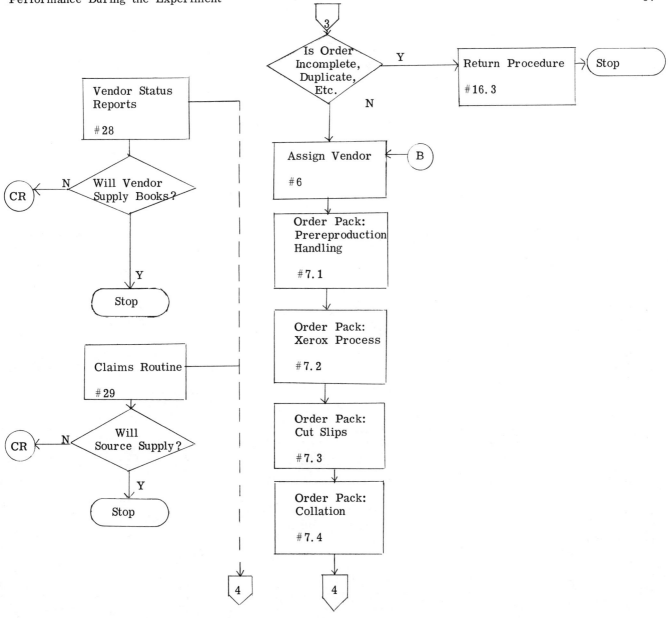

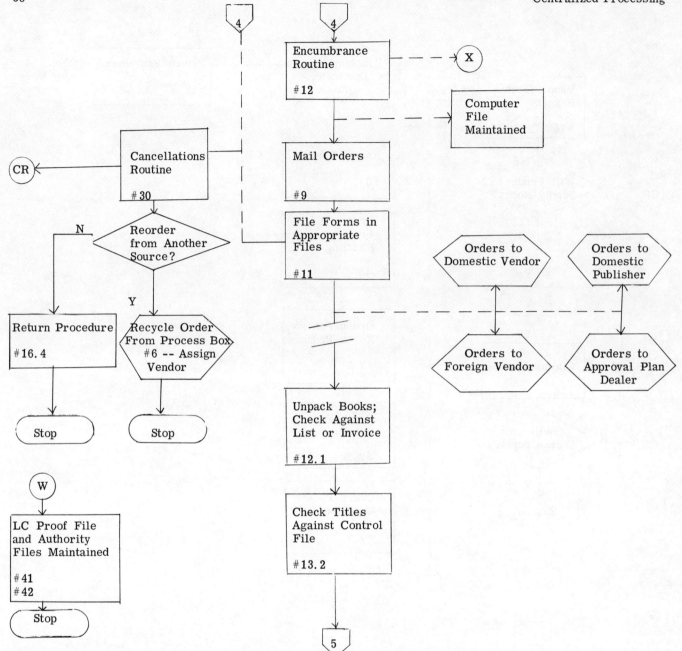

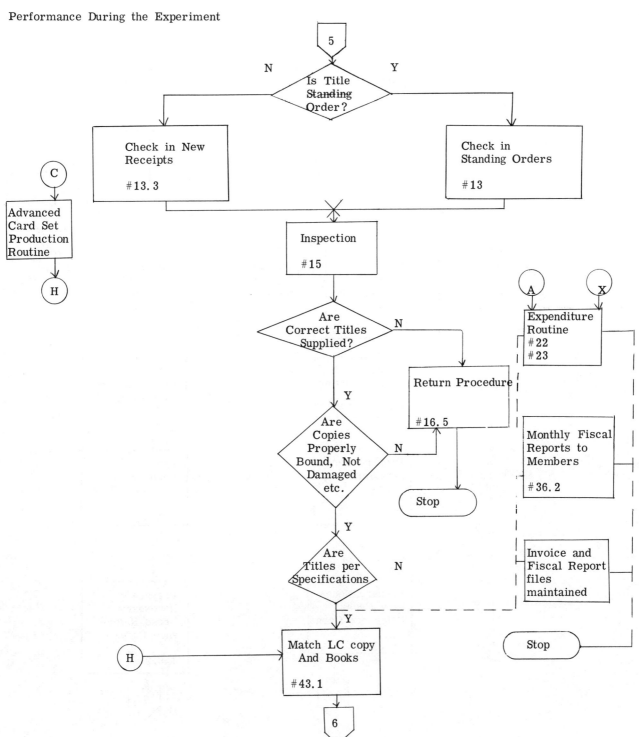

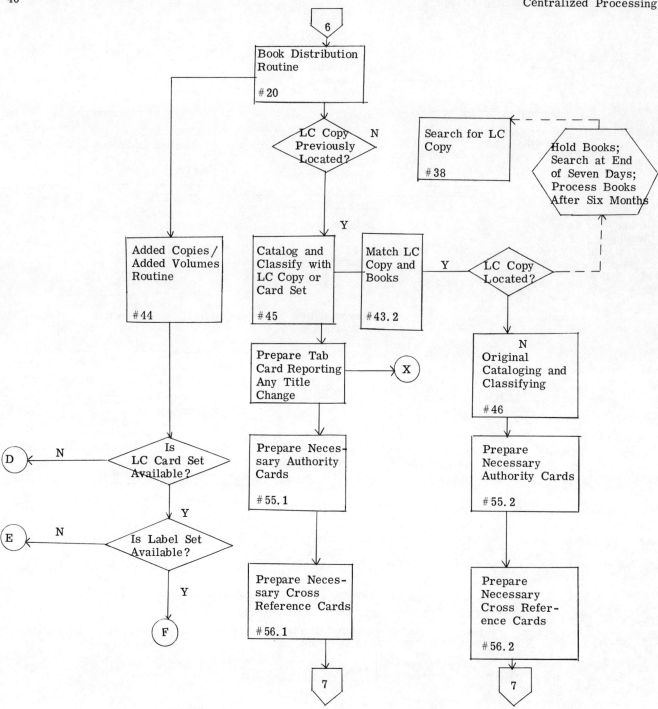

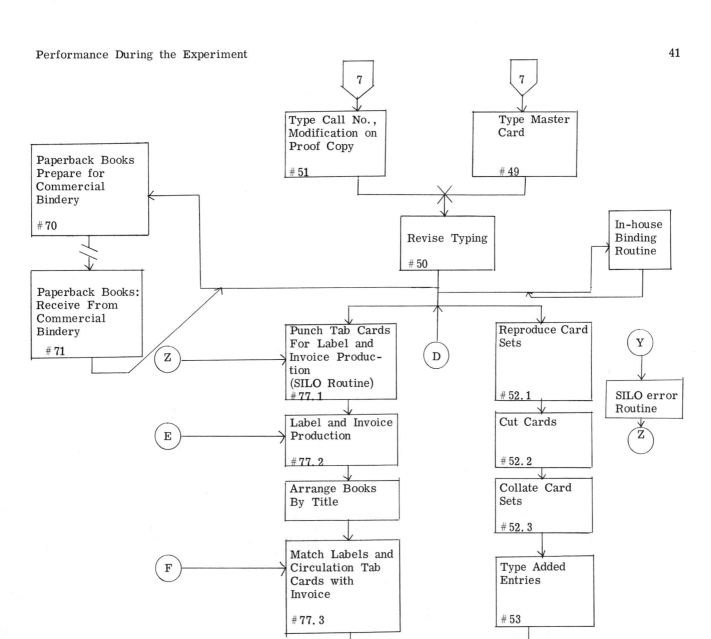

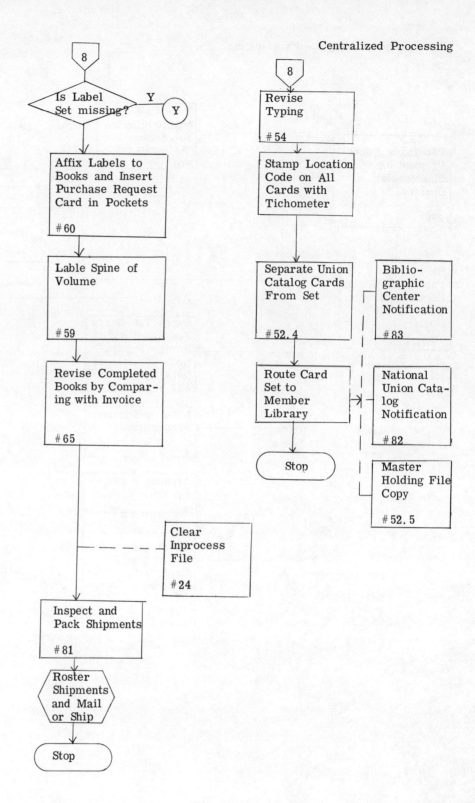

Figure 2.7

LABOR (L)

Unit Cost Calculation for Technical Processing Activities Proportioned by Frequency
Acquisitions

KEY:

AF = Another function incorporated this activity at the Center.
NA = Not applicable (not performed at the Center).
( )= Simulated data
P = Performed in parallel for C.U. non-specification items.

u = Performed for C.U. books only
m = Performed at most libraries for CALBPC orders
+ = Standardizing factor (1.4771)
d = Data taken from the diary study at C.U. in Phase I
f_1 = Student
f_2 = Clerk II

f_3 = Clerk III
f_4 = Library Assistant I
f_5 = Library Assistant II
f_6 = Library Assistant III
f_7 = Assistant Librarian
f_8 = Associate Librarian
f_9 = Senior Librarian

Code	Activity Description	P	a Observed Mean Time	b Personal Rating Factor	c Standard Time	d Frequency	e Proportioned Time	f Category of Worker	g Wage/Minute	h Cost of Activity
1.	Open, sort and distribute incoming mail.	P	.249	1.07	0.393	0.529	.208	2	.0364	.0076
2.	Review book order requests; review selection media.	P	u,m							
3.	Select titles to be ordered.	P	u,m							
4.	Type library order request card.	P	u,m							
5.1	Search and verify bibliographic information.	P	3.489	1.10	5.669	0.529	2.999	6	.0531	.1592
5.2	Return non-specification orders to member libraries.	P	(.300)	1.00	0.443	0.007	.003	7	.0711	.0002
6.	Assign vendor.	P	.063	1.10	0.099	0.522	.052	8	.0884	.0046
7.	Prepare multiple order record.	P	.580	1.10	0.942	0.522	.492	5	.0490	.0241
8.	Type purchase requisition, etc.	P	NA,u							
9.	Mail requests.	P	.112	1.05	0.174	0.522	.091	2	.0364	.0033
10.	Burst forms.	P	NA							
11.	File forms in Appropriate files.	P	.324	1.15	0.549	0.522	.287	5	.0490	.0141

+ Standardizing Factor: 1.4771

Figure 2.7 (Continued)

LABOR (L)
Unit Cost Calculation for C.A.L.B.P.C. Activities

Acquisitions

Code	Activity Description	P	a Observed Mean Time	b Personal Rating Factor	c Standard Time	d Frequency	e Proportioned Time	f Category of Worker	g Wage/ Minute	h Cost of Activity
12.1	Keypunch encumbrances.	P	.160	1.15	0.272	0.522	.142	3	.0404	.0057
12.2	Verify encumbrances.	P	.121	1.05	0.188	0.522	.098	3	.0404	.0040
13.1	Unpack books; check against packing list or invoice. Check outstanding order file.	P	5.200	1.08	8.295	0.892	7.399	2	.0364	.2693
13.2	Unpack "processing-only" books.	P	(.812)	1.08	1.295	0.108	.140	2	.0364	.0005
14.	Check in serials on Kardex.	P	.483	1.10	0.784	0.258	.202	4	.0462	.0093
15.	Collate books.	P	.311	1.20	0.551	0.892	.491	2	.0364	.0179
16.	Book return procedure (incorrect shipment, defective copy, approval books).	P	6.924	1.08	11.046	0.006	.066	6	.0531	.0035
17.	Book accessioning routine.		NA							
18.	Write sourcing information.		NA							
19.	Prepare gift record form.	P	u							
20.	Book distribution routine.	P	.191	1.07	0.301	1.000	.301	2	.0364	.0110
21.	Prepare receiving report.		NA							
22.	Prepare vendor invoices for payment.	P	.334	1.08	0.533	0.892	.475	6	.0531	.0252
23.1	Keypunch expenditures.	P	.143	1.10	0.232	0.892	.207	3	.0404	.0084
23.2	Verifying expenditures.	P	.086	1.05	0.133	0.892	.119	3	.0404	.0048

+ Standardizing Factor: 1.4771

Figure 2.7 (Continued)

LABOR (L)
Unit Cost Calculation for C.A.L.B.P.C. Activities

Acquisitions

Code	Activity Description	P	a Observed Mean Time	b Personal Rating Factor	c Standard Time	d Frequency	e Proportioned Time	f Category of Worker	g Wage/Minute	h Cost of Activity
24.	Clear in-process file.	P	.302	1.05	0.468	1.000	.468	1	.0262	.0123
25.	File forms, etc., in completed records or discard.	P	.369	1.10	0.600	1.000	.600	1	.0262	.0157
26.	Requestor notification routine.	P	u,m							
27.	Periodic accessions list routine.									
28.	Vendor status routine.	P	.985	1.15	1.669	0.158	.264	3	.0404	.0107
29.	Claims routine.	P	3.264	1.10	5.303	0.037	.196	3	.0404	.0079
30.	Cancellations routine.	P	1.864	1.15	3.167	0.007	.022	3	.0404	.0009
31.	Out-of-print order routine.	P	u,m							
32.	Process inquiries.	P	10.208d	1.10	16.587	0.015	.249	6	.0531	.0132
33.	General typing – correspondence, etc. (specify).	NA								
34.	General revision (specify).	NA								
35.1	Sorting tab cards.	P	.013	1.05	0.021	1.000	.021	2	.0364	.0008
35.2	Prepare a computer run.	P	.005	1.05	0.007	1.000	.007	3	.0404	.0003
35.3	Check in computer run.	P	.066	1.10	0.108	1.000	.108	3	.0404	.0044
35.4	Keypunch title changes.	P	2.255	1.00	3.331	0.006	.020	3	.0404	.0008
36.	Bi-monthly accounting reports to members.	AF								

Acquisitions   Sub-total   .6397

+ Standardizing Factor: 1.4771

Figure 2.7 (Continued)

LABOR (L)

Unit Cost Calculation for Technical Processing Activities

Cataloging

Code	Activity Description	P	a Observed Mean Time	b Personal Rating Factor	c Stan- dard Time	d Fre- quency	e Propor- tioned Time	f Cate- gory of Worker	g Wage/ Minute	h Cost of Activity
37.	Sort books, assign and distribute.	P	4.894	1.05	7.591	1.000	7.591	6	.0531	.4031
38.	Search for LC copy; verify bibliographic information.	P	.895	1.10	1.453	0.344	.500	6	.0531	.0266
39.1	Advanced card production: C. U. instruction slips.	P	.436	1.10	0.709	0.623	.442	2	.0364	.0161
39.2	Advanced card production: member library instruction slips.	P	.952	1.10	1.547	0.762	1.179	6	.0531	.0626
40.	Receive and arrange LC cards.		NA							
41.1	Receive and arrange LC proof slips or proof sheets.	P	.171d	1.10	0.278	3.017	.839	1	.0262	.0220
41.2	Stamp date and destination code on verso of master cards.	P	.101	1.10	0.162	2.188	.354	2	.0364	.0129
42.	File LC copy. (cards or proof)	P	.244	1.15	0.415	2.188	.908	1	.0262	.0238
43.	Match LC cards or proof copy and books.	P	.290	1.15	0.493	0.226	.111	2	.0364	.0040
44.	Added copies/added volumes routine.	P	.373	1.09	0.601	0.661	.397	5	.0498	.0194
45.	Catalog and classify with LC cards/copy.	P	1.510	1.05	2.343	0.226	.530	6	.0531	.0281
46.	Original cataloging and classifying.	P	14.081d	1.10	22.879	0.113	2.585	8	.0884	.2285
47.	Shelf Listing (for 44, 45, and 46).	P	u,m							

+ **Standardizing Factor 1.4771**

Figure 2.7 (Continued)

LABOR (L)

Unit Cost Calculation for C.A.L.B.P.C. Activities

Cataloging

Code	Activity Description	P	a Observed Mean Time	b Personal Rating Factor	c Standard Time	d Frequency	e Proportioned Time	f Category of Worker	g Wage/Minute	b Cost of Activity
48.	Type complete card sets.	P	NA							
49.	Type master card.	P	1.304	1.18	2.273	0.113	.257	2	.0364	.0094
50.	Revise master card.	P	.270	1.10	0.439	0.113	.050	4	.0462	.0023
51.	Type modification on a card or proof slip.	P	.155	1.10	0.251	0.226	.057	2	.0364	.0021
52.1	Reproduce cards sets (other than typing). Sort cards into sets.	P	1.489	1.10	2.419	0.672	1.626	3	.0404	.0657
52.2	Sort card sets by member or departmental library & stamp location code on each card.	P	.959	1.10	1.558	0.672	1.047	2	.0364	.0381
53.	Type call number, added entries.	P	.821	1.05	1.273	0.672	.855	2	.0364	.0311
54.	Revise typing on card sets.	P	.479	1.10	0.778	0.672	.523	4	.0462	.0242
55.	Prepare authority cards.	P	1.168	1.00	1.725	0.010	.017	2	.0364	.0006
56.	Prepare cross-reference cards.	P	1.648	1.10	2.678	0.031	.083	2	.0364	.0030
57.	Prepare circulation card.	A.F.								
58.	Prepare book pocket.									
59.	Apply date due slip and spine label.	P	.546	1.15	0.928	1.000	.928	1	.0262	.0243
60.1	Match label sets and invoices to books.	P	.427	1.05	0.662	1.000	.662	2	.0364	.0241
60.2	Burst label sets and affix pockets.	P	.704	1.15	1.196	1.000	1.196	1	.0262	.0313

+ Standardizing Factor: 1.4771

Figure 2.7 (Continued)

LABOR (L)

Unit Cost Calculation for C.A.L.B.P.C. Activities

Cataloging

Code / Activity Description	P	a Observed Mean Time	b Personal Rating Factor	c Standard Time +	d Frequency	e Proportioned Time	f Category of Worker	g Wage/ Minute	h Cost of Activity
60.3 Inspect pockets and remove flags.	P	.279	1.10	0.453	1.000	.453	1	.0262	.0119
61. Affix biographical and review material in book.		NA							
62. Stamp property marks.	P	u,m							
63. Affix plastic jacket to book.		NA							
64. Paperback books — in house binding routine.	P	2.618	1.00	3.867	0.062	.240	3	.0404	.0097
65. Revise completed books before forwarding.	P	.127	1.15	0.216	1.000	.216	3	.0404	.0087
66. Sort and alphabetize shelf list and all catalog cards.	P	NA, u,m							
67. File shelf list and all catalog cards.	P	NA, u,m							
68. Revise filing of shelf list and all catalog cards.	P	NA, u,m							
69. Route card sets to departmental or member libraries.	P	.437u	1.05	0.678	1.000	.678	2	.0364	.0247
70. Paperback books — bindery routine (preparation).	P	2.724	1.05	4.224	0.079	.334	3	.0404	.0135
71. Paperback books — bindery routine (receiving).	P	.685	1.10	1.114	0.079	.009	3	.0404	.0004
72. Catalog maintenance (Other than filing).	P	NA, u,m							
73. General typing (specify).		NA							
74. General revision (specify).		NA, u,m							

+ Standardizing Factor: 1.4771

Figure 2.7 (Continued)

LABOR (L)

Unit Cost Calculation for C.A.L.B.P.C. Activities

Cataloging

Code	Activity Description	P	a Observed Mean Time	b Personal Rating Factor	c Standard Time	d Frequency	e Proportioned Time	f Category of Worker	g Wage/ Minute	h Cost of Activity
75.	General filing (specify).		NA, u,m							
76.	Other cataloging activities not listed above (specify).		NA, u,m							
77.1	Distribution of books to pre-keypunch staging area.	P	.056	1.05	0.087	1.000	.087	4	.0462	.0040
77.2	Keypunch SILO cards.	P	.419	1.10	0.681	1.000	.681	3	.0404	.0275
77.3	SILO error routine.	P	.974	1.05	1.511	0.108	.163	2,4,7	.0512*	.0083
78.	Arrange books by library.	P	.240	1.10	0.390	1.000	.390	1	.0262	.0102
79.	Invoice/shipping list production.		A.F.							
80.	Billing.		A.F.							
81.1	Pack member library books.		.205	1.10	0.334	0.146	.049	4	.0462	.0023
81.2	Inspect shipments and mail out.		.433	1.10	0.703	0.146	.103	2	.0364	.0037
82.	Union catalog (arrange and file).		NA							
83.	Bibliographic Center notification.		A.F.							
	Sub-Total									1.24
	Acquisitions									0.64
	Cataloging									1.24
	ΣL									1.88

* Average of the three wage rates.

Times still lacking were obtained by averaging the observed times gathered at other libraries in the study. Times calculated by this last method are distinguished by parentheses. (See Figure 2.7)

Activity Descriptions

The eighty-three tasks on the labor chart are not all performed at the Center. The major task additions relate to data processing and shipping activities. Other tasks performed at C.U. in 1967 but which were subsequently changed were reanalyzed. Since C.U. essentially wears two hats--serving the University library system as well as the libraries of participating institutions-- the individual activities on the labor chart were keyed two ways:

> p = performed in parallel for C.U. books which fall outside the CALBPC specifications, and
>
> u = performed for C.U. books only.

An "m" was used to identify those tasks that, although not performed at the Center, are typically performed at member libraries to complete the processing cycle. An estimate of the cost of these additional local tasks has been updated from Phase I-II and is provided in Figure 2.16. A ten percent cost of living increase has been used to modify the 1967 figures.

Frequencies (See column d)

All labor functions for each library were evaluated to determine to what extent a given function was performed for each book moving through the system. The Frequency Computation Chart in Figure A2.28 summarizes the statistical ratios with which the frequency percentages are obtained. The source of and the actual statistics employed are cited in Figure A2.29. The total of volumes processed (81071) is based on Figure A2.3, "Processing Center Cataloging Workloads." Figure A2.30 relates these statistics to the labor chart tasks list and shows the actual calculation of the frequencies. Not all books are subjected to the same functions 100% of the time, so that a frequency of less than 1.00 had to be established. Proportions such as gift books compared to purchases, hardbacks to paperbacks, added volumes compared to new titles, all affect the frequency with which a function is performed. Percentages based on the statistics collected were calculated and entered on the labor chart. For example, for every book a SILO card is keypunched (Activity #77.2), therefore, the frequency is 1.00. In contrast, the claims routine (Activity #29) was used for only 3.7% of the books during Phase III; therefore, .037 is entered in the frequency column. A few tasks such as #41.1 (Receive and Arrange LC Cards) occur more than once relative to the total volumes processed; therefore, Activity #41.1 has a frequency of 3.017, meaning that three proof cards are handled for every volume processed.

Personal Rating Factor (See column b)

The rating factor for each function was recorded on the time sheet as the time observations were taken to indicate the extent to which the person was performing normally though under observation. At the same time, each function was keyed according to one of nine categories of personnel performing the function.

Standardizing Factor (+)

Voos has listed the following elements which affect labor productivity and which are difficult to obtain through direct time observations and diary study data.[11] These elements are:

unproductive time	16.3%
supervision	6.5%
administration	3.8%
instruction	5.7%
p =	32.3%

The standardizing factor was computed from the formula:[12]

$$e = \frac{100}{100-p} \quad \text{where } p = 32.3;$$

$$e = 1.4771.$$

Standard Times (See column c)

Standard times for each activity were calculated by multiplying the observed mean time (a) by the personal rating factor (b) and standardizing factor (+).

Wages-per-minute (See column g)

Full-time Employees (Clerk II to Senior Librarian):

Salary data for the Center is represented in Figures A2.34 to A2.38. There are 260 theoretical work days in the year (5 days per week x 52 = 260). However, the actual work days were calculated at 239 because of:

Annual Leave	10
Legal Holidays	11
Total	21

Therefore, 260 - 21 = 239 actual work days. Two hundred and thirty-nine days converts to 114,720 man minutes (239 x 8 hours per day x 60 minutes per hour).

Although annual leave for the supervisor is 22 days rather than 10 days, they are represented infrequently on the labor chart. For this reason, 10 days was used uniformly throughout.

For each wage category, the gross salary paid monthly was divided by the number of slots in that category to obtain the average monthly wage. This average was multiplied by 12 to obtain an estimated average annual salary expenditure. The average annual salary was then divided by the man year expressed in minutes (114,720) to arrive at the wage-per-minute per category.

Student Employees:

Since student employees are paid at four hourly wage rates, it was necessary to compute a weighted average rate by taking the percentage of students represented in each rate, multiplying the rate by its percentage of use, then adding the products together to obtain a weighted hourly wage

of 1.57. (See Figures A2.36 and A2.37)

Proportioned Time (See column e of Figure 2.7)

The standard time (c) multiplied by the frequency percentage (d) produced the proportioned time (e). In other words, the time of each activity is modified relative to its importance in the overall workload.

Unit Labor Cost per Function (See column h)

The unit cost obtained for each function was calculated by multiplying the value for proportioned time (e) by the wages per minute (g).

Total Unit Labor Cost (See column h)

The total unit labor cost was calculated by summing the unit costs for each function. (See Figure 2.7)

Unit Supply Cost (S) (See Figure A2.39)--

Unit costs of individual supply items were summed.

Unit Overhead Cost (O)

Two categories of overhead were considered: equipment and institutional.

Equipment Overhead (O_e) (See Figure A2.40 and 2.8)

$$O_e = \frac{O_p + O_r + O_d}{P}$$

Equipment overhead was calculated as the sum of the funds spent on new equipment (O_p) during the year prorated over a use period of one year according to the expected life span, the rental charges and contractural charges for equipment (O_r), and the amount of depreciation allowance (O_d) on equipment for the year considered. This sum was divided by the total volumes processed (P) during 1969 to obtain the equipment overhead per book. The key to the symbols is as follows: (cont. on p. 53)

Figure 2.8

EQUIPMENT OVERHEAD (O_e)

Capital Outlay, 1969	Life Span in Years	O_p Equipment Cost in 1969	O_r Contractual Services	O_d Depreciation per Year	P Total # of Books Processed During 1969	$O_p + O_r + O_d$	O_e Equipment Overhead per Book
$1890.35	20	$189.04	$13,807.19	$465.19*	81,071	$14,461.42	$0.1784

*Depreciation from Leonard, Centralized Book Processing, p. 69, for Library #8 (1967 data).

INSTITUTIONAL OVERHEAD (O_i)*

O_{i-u} Institutional Overhead in Dollars per Square Foot	X Total Square Footage	O_{i-t} Total Institutional Overhead Cost	P Total # of Books Processed During 1969	O_i Institutional Overhead per Book
$0.9615**	12,182.85	$11,713.81	81,071	$0.1445

*Source: Leonard, Centralized Book Processing, p. 74, for Library #8 (1967 data).
**$.9071 increased by 6% for cost of living.

UNIT OVERHEAD COST (O)

O_e Equipment	O_i Institutional	O Total
$0.1784	$0.1445	$0.3229

O_e = overhead on equipment,

O_p = equipment cost per anuum,

P = total books processed in 1969,

c = capital outlay for equipment for technical processes in 1969,

l = estimated life span of the equipment purchased,

$$O_p = \frac{c}{l},$$

O_r = contract services (such as Xerox) per annum (prorate if such equipment is shared with another department), and

O_d = depreciation in dollars per annum on equipment held prior to 1969.

Equipment overhead per book and the institutional overhead were summed to yield the total unit overhead cost. (See Figure 2. 8)

Unit Transportation Cost (T)

Figure 2. 9

TRANSPORTATION (T)

j	t	ha	t_c	T
8730	39. 1946	.0421	1. 5238	.0508

Key:

j = total feet recorded on flow chart

$t = \dfrac{j}{241.2}$ = time in minutes required for transportation (241. 2) feet per minute is the speed of the average worker)

h_a = weighted average wage per minute from Table

t_c = total transportation cost in dollars per minute

$T = \dfrac{t_c}{30}$ (30 is used as the batching factor)

Definition

Transporation is defined as the cost associated with the distance a book moves through the system.

Rate of walking speed for the average worker (s), and the sum of the feet recorded in the distance column on each flow chart were calculated (j). On the basis of times observations, the rate of speed of the average worker in feet per minute was calculated to be 241. 2 feet (s = 241. 2 feet per minute).

Total Transportation Cost in Dollars

The total distance (j) divided by 241. 2 (s) yielded the number of minutes required for transportation (t).

$$t = \frac{j}{s}$$

A weighted wage rate (ha) to use with the transportation factor (See Figure A2. 41) was obtained by first calculating the percentage of the labor force represented in each wage category, then multiplying each wage rate by the appropriate percentage. The products were summed to obtain the weighted average wage per minute.

The total transportation cost in dollars (t_c) was calculated by multiplying the minutes of transportation by the weighted average wage per minute (ha) from Figure A2. 41 used in transportation (t).

Unit Transportation Cost (See Figure 2.9)

$$t_c = t \cdot ha$$

A sample study of the number of books transported on a book truck at various times of the day and on different days yielded a "batching" factor of 30, i. e. an average of 30 books are transported at one time.

Therefore, the unit transportation cost (T) was obtained by dividing the total transportation cost (t_c) by 30.

$$T = \frac{tc}{30}$$

Unit Binding Cost (Prorated) for Paperbacks (B) (See Figure 2.10)

A paperback is defined as a commercially published monograph or a title in

Figure 2.10

BINDING STATISTICS (B)

February - December 1969

Institution	Volumes with Pamphlet Binding	Volumes with Commercial Binding	Total Volumes Processed	% Pam. Bound	% Com. Bound
A.S.C.	34	56	1470	2.31	3.81
C.S.C.	94	178	2946	3.19	6.04
C.S.M.	11	34	875	1.26	3.89
C.S.U.	211	396	3373	6.26	11.74
C.U.	4652	5632	69255	6.72	8.13
M.S.C.	63	138	3152	2.00	4.38
Total Volumes	5065	6434	81071	6.25	7.94
Unit Cost	$ 1.15	$ 2.35			
% of Volumes Bound	6.25	7.94			
Weighted Unit Cost	$ 0.0719	$ 0.1866			
Total Weighted Unit Cost for Binding			$ 0.2585		

a monographic series that arrives from the vendor bound in a paper cover.

The charge for in house binding is $1.15, for commercial binding $2.35. The percentage of CALBPC specification books bound by each method is reported in Figure 2.10. Therefore, the unit charge was prorated according to use and two weighted unit costs were summed to obtain the total weighted unit cost for binding.

The out of house binding figure is slightly high because some commercial binding was of the Permabind quality ($1.25). However, the in house binding charge is probably too low because the Center was using materials provided gratis from the University Bindery when it closed in 1968.

Total Unit Processing Cost (C) (See Figure 2.11)

The summation of the costs for Labor (L), supplies (S), overhead (O), transportation (T), and binding (B) produced the Unit Processing Cost (C).

$$C = L + S + O + T + B$$

Processing Fees Calculated According to the Type of Product

The foregoing has described the calculation of an overall unit cost based upon the modeling of each individual activity in the process by the frequency of its occurrence. Labor calculated without regard to frequency is reported on Figure A2.42.

If the frequency is removed, the unit cost thus computed can become the basis for deriving a fee schedule based upon the level of difficulty and type of material processed, or for other purposes. Six cataloging product classes were selected:

1. Basic - those tasks which must be performed on every book whether it be purchased and cataloged, or simply cataloged.

2. Prorated - those tasks which occur very infrequently, but for which a state of readiness must be maintained such as inquiries and cancellations.

3. Mass cataloging with initial copy available - a master card with call number is in the master file.

   a) processing only
   b) purchasing and processing

4. Mass cataloging with no initial copy available - it may be necessary to search several times for a proof card.

   a) processing only
   b) purchasing and processing

5. Original cataloging - no existing copy located; therefore a master card is created for the title in question.

   a) processing only
   b) purchasing and processing

6. Binding - this applies only when a book has received binding attention.

   a) in house - pamphlet binding
   b) commercial - preparation for sending the book to an outside binder and checking it back in. Note: for any title known to be a paperback, the order is placed through a paperback book jobber to save handling at a later date.

Figure 2.11

SUMMARY OF UNIT COST FACTORS

	L	S	O	T	B	C
Phase III	1.88	.12	.32	.05	.26	2.63
Predicted in Phase I*	2.35	.29	.31	.06	.09	3.10

* Leonard, p. 139

KEY:

L	Labor Cost	T	Transportation Factor
S	Supplies	B	Pamphlet and Commercial Binding
O	Overhead (Equipment and Institutional)	C	Cost of Processing per Volume

Figure 2.12

LABOR (L)

Unit Cost Calculation for Technical Processing Activities by Cataloging Class

Acquisitions

KEY:
O = Processing only
Pur = Purchase and Process
f_1 = Student
f_2 = Clerk II
f_3 = Clerk III

f_4 = Library Assistant I
f_5 = Library Assistant II
f_6 = Library Assistant III
f_7 = Assistant Librarian
f_8 = Associate Librarian
f_9 = Senior Librarian

Code	Activity Description	Cataloging Class								e Standard Time	f Category of Worker	g Wage/Minute	h Cost of Activity
		1 Basic	2 Pro-rated	3 Mass cat. with initial copy avail.		4 Mass cat. no initial copy avail.		5 Original Cat.					
				O	Pur	O	Pur	O	Pur				
1.	Open, sort and distribute incoming mail.			X	X		X		X	0.393	2	.0364	.0143
2.	Review book order requests; review selection media.												
3.	Select titles to be ordered.												
4.	Type library order request card.												
5.1	Search and verify bibliographic information.	X								5.669	6	.0531	.3010
5.2	Return non-specification orders to member libraries.	X								0.443	7	.0711	.0315
6.	Assign vendor.				X		X		X	0.099	8	.0884	.0088
7.	Prepare multiple order record.	X								0.942	5	.0490	.0462
8.	Type purchase requisition, etc.												
9.	Mail requests.				X		X		X	0.174	2	.0364	.0063
10.	Burst forms.												
11.	File forms in Appropriate files.	X								0.549	5	.0490	.0269

Figure 2.12 (Continued)

LABOR (L)
Unit Cost Calculation for C.A.L.B.P.C. Activities

Acquisitions

Code / Activity Description	Cataloging Class					Standard Time	Category of Worker	Wage/Minute (g)	Cost of Activity (h)
	1 Basic	2 Pro-rated	3 Mass cat with initial copy avail. (O Pur)	4 Mass cat no initial copy avail. (O Pur)	5 Original Cat. (O Pur)	(f)			
12.1 Keypunch encumbrances.	X					0.272	3	.0404	.0110
12.2 Verify encumbrances.	X					0.188	3	.0404	.0076
13.1 Unpack books; check against packing list or invoice. Check outstanding order file.			X	X	X	8.295	2	.0364	.3019
13.2 Unpack "processing-only" books.			X	X	X	1.295	2	.0364	.0471
14. Check in serials on Kardex.	X					0.784	4	.0462	.0362
15. Collate books.	X					0.551	2	.0364	.0200
16. Book return procedure (incorrect shipment, defective copy, approval books).		X				11.046	6	.0531	.5865
17. Book accessioning routine.									
18. Write sourcing information.									
19. Prepare gift record form.									
20. Book distribution routine.	X					0.301	2	.0364	.0110
21. Prepare receiving report.									
22. Prepare vendor invoices for payment.			X	X	X	0.533	6	.0531	.0283
23.1 Keypunch expenditures.	X					0.232	3	.0404	.0094
23.2 Verifying expenditures.	X					0.133	3	.0404	.0054

Figure 2.12 (Continued)
LABOR (L)
Unit Cost Calculation for C.A.L.B.P.C. Activities

Acquisitions

Code / Activity Description	Cataloging Class									Standard Time	f Category of Worker	g Wage/ Minute	h Cost of Activity
	1 Basic	2 Pro-rated	3 Mass cat. with ini-tial copy avail		4 Mass cat. no ini-tial copy avail		5 Original Cat.						
			O	Pur	O	Pur	O	Pur					
24. Clear in-process file.	X								0.468	1	.0262	.0123
25. File forms, etc., in completed records or discard.	X								0.600	1	.0262	.0157
26. Requestor notification routine.												
27. Periodic accessions list routine.												
28. Vendor status routine.		X							1.669	3	.0404	.0674
29. Claims routine.		X							5.303	3	.0404	.2142
30. Cancellations routine.		X							3.167	3	.0404	.1279
31. Out-of-print order routine.												
32. Process inquiries.		X							16.587	6	.0531	.8808
33. General typing — correspondence, etc. (specify).												
34. General revision (specify).												
35.1 Sorting tab cards.	X								0.021	2	.0364	.0008
35.2 Prepare a computer run.	X								0.007	3	.0404	.0003
35.3 Check in computer run.	X								0.108	3	.0404	.0044
35.4 Keypunch title changes.	X								3.331	3	.0404	.1346
36. Bi-monthly accounting reports to members.												

Figure 2.12 (Continued)

LABOR (L)

Unit Cost Calculation for Technical Processing Activities

Cataloging

Code	Activity Description	1 Basic	2 Pro-rated	3 Mass cat. with initial copy avail. O	3 Pur	4 Mass cat. no initial copy avail. O	4 Pur	5 Original Cat. O	5 Pur	Standard Time	Category of Worker	Wage/Minute	Cost of Activity
37.	Sort books, assign and distribute.	X								7.591	6	.0531	.4031
38.	Search for LC copy; verify bibliographic information.				X				X	1.453	6	.0531	.0772
39.1	Advanced card production: C. U. instruction slips.									0.709	2	.0364	.0258
39.2	Advanced card production: member library instruction slips.			X	X					1.547	6	.0531	.0821
40.	Receive and arrange LC cards.												
41.1	Receive and arrange LC proof slips or proof sheets.	X								0.278	1	.0262	.0073
41.2	Stamp date and destination code on verso of master cards.	X								0.162	2	.0364	.0059
42.	File LC copy. (cards or proof)	X								0.415	1	.0262	.0109
43.	Match LC cards or proof copy and books.			X	X			X	X	0.493	2	.0364	.0179
44.	Added copies/added volumes routine.			X	X					0.601	5	.0490	.0294
45.	Catalog and classify with LC cards/copy.					X	X			2.343	6	.0531	.1244
46.	Original cataloging and classifying.							X	X	22.879	8	.0884	2.0225
47.	Shelf Listing (for 44, 45, and 46).												

Figure 2.12 (Continued)
LABOR (L)
Unit Cost Calculation for Technical Processing Activities

Cataloging

Code	Activity Description	1 Basic	2 Pro-rated	3 Mass cat with initial copy avail. O / Pur	4 Mass cat no initial copy avail. O / Pur	5 Original Cat. O / Pur	Standard Time	f Category of Worker	g Wage/Minute	h Cost of Activity
48.	Type complete card sets.									
49.	Type master card.					X X	2.273	2	.0364	.0827
50.	Revise master card.					X X	0.439	4	.0462	.0203
51.	Type modification on a card or proof slip.	X					0.251	2	.0364	.0091
52.1	Reproduce cards sets (other than typing). Sort cards into sets.	X					2.419	3	.0404	.0977
52.2	Sort card sets by member or departmental library & stamp location code on each card.	X					1.558	2	.0364	.0567
53.	Type call number, added entries.	X					1.273	2	.0364	.0463
54.	Revise typing on card sets.	X					0.778	4	.0462	.0359
55.	Prepare authority cards.		X				1.725	2	.0364	.0628
56.	Prepare cross-reference cards.		X				2.678	2	.0364	.0975
57.	Prepare circulation card.									
58.	Prepare book pocket.									
59.	Apply date due slip and spine label.	X					0.928	1	.0262	.0243
60.1	Match label sets and invoices to books.	X					0.662	2	.0364	.0241
60.2	Burst label sets and affix pockets.	X					1.196	1	.0262	.0313

Figure 2.12 (Continued)
LABOR (L)
Unit Cost Calculation for Technical Processing Activities

Cataloging

Code	Activity Description	Cataloging Class											Standard Time	Category of Worker	Wage/ Minute	Cost of Activity
		1 Basic	2 Pro-rated	3 Mass cat. with initial copy avail.		4 Mass cat. no initial copy avail.		5 Original Cat.						f	g	h
				O	Pur	O	Pur	O	Pur							
60.3	Inspect pockets and remove flags.	X											0.453	1	.0262	.0119
61.	Affix biographical and review material in book.															
62.	Stamp property marks.															
63.	Affix plastic jacket to book.															
64.	Paperback books — in house binding routine.												3.867	3	.0404	.1562
65.	Revise completed books before forwarding.	X											0.216	3	.0404	.0087
66.	Sort and alphabetize shelf list and all catalog cards.															
67.	File shelf list and all catalog cards.															
68.	Revise filing of shelf list and all catalog cards.															
69.	Route card sets to departmental or member libraries.	X											0.678	2	.0364	.0247
70.	Paperback books — bindery routine (preparation).												4.224	3	.0404	.1706
71.	Paperback books — bindery routine (receiving).												1.114	3	.0404	.0450
72.	Catalog maintenance (Other than filing).															
73.	General typing (specify).															
74.	General revision (specify).															

Figure 2.12 (Continued)

LABOR (L)

Unit Cost Calculation for Technical Processing Activities

Cataloging Code / Activity Description	Cataloging Class					Standard Time	Category of Worker (f)	Wage/ Minute (g)	Cost of Activity (h)
	1 Basic	2 Pro-rated	3 Mass cat. with initial copy avail. (O Pur)	4 Mass cat. no initial copy avail. (O Pur)	5 Original Cat. (O Pur)				
75. General filing (specify).									
76. Other cataloging activities not listed above (specify).									
77.1 Distribution of books to pre-keypunch staging area.	X					0.087	4	.0462	.0040
77.2 Keypunch SILO cards.	X					0.681	3	.0404	.0275
77.3 SILO error routine.	X					1.511	2,4,7	.0512*	.0774
78. Arrange books by library.	X					0.390	1	.0262	.0102
79. Invoice/shipping list production.									
80. Billing.									
81.1 Pack member library books.	X					0.334	4	.0462	.0154
81.2 Inspect shipments and mail out.									
82. Union catalog (arrange and file).	X					0.703	2	.0364	.0256
83. Bibliographic Center notification									
Total	1.6323	2.0371	a	b c d	e f				

a – .1765
b – .4607
c – .2666
d – .5791
e – 2.2677
f – 2.5802

* Average of the three wage rates.

In Figure 2.12 each activity was identified according to cataloging class. Standard times and unit costs were then summed for each class.

The exception labor activities without regard to frequency totaled $2.04. This charge would be inappropriate to apply to any given book because these activities occur infrequently. To arrive at a just charge for these "labor overhead" items, the unit cost, including frequency, was transferred from Figure 2.7 and summed in Figure A2.43. The prorated charge of $.0398 was carried forward to the Labor Fee Schedule as Class 2.

The total standard processing time for Classes 3-6 are the basic time (Class 1) plus the time of any of the other selected classes. Class 2 was omitted from the time summation. The total unit cost of any class includes those of the basic (Class 1), a prorated Class 2 plus one of the Classes in the 3-5 series, plus Class 6 (type of binding), if applicable.

On Figure 2.14 the Recommended Processing Fees incorporate the unit labor charge from Figure 2.13 plus supplies, overhead, and transportation charges. The binding charge would be additional to any of the Class 1-5 total charges.

One additional cost to those libraries utilizing the Interlibrary Loan Courier would be the shipping charge. Based on $1.00 per box and an average of 20 books per box, the cost is $.05. Fourth class insured mail was used for Adams State part of the time and a trucking firm part of the time during Phase III.

The libraries belonging to the Courier System pay their shipping charges incurred by CALBPC participation directly to C.S.U., which administers the courier system, only once per year (September for the previous fiscal year). The method of prorating is now in the process of change. The cost of $.05 per book is at best an estimate and will have to be revised next September.

Mailings to libraries not members of the courier were facilitated by the use of a blanket university-wide insurance policy. This policy was dropped, however, because so few claims were ever levied against it. It has not been decided whether the Center will take out a policy covering its own mailings.

It is interesting to note that fees for Cataloging Classes 3b, 4b, and 5b are significantly higher than for Classes 3a, 4a, and 5a. The reason is that purchasing and processing as opposed to processing only includes several extra activities, such as #1, the initial mail sort; #6, assigning a vendor; #9, mailing purchase requests; and #22, preparing vender invoices for payment. In short, the procurement steps are an integral part of the fee computation in the purchase and process class and inevitably increase the cost.

The Importance of Frequency Data to the Understanding of Cost Calculations -- The first unit labor cost was computed with careful consideration to the frequency of occurrence of each task within the CALBPC system. In order that the activities be weighted by their relative importance to the overall operation, each standard time was multiplied by the percentage (expressed in a decimal fraction) of real time in which the activity is likely to occur.

For instance, according to Figure 2.7, Activity #1, "open, sort and distribute mail," occurs 52.9% of the time; that is, 52.9% of the volume load handled by the Center involves this activity. Consequently, the standard time of .393 minutes is proportioned to .208 minutes with a resulting unit cost of $.0076. If the frequency had not been used as a factor, the time would have remained .393 minutes and the cost would have been $.0143, as shown in Figure A2.42, an increase in cost of $.0067. A more startling example is #46, original cataloging, which is reported in Figure 2.7 as having a standard time of 22.87 minutes and a frequency of 11.3% in the system. The proportioned time is reduced to 2.585, therefore resulting in a unit cost of $.228. With the frequency factor omitted, the cost increased to $2.00--a difference of $1.79.

Of course, if a book received original cataloging, that special activity has to be paid for. The frequency proportioning or "modeling" in Figure 2.7 is useful as an administrative conception or model of the total operation, but not useful as a

Figure 2.13

LABOR FEE SCHEDULE FOR MEMBER LIBRARIES

Cataloging Class	Standard Time	Unit Cost	Total Time (Class 1[+])	Fee Schedule (Class 1 & 2[+])
1. Basic	37.163	1.63		
2. Prorated tasks	42.175	.04		
3. Mass cataloging with copy				
a. Processing only	3.936	.18	41.099	1.85
b. Purchasing and processing	12.135	.49	49.298	2.16
4. Mass cataloging without copy				
a. Processing only	5.584	.27	42.747	1.94
b. Purchasing and processing	13.783	.58	50.946	2.25
5. Original cataloging				
a. Processing only	28.832	2.27	65.995	3.94
b. Purchasing and processing	37.031	2.58	74.194	4.25
6. Binding				
a. In-house (Activity #66)	3.867	.16		
b. Commercial (Activities #71 and 72)	5.338	.22		

Figure 2.14

RECOMMENDED PROCESSING FEES
BY CATALOGING CLASS

Labor	Total *	Supplies	Overhead	Transportation	Binding	Total Fee
Uniform charges		.12	.32	.05	optional	
1. Basic	1.63					
2. Prorated tasks	.04					
Class charges						
3. Mass cataloging with copy						
a. Processing only	.18					2.34
b. Purchasing and processing	.49					2.65
(1.85 / 2.16)	1.85 / 2.16					
4. Mass cataloging without copy						
a. Processing only	.27	1.94				2.43
b. Purchasing and processing	.58	2.25				2.74
5. Original cataloging						
a. Processing only	2.27	3.94				4.43
b. Purchasing and processing	2.58	4.25				4.74
6. Binding						
a. In-house (Activity #66)	.16				1.25	1.41
b. Commercial (Activity #71 and 72)	.22				1) 1.25 2) 2.35	1.47 2.57
Shipping/Postal charges						.05

* Class charge plus basic and prorated charges

1) Permabinding   2) Scholarly binding

Figure 2.15

SUMMARY OF CHANGES IN UNIT LABOR COST
(Minimum Change Reported: Five Cents)

Code	Activity Description	Between CU-1967 and CALBPC 1969: Amount Increased or Decreased	Reason	Between CALBPC 1967 and CALBPC 1967: Amount Increased or Decreased	Reason
6.	Assign vendor	-.52	c		
11.	File forms in appropriate files.	-.46	a	-.06	e
13.	Unpack books.	+.07	d		
22.	Prepare vendor invoices for payment.			-.45	b,c
25.	File forms, etc., in completed records or discard.			-.20	b
34.	General revision (specify)	-.31	a		
37.	Sort books, assign and distribute.	+.13	d	+.40	f
38.	Search for LC copy; verify bibliographic information.	-.07	c		
43.	Match LC cards or proof copy and books.	-.09	a,c		
44.	Added copies/added volumes routine.	-.19	a		
45.	Catalog and classify with LC cards/copy.	-.08	a,c	+.06	d
46.	Original cataloging and classifying.	-.23	a,c		
47.	Shelf listing (for 44, 45, and 46).	-.15	a		

Figure 2.15 (Continued)

SUMMARY OF CHANGES IN UNIT LABOR COST
(Minimum Change Reported: Five Cents)

Code	Activity Description	Between CU-1967 and CALBPC 1969 Amount Increased or Decreased	Reason	Between CALBPC-1967 and CALBPC 1967 Amount Increased or Decreased	Reason
49.	Type master card.	-.06	a		
52.	Reproduce card sets.	-.15	e		
53.	Type call number, added entries.			-.18	e
55.	Prepare authority cards.			-.06	a,b
56.	Prepare cross-reference cards.			-.10	a,b
59.	Apply date due slip and spine label.	-.08	e		
66.	Sort and alphabetize shelf list and all catalog cards.	-.25	a,b		
68.	Revise filing of shelf list and all catalog cards.	-.11	a,b		

	Reasons	a b c d e		a b c d e	
	Times used	10 2 5 2 2		2 4 0 1 3	

basis for determining fees for work actually performed on each volume when accounted for
separately.   Hence, Figure A2.42 becomes the
reference for a third table (Figure 2.12) for calculating labor cost by cataloging class or type of
product handled.

Unit Cost Changes -- Between the Phase I-
II simulated cost analysis and that of Phase III,
there was an important decrease in the labor
cost--from $2.35 to $1.88, or a difference of
$.47 per volume.   Supplies also decreased in
cost from $.29 to $.12 per volume, probably
due to the fact that the C.U. supplies figure was
used in the CALBPC simulation.   C.U. supplies
would include items used in that library generally,
not just in the processing of CALBPC specification
items.   Binding increased from $.09 to $.26, re-
flecting an increase not only in the cost of these
services, but an increase in the publication of
titles in paperback form.

The overall unit labor cost for C.U. (1967),
CALBPC Simulated (1967), and CALBPC Phase III
(1969) totaled $3.57, $2.35, and $1.88 respective-
ly.   Because C.U. is the host institution for the
Center and because labor is the most important
single factor in cost, the investigator prepared a
unit cost comparison chart (Figure A2.44) to
analyze the reasons for the increase or decrease
in cost of activities which had changed by at least
five cents between the first study (C.U.) and the
third study (Phase III).   Also analyzed were
changes occurring between the second study
(CALBPC Simulated) and the third study.   The
results of this analysis are summarized in Figure
2.15.

The reason for a sizeable reduction in labor
cost at C.U. between Phase I and Phase III is primarily due to the report of non-specification activities, i.e., monographic serials, microforms,
etc., and frequencies on C.U.'s chart in the first
study.   A second reason is simplification of certain tasks due to strict adherence to the CALBPC
specifications.

As to changes between the simulated labor

chart of Phase I for the Center and the Phase III
chart, the most important reason is that parts of
the activity are actually being performed locally.
This means that the simulated labor chart erred in
design in these cases.   Almost as important is the
change due to simplification of the manual procedures in Phase III or a conversion of them to
a machine function.

The labor cost comparison chart demon-
strates that the Center in actual operation followed the basic path predicted in Phase I-II, both
in the manually calculated "simulated cost analysis"
and in the mathematical model.[13, 14]

The predicted overall unit cost by the manual
calculation based on 1967 figures was $3.10,
whereas the mathematical model total was $2.96
at an operating level of 130,000 volumes.   The
mathematical model predicted $2.69 as the unit
cost between the 69 and 92K volume levels.   The
cost analysis of Phase III totaled $2.63 based on a
volume level of 81,000 in 1969.   Therefore, the
unit cost of $2.63 for Phase III supports the
hypothesis that as the volume level increases, the
unit cost decreases.

As both the Center and its member libraries
become more efficient in their participation in
centralized processing and the volume level increases, it is reasonable to have confidence in the
cost predictions of the math model used in the
Phase I-II.[15]   The result of the cost analysis of
Phase III is a very positive endorsement of
CALBPC as a cost beneficial alternative to
strictly local processing in Colorado.

Estimated Unit Savings via Centralized
Processing -- Taking the 1967 member library unit
cost figures plus $2.63 as the weighted unit cost
per volume at the Center during 1969, the investigator estimated the unit savings to member libraries in their use of centralized processing.   As
indicated in Figure 2.16, the 1967 amounts were
increased by ten percent to reflect the rise in the
cost of living.   Column e shows a range in unit
savings from $.14 for Library 4 to $5.13 for Library 3, with an average savings of $2.09.

Figure 2.16

ESTIMATED UNIT SAVINGS TO MEMBER LIBRARIES THROUGH
THE USE OF CENTRALIZED PROCESSING

Library	Unit Cost of Functions Retained by Library in 1967*	Estimated Unit Cost in 1969 Using a 10% Cost of Living Increase	Use of CALBPC (c) Unit Cost in 1969 Plus CALBPC's Unit Cost of 2.630 (b)	Unit Cost of Local System in 1967*	Unit Cost of Local System in 1969 Using a Cost of Living Increase of 10%	Unit Savings Via Use of CALBPC
		a	a + b = c		d	d - c = e
1	.513	.564	3.194	3.550	3.905	0.71
2	.677	.745	3.375	5.870	6.457	3.08
3	.658	.724	3.354	7.710	8.481	5.13
4	.922	1.114	3.744	3.530	3.883	0.14
5	.230	.253	2.883	4.160	4.576	1.69
6	.484	.532	3.162	4.490	4.939	1.78

X = 2.09

*Figures cited from Leonard, ibid., p. 14.

Many of the new members of the Center are small volume level participants, as was Library 3 during Phase III; therefore, it seemed reasonable to include $5.13 in computing the average of estimated savings per volume processed through the Center.

Notes

1. Lawrence E. Leonard, Joan M. Maier, Richard M. Dougherty, Centralized Book Processing (Metuchen, N.J.: Scarecrow Press, 1969), p. 27.

2. The universe of titles analyzed for imprint date was 23,440; the random sample size was 2,441.

3. Leonard, ibid., p. 244-5.

4. Ibid.

5. The slight difference in the data in Figures A2.11 and A2.12 was caused by the fact that the data in Figure A2.11 includes books ordered beginning February 1, 1969; whereas the data in Figure A2.12 includes 5,000 items ordered between January 22-31, 1969.

6. Ibid., Figure 2.8.

7. Ibid., p. 32. (The data cited in this figure were based on the data collected in the Phase I-II studies. The methodologies used in both studies were the same.)

8. George A. Ferguson, Statistical Analysis in Psychology and Education 2nd ed. (New York: McGraw-Hill, 1966), p. 145.

9. The language analysis refers to the language of the text. Western European refers to those countries in the NATO alliance except for the Scandinavian countries. Eastern Europe refers to the Iron Curtain countries including Russia. The Orient includes Near East countries such as Turkey and Arabia as well as China, Japan, and the Phillipines. Examples of other languages are African dialects, Polynesian, Eskimo, etc.

10. Richard M. Dougherty, "The Colorado Academic Library Book Processing Center: Immediate Prospects and Problems," The Colorado Academic Library 5:2 (Spring, 1969), p. 3-8.

11. Henry Voos, "Standard Times for Certain Clerical Activities in Technical Processing," Ph.D. Thesis, Rutgers, The State University, New Brunswick, New Jersey (1964), p. 94.

12. Richard M. Dougherty and Fred J. Heinritz, Scientific Management of Library Operations (New York: Scarecrow Press, 1966), p. 113.

13. Leonard, Centralized Book Processing, p. 134-8.

14. Ibid., p. 206-7.

15. Ibid.

Chapter III

DESCRIPTION AND EVALUATION OF THE PROCESSING SYSTEM COMPONENTS

The Accounting Subsystem

Before the Center could begin operations, a multi-purpose accounting/reporting system had to be designed, programmed, and field tested. Even under normal conditions, this was not a simple job; but these were not normal times at the Center. CALBPC had been without the services of a systems analyst since February, 1968. The new incumbent did not assume his duties until October, 1968.

His first job, with little more than a day or two of reflection, was to begin work on the accounting project. The system was to be operable by the beginning of January, 1969. This was an impossible goal in light of the manpower resources available to the Center. Consequently, the Center purchased programming support from the University of Colorado's Administrative Systems Department. In all, four programmers worked on the design and programming of the system, three of whom had no previous library experience, but fortunately, one of the four had extensive knowledge of the requirements of a business accounting system. In spite of the severe time constraints, the first run was completed on January 2, 1969.[1]

The accounting subsystem was designed to perform a variety of functions. (See Figure 3.1 for an overview of the system) Most importantly, the system performed the traditional bookkeeping functions of recording encumbrances, expenditures, and free balances. To accomplish these tasks, two major records were created. The first was termed "School Update." (5) This record contains a summary of accounting information for each school arranged by fund and account. An example of a School-Update report is shown in Figure 3.2. One feature of the software package was that it permitted a school to overencumber a fund up to a pre-agreed upon percentage. That is, if a library wished to continue ordering materials even though the total encumbrances produced a minus free balance, this was possible. Some schools did not choose to use this feature, but others found it beneficial since ten to fifteen percent of the titles ordered were not received during the current fiscal year, or not received at all. This feature provides additional flexibility to the system. However, the School-Update software will not permit an overexpenditure in a fund. A "fund" refers to a library departmental allocation, i.e., history, anthropology, English, mathematics, etc. An "account" is the term used by the University to designate a legally established fund. For example, the history, English, anthropology funds are all part of account 3201-01-03. Readers should keep in mind the distinction between an account and a fund. For the failure of the system designers to distinguish between this seemingly innocuous difference served to illustrate the importance of involving users in the design of automated systems. We will return to this problem later in the chapter.

The second major program was termed "Book Update." This file records individual transactions arranged by fund within each school. (See Figure 3.3) The Book Update data are used in conjunction with the shipping, invoice, labeling, software (SILO) to generate book cards, book pockets, and spine label sets. The Book Update data can also be used to list orders reported delayed or cancelled by vendors. Since the Book Update record includes vendor information as well as the date of order, claims can be generated also as a by-product. Programs were written to maintain a vendor code address file; however, this routine has not yet been used. (5, 8)

Figure 3.1

CALBPC System Overview

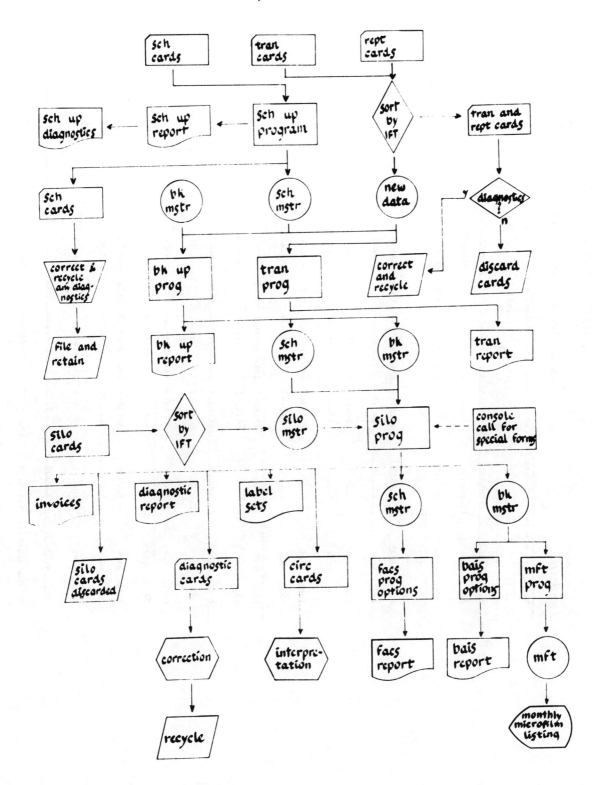

Figure 3.2

SCHOOL MASTER LISTING

03/17/70	SCHOOL MASTER LISTING								PAGE 19
SCHOOL	BINDING BUD	BINDING EXP	PROCESS BUD	PROCESS EXP	LOCAL BUD	LOCAL ENC	LOCAL EXP	LOCAL BAL	COMBINED BAL
STATE	403.25	128.95	5,191.40	2,437.30	0.00	0.00	0.00	0.00	14,542.27

FUND NAME	BUDGET	EXPENSES	ENCUMBRANCES	FREE BALANCE
500 LIB-G	12,228.59	11,823.87	1,249.00	844.28-
FUND NAME	BUDGET	EXPENSES	ENCUMBRANCES	FREE BALANCE
510 BIO-S	900.00	670.93	143.13	85.94
FUND NAME	BUDGET	EXPENSES	ENCUMBRANCES	FREE BALANCE
520 ENG	700.00	262.36	320.36	116.34
FUND NAME	BUDGET	EXPENSES	ENCUMBRANCES	FREE BALANCE
530 FASCI	666.50	436.46	290.47	60.93-
FUND NAME	BUDGET	EXPENSES	ENCUMBRANCES	FREE BALANCE
540 HUM	600.00	193.97	449.30	43.27-
FUND NAME	BUDGET	EXPENSES	ENCUMBRANCES	FREE BALANCE
550 PHSCI	700.00	379.22	347.64	26.86-
FUND NAME	BUDGET	EXPENSES	ENCUMBRANCES	FREE BALANCE
560 REF	1,490.00	16.19	44.50	1,341.31
FUND NAME	BUDGET	EXPENSES	ENCUMBRANCES	FREE BALANCE
570 SOC-S	7,530.00	1,215.28	2,277.18	4,037.54
FUND NAME	BUDGET	EXPENSES	ENCUMBRANCES	FREE BALANCE
580 AELON	1,490.00	113.50	168.59	1,117.91
FUND NAME	BUDGET	EXPENSES	ENCUMBRANCES	FREE BALANCE
590 EL	500.00	0.03	441.50	58.50
SCHOOL TOTAL	26,624.59	15,110.72	5,731.67	5,782.20

Figure 3.3

BOOK UPDATE SUMMARY

03/17/70

BOOK UPDATE SUMMARY

FUND	FD NME	FD PER	FD BK BUD	FD BK EXP	FD BK ENC	FD BK BAL	SCHOOL BUD	SCHOOL EXP	SCHOOL ENC	SCHOOL BAL
170	GEOG	200	135.84	44.04	90.00	137.64	1,179,442.76	843,233.64	143,137.63	336,209.12
172	GEOL	200	5,491.33	1,324.47	3,219.03	6,439.16	1,179,442.76	843,264.14	143,731.10	336,178.62
176	HARR	200	5,000.00	3,526.84		6,473.16	1,179,442.76	843,264.14	143,731.10	336,178.62
180	HIST	500	6,971.44	7,931.69	6,491.21	30,434.30	1,179,442.76	343,264.14	143,872.40	336,178.62
202	HUM	200	199.48	199.48		199.49	1,179,442.76	843,264.14	143,872.40	336,178.62
205	IAR	500	14.09	11.03	11.19	51.23	1,179,442.76	843,264.14	143,872.40	336,178.62
206	JCUR	200	301.46	276.96	24.50	301.46	1,179,442.76	843,264.14	143,872.40	336,178.62
210	LW/S	200	60,000.00	58,024.39		61,975.61	1,179,442.76	843,926.11	143,872.40	335,516.65
211	LING	200	307.34	280.71	32.50	301.47	1,179,442.76	843,926.11	143,872.40	335,516.65
212	LIT	200	16,443.05	11,501.51	3,923.20	17,461.39	1,179,442.76	844,064.78	143,748.53	335,377.98
218	MATH	200	5,093.47	3,242.40	2,267.35	4,677.19	1,179,442.76	844,081.43	143,918.02	335,361.33
220	MC&D	200	77.75	52.75	25.00	77.75	1,179,442.76	844,081.43	143,918.02	335,361.33
230	ML/F	500	500.75	427.64	308.46	1,767.65	1,179,442.76	844,081.43	143,918.02	335,361.33
232	ML/G	500	33,595.15	22,258.20	21,974.57	123,742.98	1,179,442.76	844,293.72	143,776.63	335,149.04
236	ML/I	200	1,458.53	339.72	1,117.25	1,460.09	1,179,442.76	844,293.72	143,776.63	335,149.04
238	ML/O	200	71.05	43.55	32.50	66.05	1,179,442.76	844,293.72	143,781.63	335,149.04
240	ML/R	200	236.47	192.74	40.23	239.97	1,179,442.76	844,293.72	143,781.63	335,149.04
244	ML/S	500	1,477.82	1,431.26	223.81	5,734.03	1,179,442.76	844,293.72	143,781.63	335,149.04
250	MUSM	200	2,083.77	1,456.89	830.22	1,880.43	1,179,442.76	844,293.72	143,794.88	335,149.04
252	MSIC	200	12,032.44	6,507.56	3,641.43	11,915.45	1,179,442.76	844,300.28	143,793.13	335,142.48
253	MR	200	1,110.77	427.18	89.84	1,704.52	1,179,442.76	844,300.28	143,793.13	335,142.48
255	NJC	500	3.25		3.25	13.00	1,179,442.76	844,300.28	143,793.13	335,142.48
260	PHAR	200	108.27	33.77	74.50	108.27	1,179,442.76	844,300.28	143,793.13	335,142.48
262	PHIL	200	61.25	61.25		61.25	1,179,442.76	844,300.28	143,793.13	335,142.48
264	PE/M	200	1.45	1.45		1.45	1,179,442.76	844,300.28	143,793.13	335,142.48
266	PE/W	200	9.25	6.25	3.00	9.25	1,179,442.76	844,300.28	143,793.13	335,142.48
268	PHYS	200	325.23	296.68	26.55	325.23	1,179,442.76	844,300.28	143,793.13	335,142.48

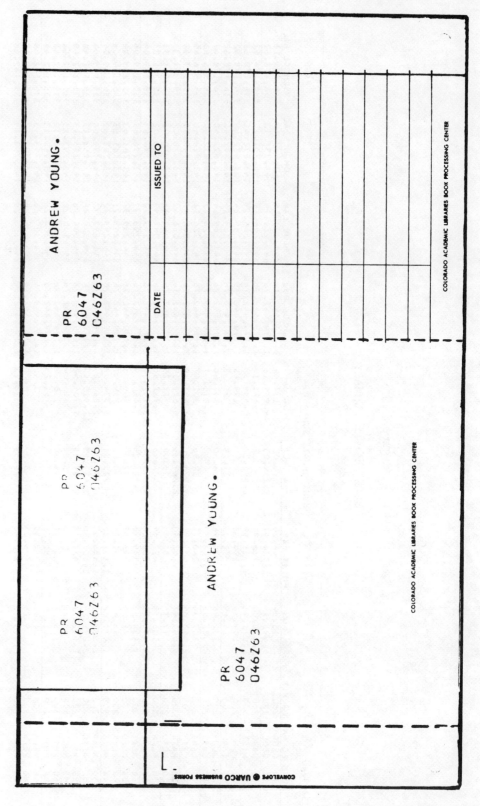

Figure 3.4

CIRCULATION CARD/POCKET/LABEL SET
(Original Form)

Figure 3.5

REVISED CIRCULATION CARD WITH MATCHING POCKET/LABEL SET

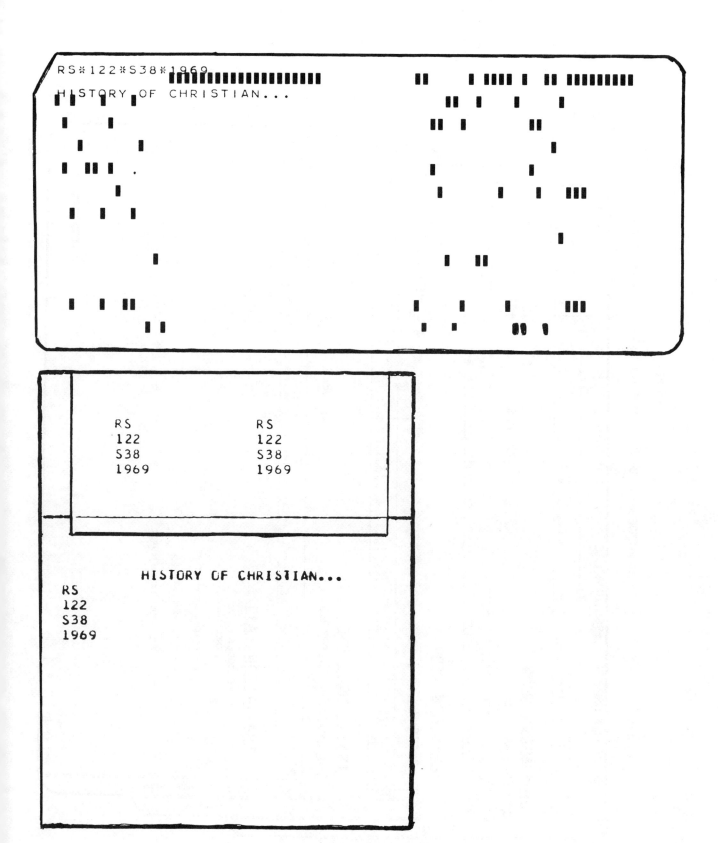

Figure 3.6

TRANSACTION CARD USED IN FOUR TYPES OF EXPENDITURES

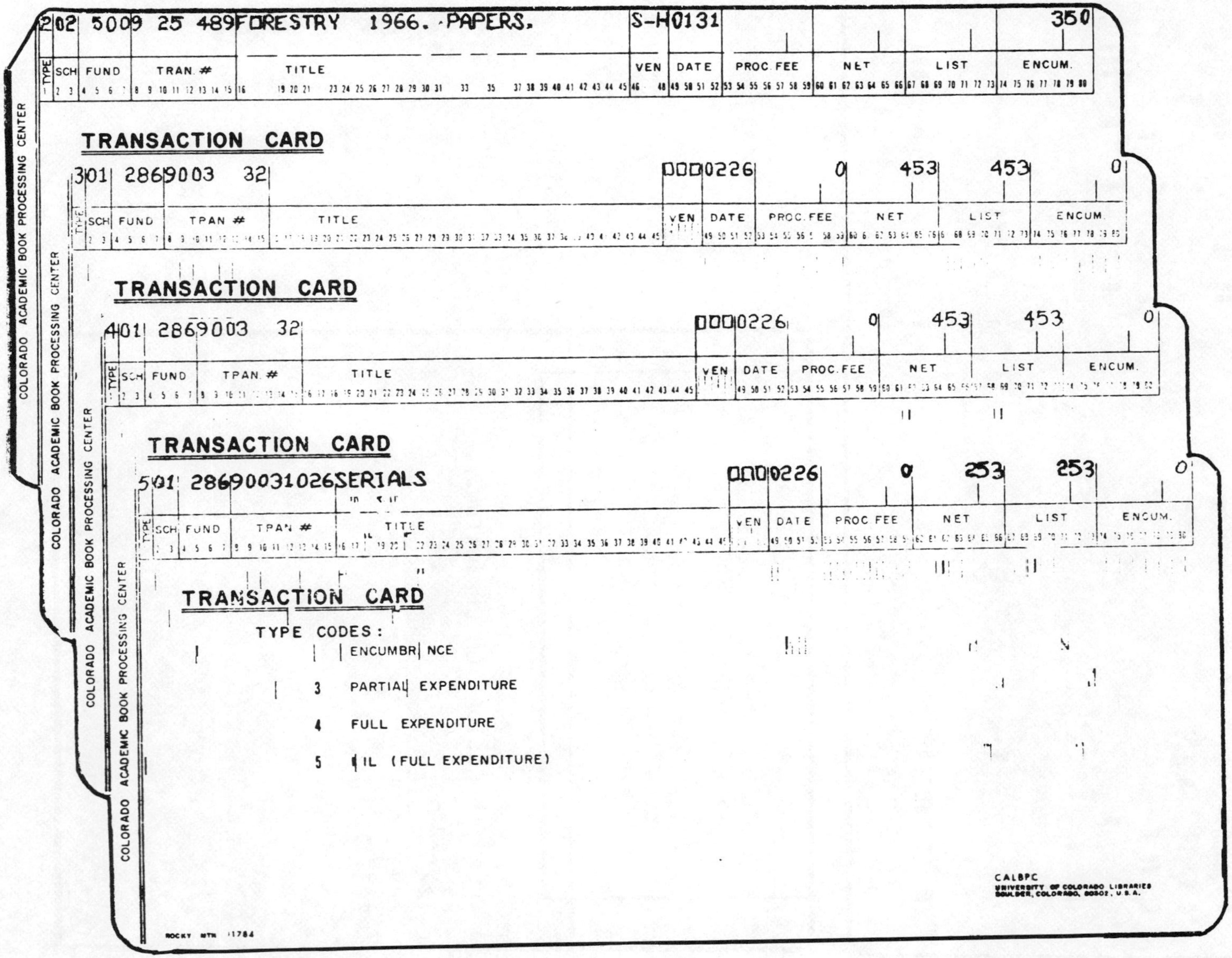

Sample of Partial expenditure

Sample of a full expenditure

Sample of Nil

Figure 3.7

THE REPORT CARD: SAMPLE FUNCTIONS

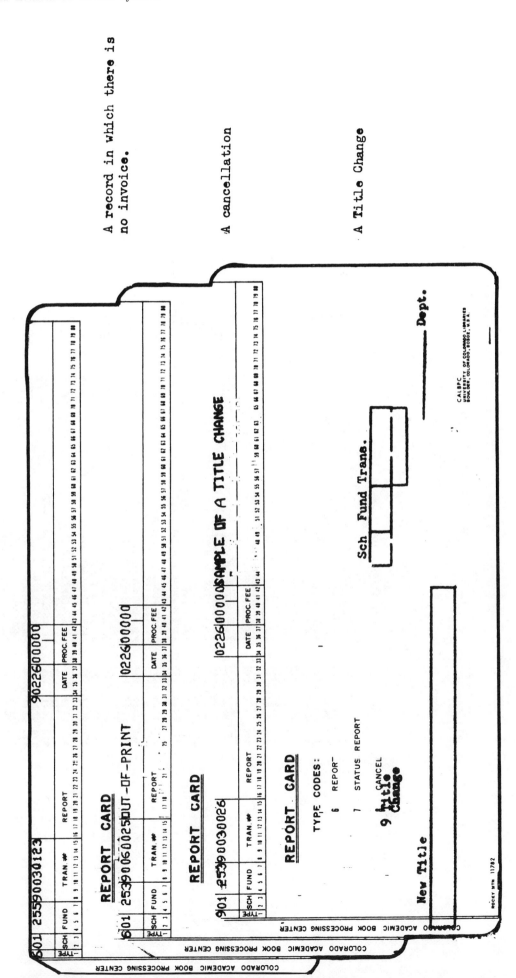

Figure 3.8

INVOICE/SHIPPING DOCUMENT

COLORADO ACADEMIC LIBRARIES BOOK PROCESSING CENTER

INVOICE   INVOICE DATE   03/17/70   PAGE 1

COLORADO STATE UNIVERSITY   (02)

TRANS NO	TITLE IDENTIFICATION	LIST	NET	PROC CHG	BIND
500 C072 1C11	CRPRCCFEE-HUSBANCKY...	.00	.00	2.15-	.00
500 9C22 C551	EASTER SEAL GUIDE TO SPECIAL	1.50	1.50	.00	2.35
500 9C52 0C37	HOW TO USE THE THREE-POINT REV	3.95	3.95	.00	2.35
500 9C55 0172	PROCEEDINGS.	11.00	11.00	.00	.00
500 9C63 05C1	JEFFERSONIAN DEMOCRACY	.00	1.31	.00	.00
500 9C85 0559	CONCERNING THE ART OF	.00	.78	.00	.00
500 9093 C1C6	LA DEMOGRAFIA Y LOS	.00	2.00	.00	2.35
500 9146 0316	LE VOYAGE DU ORIENT	3.10	3.10	.00	2.35
500 9196 1289	SMALLWOOD.	.00	.00	.00	.00
500 9157 1079	COMPORTEMENT DES PILIEUX	.00	.00	.00	.00
500 9159 1C51	VVVINVVE	.00	.00	.00	.00
500 9237 1249	BOOKS AND PUBLISHING	.00	.00	.00	.00
500 9323 CC64	DICTIONARY OF GREEK...	125.00	125.00	1.85	.00
500 9323 0084	DICTIONARY OF GREEK...	.0C	.00	.00	.00
500 9323 0C84	DICTIONARY OF GREEK...	.00	.00	.00	.00
500 9323 0182	EASTERN ELEMENTS...	.00	15.39	1.85	.00
510 9310 G03b	OPERATIVE TECHNIC IN GENERAL	22.00	18.70	2.35	.0C
520 9311 C145	EXPLANATORY HANDBOOK...	.00	2.40	3.95	.00
530 CC09 CCC5	PSYCHOPHYSIOLOGIE.2	14.50	14.50	2.35	.00
530 C028 C037	PLANG PUXGX CV IFFZOL	18.00	18.00	3.95	.00
540 0C21 0014	FRANKFURTER...	4.95	4.95	1.85	.00
540 CC27 C188	RICHARD STRAUSS...	7.50	7.50	2.35	.00
540 0C27 C194	RUSSINE E SAGGI...	9.65	9.65	2.35	.00
540 9351 0279	THE CUISIDER	1.25	1.00	1.85	.00
540 9351 C297	BRONZEVILLE BOYS...	3.95	2.45	1.85	.00
540 9351 G335	GIOVANNI'S ROOM	4.50	3.00	1.85	.00
550 0C37 C441	INTRO TO ORGANIC...	9.95	8.95	2.35	.00
550 0C37 C442	INTRO TO THE STRUCTURE	16.50	14.85	1.85	.00
570 0C09 0015	EINE VERPASSTE...	1.45	1.45	2.35	2.35
570 0C21 CC21	BEGEGNUNG EUROPAS...	10.25	10.25	2.35	.0C
570 0C21 0C24	GESCHICHTE DES DEUTSCHEN	6.20	6.20	2.35	.00
570 0C27 0187	RICHTLINIEN...	1.45	1.45	1.85	.00
570 9311 0220	FOUNDING OF THE ROMAN EMPIRE	5.00	4.40	3.95	.00
570 9326 0494	ENGLISH CHAIRS	.00	2.24	3.95	2.35
570 9329 0247	SWORDS AGAINST CARTHAGE	4.50	3.96	1.85	.00
570 9354 0053	POLITISCHER RADIKALISMUS	1.70	1.70	2.35	2.35

LIST, NET, PROC CHARGES FOR BELOW IFT WILL APPEAR WHEN THE ORDER IS FULLY EXPENDED.

590 0028 0129	LECTURA EN VOZ ALTA	.00	.00	.00	.00

LIST, NET, PROC CHARGES FOR BELOW IFT WILL APPEAR WHEN THE ORDER IS FULLY EXPENDED.

590 0028 0167	AMOR Y EXTASIS	.00	.00	.00	.00

		SUB 287.85	301.63	51.50	16.45

TOTAL   369.58

Figure 3.9

DIAGNOSTIC CODES 10/2/69

message	reason
code 1	Blank IFT (Institution-Fund-Transaction) number or not a valid school code 01-06.
code 2	Missing message or date on cancel card.
code 3	Missing message or date on message card.
code 4	Invalid type code.
code 5	One a type 3, 4, 5 no net expense.
code 6	On a type 2 empty data field.
code 7	On a type 5 empty data field or net field.
code 8	Duplicate card.
code 9	Card sequence error.
code 10	Book Master out of sequence, program stopped; action resequence tape.
code 11	Invalid card in the add routine BKMCTHLI.
code 12	Trying to add with BLDSW on.
code 13	Invalid fund on Add record.
code 14	School Master out of sequence.
code 15	Cards out of sequence; program stopped; action resequence tape.
code 16	Processing budget exceeded.
code 17	Exceeding definition of (%), budget must be greater than encumbrances plus expenses.
code 18	Fund budget exceeded.
code 19	Invalid card type against a tap record.
code 20	Processing budget exceeded.
code 21	Trying to cancel something other than an encumbrance.
code 22	Exceeded processing budget.
code 23	Exceeded code 17 definition.
code 24	
code 25	Transaction against a cancelled record.
code 26	Within $10.00 of processing budget.
code 27	Within $10.00 of binding budget.
code 28	Within $10.00 of budget (fund).
code 29	Within $20.00 of budget (expenditure and encumbrance).
code 30	
code 31	Invalid card type against tape type 2.
code 32	Conversion NIL (not-in-ledger) with a match on the file.
code 33	Invalid fund on a card.

Figure 3.10

SILO CARDS WITH ERRORS

```
008  3609323020C   JC*73*M8*1968   00000012B   00000   ***
                   THIS DOCUMENT HAS NOT BEEN EXPENDED EITHER PARTIALLY OR FULLY

009  5509329014C   QM*81*K86       00000010B   00050   **
                   NON-EXISTENT IFT

009  5509329019T   F*19*F6B4       00000010B   00050   **
                   NON-EXISTENT IFT

009  5509329020B   G*91*M424       00000010B   00000   **
                   NON-EXISTENT IFT

009  5509338024B   BT*301*C6*1963  00000022T   00050
                   THIS DOCUMENT HAS NOT BEEN EXPENDED EITHER PARTIALLY OR FULLY

010  600000060123   BT*28*C65      000000211   00050   *
                   THIS DOCUMENT HAS NOT BEEN EXPENDED EITHER PARTIALLY OR FULLY

010  6000055119S   UPDATE*9363*0175   00000022S   00000
                   NON-EXISTENT IFT

010  6009275102T   JN*955*A62      001150220   00000   *
                   PROCESSING THIS DOCUMENT WOULD ILLEGALLY OVERDRAW THIS SCHOOLS BINDING BUDGET

010  6009275103S   JS*308*M65*1966   00235021T   00050   *
                   PROCESSING THIS DOCUMENT WOULD ILLEGALLY OVERDRAW THIS SCHOOLS BINDING BUDGET

010  600931010694   J0*161T*L3      00235021T   00050   *
                   PROCESSING THIS DOCUMENT WOULD ILLEGALLY OVERDRAW THIS SCHOOLS BINDING BUDGET

010  6009315025C   CT*103*C4*1969   000000211   00000   *
                   THIS DOCUMENT HAS NOT BEEN EXPENDED EITHER PARTIALLY OR FULLY

010  600931601T6   E*185.61*876    000000211   00050   *
                   THIS DOCUMENT HAS NOT BEEN EXPENDED EITHER PARTIALLY OR FULLY

010  600932300ST   GV*1002.8*Y3*1968   00000021T   00050   *
                   THIS DOCUMENT HAS NOT BEEN EXPENDED EITHER PARTIALLY OR FULLY
```

The SILO software produces book cards, book pockets, spine label sets and invoice-shipping documents. Examples of two book card/pocket/spine label sets are shown in Figures 3.4 and 3.5. The initial book card format was designed to be used in a manual circulation system. Later the format was changed to produce a machine-readable book card. This decision was based on a cost study which showed that it would be cheaper for the local participants to type their own book cards than it would be for those libraries contemplating automated circulation systems to produce machine-readable cards locally. (92) Also, most member libraries were using circulation forms other than the book cards supplied by CALBPC. The SILO software updates the School Update and Book Update records, as well as the School Master and Book Master records during each SILO run. (The difference between the School and Book Master records and the School Update and Book Update records is that the later are listings of current transactions. The master records are composed of accumulations of all records, either current or completed, still on the tape record.)

Data are inputed to the system at a number of points. The Book Update record consisting of the institution/fund/transaction number (IFT), truncated title, vendor, and list price, if known, is inputed before a title is ordered. (See Figure 3.6) The PR is shown in Figure A3.1. The call number, processing fee charges, and book expenditure data are keypunched during the SILO input procedure. (See Figure A3.1) The IFT number is the link between the School Master and Book Master records. If the IFT number is incorrectly keypunched the SILO software will print a book card/pocket/label set for the wrong title, or an error message warning of "an nonexistent IFT" will be printed. Another product of the SILO processing is an invoice document which includes list price, net price, processing charge and binding cost. (See Figure 3.8) Copies of the invoice document also serve as the shipping list.

A variety of diagnostic codes are built into the SILO software package. A list of the codes is shown in Figure 3.9. The diagnostics point out not only errors such as an invalid use of symbols, but also warnings that a fund is about to be exhausted. See Codes 26, 27, 28, and 29. Codes 2, 3, and 4 signal the use of invalid characters. A sample listing of several error messages is shown in Figure 3.10. Routines have also been devised to permit inputing of data to change records such as title changes and changes in expenditure information. Changes are inputed using the SILO input card shown in Figure A3.1 (90)

Another software package produces a variety of reports as by-products of the accounting subsystem. These include the Fund Accounting Summary, FACS (See Figure 3.11), the Balance and Invoice Summary, BAIS (See Figure 3.12), and a total dump of the Book Master tape. The total dump enables a library to identify outstanding transactions. (See Figure 3.13) (5)

Accounting Subsystem Modifications

Has the accounting subsystem performed the jobs for which it was intended? The answer is a qualified yes; however, like most new systems, the going has not always been smooth. Readers should keep in mind that none of those involved in the design of the accounting system had ever been involved with a multi-institutional processing center. All could agree that the most important objective was to provide tight fiscal controls to keep track of state funds. But beyond that objective it was not clear as to what the system should do, and which features would prove most useful. It was not until the system had been operable for some time that the designers, with a clarity of hindsight, could see their mistakes.

Expenditure/Labeling Interface -- The SILO software will not generate book card/pocket/label sets unless the Book Master record indicates that a transaction has been expended. This safeguard was intended to guarantee the integrity of the accounting data. While the integrity of the system was maintained, the safeguard produced an undesirable side effect. No one anticipated that on occasion books would be ready for labeling and shipment before the invoice was cleared for

Figure 3.11

COLORADO ACADEMIC LIBRARY BOOK PROCESSING CENTER

BAIS OPTION REPORT 1   03/17/76
COLORADO STATE UNIVERSITY

**** FUND 500

T SC CO. NUMBER	FN TRAN. TITLE / LC CLASS. NUMBER	VEN CD. / ENEX DATE	BIND FEE	PROC FEE	NET FEE	LIST FEE	ENCUM FEE	REPORT	RPT. MO DATE S F
302 5000C48	1073 KENSINGTON RUNE STONE	MON 0225	.00	.00	4.30	4.50	.00		1
302 5000C58	1153 POSTAGE	RTZ C304	.00	.00	2.46	.00	.00		1
302 5000072	1011 CRPROCFEE-HUSBANDRY... UPDATE*9024*0171	COO 0313 / 0213	.00	2.10	.00	.00	.00		1
102 5009034	0140 LEGAMC PQ*8097*C2914	S-H 0213 / 0916	2.35	.00	.00	.00	3.50		9 0304 11
302 5009C34	0145 DETRAS	S-H 0312	.00	.00	2.25	.00	1.50		9 0304 11
302 5009048	0056 EL FUEGO SOMBRIO	S-H 0312	.00	.00	6.75	.00	3.75		9 0304 11
102 5009050	0276 CUENTOS DEL DIS PQ*7297*V4L8*1962	S-H 0224 / 0718	2.35	.00	.00	.00	2.00		9 0304 11
102 5009050	0278 ZENAIDA, NOVELA RT*86*R6*C.1	S-H 0224 / 0728	.00	.00	.00	.00	1.50		9 0304 11
102 5009051	CC47 OBRA LITERARIA PQ*7297*R383*1967*L1	S-H 0224 / 0526	.00	.00	.00	.00	3.50		9 0304 11
102 5009051	0056 AGUECA PQ*8549*87A7*1968	S-H 0224 / 0718	2.35	.00	.00	.00	2.25		9 0304 11
102 5009051	0060 LA GENERACION DE LAS PQ*8098*12*L3C4*1966	S-H 0224 / 0916	2.35	.00	.00	.00	4.00		9 0304 11
302 5009052	0C31 DEMOGRAPHIC INFORMATION	MAK 0316	.00	.00	10.95	10.95	2.50		1
102 5009052	0105 LLOVIA ROJA, PQ*7297*G7415	S-H 0225 / 0826	2.35	.00	.00	.00	1.20		9 0304 11
102 5009055	0211 BARBARA PQ*8097*S3B3	S-H J226 / 0916	2.35	.00	.00	.00	2.75		9 0304 11
102 5000C55	0212 ANTOLOGIA DE PQ*8097*S56AB	S-H 022b / 0916	2.35	.00	.00	.00	1.50		9 0304 11
302 5009CE3	0501 JEFFERSONIAN DEMOCRACY	UNC 0304 / 0109	.00	.00	1.31	.00	2.50		9 0228 11
402 5009063	0502 RUSSIAN THINKERS AND	AMB 0307	.00	.00	.00	.00	3.75	OUT-OF-PRINT	0304 1
362 5009C7C	0133 THE SALT WATER AQUARIUM	BIO 0226	.00	.00	8.30	.00	6.00		1
102 5009072	0130 PATERNIDAD PQ*7297*U4P3	S-H 0314 / 0718	2.35	.00	.00	.00	1.25		9 0304 11
102 5009072	0132 LA TRAGEDIA DE VIVIR PQ*7298*3*0717	S-H 0314 / 0718	2.35	.00	.00	.00	1.25		9 0304 11
102 5009072	0133 PABLO NERUDA PQ*8097*N478	S-H 0314 / 1021	.00	.00	.00	.00	6.75		9 0304 11
102 5009073	0386 RECUEIL DE DOCUMENTS	S-H 0317	.00	.00	.00	.00	4.00		9 0304 11
462 5009078	0059 COMMUNITY AND RACIAL	B-D 0320	.00	.00	.00	.00	7.50	OUT-OF-PRINT	0304 1
302 5009C9C	0360 GAS EISERNE JAHR	G 0312	.00	.00	.00	.00	.00		1

Key:
BAIS =
T   = Type of Transaction
SC = School Code
FN = Fund Number Code
CD

VEN = Vendor
CD
ENEX = Encumbrance or
DATE   Expended Date

RPT = Date of Report
DATE
M   = Message
S   Flag

B = BAIS/FACTS cycle, a "1"
F   means uncycled; "2"
     means cycled

Figure 3.12

FUND ACCOUNTING SUMMARY (FACS) REPORT

COLORADO ACADEMIC LIBRARY BOOK PROCESSING CENTER

FACS REPORT   03/17/7C

ACAMS STATE COLLEGE

| FACSBINDING | 441.80 | 17.60 | 424.20 |
| PROCESS | 5,000.00 | 1,430.30 | 3,569.70 |

FUND	BUDGET	EXPEND	ENCUM.	FREE BAL.	LOCAL BUD.	LOCAL EXP.	LOCAL ENC.	LOCAL F.B.	COMB F.B.
250 LIB/G	20,130.20	16,901.47	3,035.98	15,112.75	.00	.00	.00	.00	15,112.75
255 ART	416.71	295.92	107.30	13.49	.00	.00	.00	.00	13.49
260 BUS	550.00	4.00.37	4.00	344.03	.00	.00	.00	.00	344.03
265 EDUC	1,088.14	1,025.22	47.45	15.47	.00	.00	.00	.00	15.47
270 GRD-S	200.00	33.24	.00	166.76	.00	.00	.00	.00	166.76
275 IND-A	85.97	60.21	36.85	11.39-	.00	.00	.00	.00	11.39-
280 LANG	1,218.09	1,122.71	73.20	22.18	.00	.00	.00	.00	22.18
285 PE	298.59	188.50	.00	110.09	.00	.00	.00	.00	110.09
290 SCI	914.77	649.22	117.03	387.58	.00	.00	.00	.00	387.58
295 SS	995.03	195.66	231.99	27.58-	.00	.00	.00	.00	27.58-
296 FED	360.00	359.97	93.30	95.33	.00	.00	.00	.00	95.33
FUNDS TOTAL	66,255.50	6,711.15	3,323.04	16,228.71	.00	.00	.00	.00	16,228.71

Figure 3.13

TRANDUMP: A LISTING OF ALL TRANSACTIONS SORTED AGAINST BOOKUP DURING A SINGLE COMPUTER RUN

*	**	***		Title
2	01	100	9069 9377	
2	01	100	0068 0014	WHO'S WHO IN CANADA
2	01	100	0068 0450	SMALL PRESS RECORD...
2	01	100	0069 0069	SPECIALIZED LIBRARY ...
5	01	106	0070 1025	ABEL APPROVAL CREDIT
2	01	112	0071 0182	ART OF THE EARLY RENAISSANCE
2	01	112	0071 0184	TWENTIETH CENTURY ART
4	01	112	9287 0039	
6	01	112	9339 0064	
6	01	120	0041 0124	
2	01	120	0068 0631	COMMODITY SURVEY
2	01	120	0068 0640	U.S. FOAMED PLASTIC MARKETS
2	01	120	0068 0653	RESEARCH REPORT
2	01	120	0069 0100	THE OFFICE
2	01	120	0071 0008	ESTIMATING CONSTRUCTION...
4	01	120	9282 0146	
4	01	120	9345 0173	
4	01	120	9351 0344	
4	01	120	9351 0585	
4	01	124	0007 0416	
2	01	124	0068 0272	NATURAL HISTORY OF CANTERBURY
2	01	124	0068 0624	EXTRA PHARMACOPAEIA
5	01	124	0070 1008	TEACHING
5	01	124	0071 1076	SALT WATER...
5	01	124	9345 1057	HANDBOOK OF CHEMICAL
4	01	126	0048 0402	
2	01	126	0068 0282	CPFERABKRAUCHE DER GRIECHEN
2	01	126	0068 0284	AENEAS' ARRIVAL IN LATIUM
2	01	126	0068 0649	BULLETIN
5	01	126	0070 1143	COMMENT JE CROIS
5	01	126	0071 1078	AUTOBICGRAPHY...
4	01	126	9184 0349	
4	01	126	9295 0107	
4	01	126	9295 0109	
4	01	126	9296 0157	
4	01	126	9300 0181	
4	01	126	9304 0239	
3	01	126	9304 0241	
4	01	126	9304 0243	
4	01	126	9307 0068	
4	01	126	9307 0071	
4	01	126	9307 0073	
4	01	126	9309 0345	
3	01	126	9350 0363	
3	01	126	9363 0008	
4	01	128	0013 0162	
4	01	128	0015 0310	
4	01	128	0028 0343	
4	01	128	0028 0358	
4	01	128	0633 0024	
4	01	128	0041 0158	
4	01	128	0054 0054	
4	01	128	0054 0109	
2	01	128	0068 0632	HANOVER AND PRUSSIA
5	01	128	9261 0093	
5	01	128	9286 0117	
4	01	128	9293 0226	
6	01	128	9353 0017	
4	01	128	9354 0067	
2	01	130	9350 0116	
4	01	130	9356 0123	
5	01	132	9355 0294	DANCING PALM TREE

*	**	***		Title	Date
2	01	100	0068 0430	STILL BOOK FOR WRITERS...	03/17/70
2	01	100	0068 0620	ADRESSBUCH DES...	03/17/70
2	01	100	0068 0654	FOLKLORE FELLOWS	03/17/70
2	01	106	0070 0256	LA RAZA	03/17/70
2	01	106	0072 1010	CREDIT-POSTAGE FORFEB.	03/17/70
4	01	112	0071 0183	GREEK AND ROMAN ART	03/17/70
4	01	112	9287 0037		03/17/70
4	01	112	9309 0064		03/17/70
6	01	120	0040 0213		03/17/70
6	01	120	0041 0125		03/17/70
2	01	120	0068 0633	CONFERENCE	03/17/70
2	01	120	0068 0643	SUPERVISORY MANAGEMENT	03/17/70
2	01	120	0068 0658	BIBLIOGRAPHY OF PUBLICATIONS	03/17/70
5	01	120	0070 1032	JOURNAL OF BUSINESS	03/17/70
4	01	120	9183 0805		03/17/70
4	01	120	9318 0147		03/17/70
4	01	120	9345 0177		03/17/70
4	01	120	9351 0583		03/17/70
4	01	120	9351 0566		03/17/70
2	01	124	0068 0271	AUDITORY PATHWAY	03/17/70
2	01	124	0068 0343	SYMPOSIUM ON HUMAN	03/17/70
2	01	124	0048 0655	NATIONAL FORUM	03/17/70
2	01	124	0071 0093	SCIENTIFIC INSTITUTIONS	03/17/70
4	01	124	9321 0491		03/17/70
4	01	126	0041 0151		03/17/70
2	01	126	0068 0281	VERGILIUS' VIERDE ...	03/17/70
2	01	126	0068 0283	DER PROPHET AND SEIN GOTT	03/17/70
2	01	126	0068 0285	AENEIDOS LIBRI I-IV	03/17/70
2	01	126	0069 0065	DE VERGILII ECLOGA...	03/17/70
5	01	126	0071 1077	ARTHURIAN ROMANCES	03/17/70
5	01	126	9189 1085	ON THE NATURE OF THE UNIVERSE	03/17/70
4	01	126	9189 0022		03/17/70
4	01	126	9295 0108		03/17/70
4	01	126	9296 0156		03/17/70
4	01	126	9296 0161		03/17/70
4	01	126	9301 0167		03/17/70
4	01	126	9304 0240		03/17/70
4	01	126	9304 0242		03/17/70
4	01	126	9304 0244		03/17/70
4	01	126	9307 0070		03/17/70
4	01	126	9307 0072		03/17/70
4	01	126	9307 0075		03/17/70
4	01	126	9317 0027		03/17/70
4	01	126	9350 0367		03/17/70
3	01	128	0013 0071		03/17/70
4	01	128	0013 0168		03/17/70
4	01	128	0028 0340		03/17/70
4	01	128	0030 0355		03/17/70
6	01	128	0030 0054		03/17/70
4	01	128	0040 0211		03/17/70
4	01	128	0054 0070		03/17/70
4	01	128	0054 0103		03/17/70
2	01	128	0068 0615	YOUR INCOME TAX	03/17/70
5	01	128	0070 1027	CONTEMPORARY INDIAN	03/17/70
4	01	128	9279 0289		03/17/70
4	01	128	9287 0047		03/17/70
4	01	128	9353 0014		03/17/70
6	01	128	9353 0051		03/17/70
2	01	130	0068 0013	STATE OF SOUTH AFRICA	03/17/70
4	01	130	9356 0117		03/17/70
4	01	132	0021 0032		03/17/70
5	01	132	0035 0294	DANCING PALM TREE	03/17/70

* Type of Transaction
** School Code
*** I. F. T. (Institution Fund Transaction Number)

payment. Sometimes books were processed and ready for labeling within twenty-four hours. And on occasion invoice processing was delayed because of work bottlenecks, errors, or when materials were received without invoices. In the event of a delay, the flow of books and invoices was no longer procedurally in phase.

Whenever a SILO input matched a School Master record which had not been expended, the following diagnostic was generated: "This document has not been expended either partially or fully." (31) This annoying problem occurred quite frequently. In April, there were 150 such messages, and by May, the messages had increased to 200. (83) Since we did not want to delay books until invoice processing was completed, a new transaction code was established. This code permitted production of a book card/pocket/label set but deferred payment until a later date. A processing information slip was attached to the regular accounting document so that bookkeepers knew when a book listed on an invoice had already been processed. (14)

This same exception routine was used while the University closed its financial books at the end of the fiscal year. During year end closing, all University departments hold invoices until the beginning of the new fiscal year. The CaMP Department, however, could not tolerate a three week delay in book card/pocket/label set production. Consequently, use of this exception procedure prevented a costly bottle-neck. (96)

Inability to Overexpend Funds -- As already mentioned, the accounting subsystem was designed to prevent overexpenditure in any fund. Although this feature had been clearly spelled out in the design specifications, the users of the system did not distinguish clearly between a fund and an account. One institutional account can be sub-divided into many internal fund breakdowns. For instance, Adams State College might designate a general fund, history fund, English fund, mathematics fund--all to be

charged against its book account. While the Adams State librarian might become concerned if the history fund is overexpended, the college business office will not. It watchdogs only the free balance in the book account. In other words, an institution establishes an account under which no circumstances can be overexpended, but the library may designate a series of internal fund breakdowns which can be overexpended at the discretion of the library director.

Each transaction in a fund for which the expenditures plus encumbrances was nearly equal to the budget allotment produced an error message and rejected the transaction. (71) The problem was compounded because the program logic expended dollars before it updated the encumbrance figure. This peculiarity, on occasion, created the oddity of not permitting the system to pay for books which had already been encumbered. (71, 77) One temporary stopgap was to raise the encumbrance allowance to 600, 700, or as high as 900 percent to insure that items already encumbered would not be rejected. Another stopgap was to transfer monies from one fund to another, but this alternative required permission from the school involved each time. (107)

The ultimate solution to the problem will be to permit funds to be overexpended and to change the system controls from the fund level to the institutional account level. Book selectors and bookkeepers can guard against abuse by examining the FACS report, which is generated weekly. This modification is scheduled for implementation on August 1, 1970.

Transference of Funds -- Data from the Phase I-II study showed that most schools allocated their book budgets along academic departmental lines. It was assumed that schools would expect the same capability from the Center's accounting system. Thus, the system was designed to permit each school to establish up to 99 separate funds. It was not anticipated that some schools would deposit only nominal sums--for example, a budget of $60--in some funds, or would make frequent requests that small sums such as $50 or $100 be transferred from one fund to another. (40, 41) Obviously, the proliferation of funds with small dollar amounts, coupled with the system's inability to overexpend funds, caused the error messages generated by the SILO software to mushroom. The problem was solved by agreeing that fund transfers would be initiated on no more than a quarterly basis.

Title Change Procedure -- On occasion, the form of title written on the PR form submitted by users and verified by bibliographical searchers did not match exactly the form of title printed on the title page of the book. And even though the form of title recorded on the PR form was usually based on a Library of Congress depository slip, this problem still occasionally occurred. When one of the first two or three words differed, this affected the printing on the book cards and book pockets; in such cases, users designated this an error and rejected the product. Initially, the accounting subsystem was not designed to accommodate changes in the title field. But once it became clear that some title changes would be necessary, the report card which was used to input publishers' reports and cancellations was modified to permit title changes as well. (See Figure 3.7) (105)

Dropped Book Master Records -- Not long after operations began, the Order Department began to receive error messages indicating that some records were being dropped from the tape records. Whenever this occurred, either one or all of the following problems resulted: 1) the accounting data were no longer accurate, either in the expenditure or encumbrance column; 2) attempts to expend funds against "dropped" encumbrances produced a Code 11 diagnostic message, "Invalid card in the add routine BKMCTHLI," which in turn necessitated the following exception routine. The original input transaction card and numerical slip (one copy of the order multiform) were pulled, and the item expended on a NIL (not-

in-ledger) mode, the numerical slip refiled, and the transaction card re-submitted at the next accounting run--a fairly high price to pay for a dropped record; and 3) the SILO input against a "dropped" record generated the diagnostic error message "Nonexistent IFT." (70, 80)

On three or four days, entire batches of records were dropped. These malfunctions could never be traced to one specific cause. Computer center operators mounting incorrect tapes was one major contributant. Another culprit was a program instruction which permitted the last record on each run to remain in core and thus be dropped. Inaccuracies in data transferred from the former University of Colorado accounting system may have caused some discrepancies. (In order to avoid extensive re-keypunching, all outstanding encumbrances from the former system were lumped together into one account). Some records were lost because computer center personnel misplaced the transaction cards. And finally, hardware breakdowns were the prime suspect in more than one instance.

The dilemma of dropped records has not yet been completely solved. A number of program modifications have been implemented. Center personnel now keep track of the number of transactions submitted on each processing run. And specific instructions to computer center operators accompany each batch of cards transported to the computer center.

Summary -- The bugs in the accounting system can be classified into five broad categories: 1) user failures (excessive transference of funds); 2) design failures (the failure to anticipate that books would be ready for labeling before invoices were processed; 3) software failures (leaving one record in core at the conclusion of a processing run); 4) hardware and computer operator failures (failure of tape drive read heads to function correctly or failure of machine operators to mount correct tapes; and 5) problems caused by sources external to the control of the Center (title transcription errors on Library of Congress depository

Figure 3.14

BOOK UPDATE SUMMARY

03/17/70   BOOK UPDATE SUMMARY   PAGE 1

FUND	FD NME	FD PER	FD BK BUD	FD BK EXP	FD BK ENC	FD BK BAL	SCHOOL BUD	SCHOOL EXP	SCHOOL ENC	SCHOOL BAL
100	LB	200	25,064.08	23,124.98	1,914.24	26,128.94	1,179,442.76	842,324.80	142,408.72	337,117.90
105	LBPU	200	1,915.12	437.10	27.99	2,193.14	1,179,442.76	842,324.86	142,408.72	337,117.90
106	ABEL	200	25,453.25	23,508.53	266.10	27,369.98	1,179,442.76	842,222.73	142,415.11	337,220.03
108	AFME	200	537.21	271.11		537.21	1,179,442.76	842,222.73	142,415.11	337,220.03
110	ANTH	200	147.01	130.06	16.95	147.01	1,179,442.76	842,222.73	142,415.11	337,220.03
111	ARCH	500	219.04	177.09	92.71	825.40	1,179,442.76	842,222.73	142,415.11	337,220.03
112	ART	500	15,314.90	13,506.60	1,855.97	61,211.93	1,179,442.76	842,247.82	142,378.90	337,194.94
114	AG	500	252.62	252.62	17.50	992.98	1,179,442.76	842,247.82	142,378.90	337,194.94
116	BIND	150	63,066.72	65,668.81		58,841.27	1,179,442.76	842,247.82	142,378.90	337,194.94
118	BIOL	200	351.87	298.37	33.59	331.87	1,179,442.76	842,247.82	142,378.90	337,194.94
119	BLACK	110	1,312.69			1,444.18	1,179,442.76	842,247.82	142,378.90	337,194.94

```
.........1.........2.........3.........4.........5.........6.........7.........8
401 12091B0005                               FAX0313000000000045000000000000000        MSG  CODE 11
```

FUND	FD NME	FD PER	FD BK BUD	FD BK EXP	FD BK ENC	FD BK BAL	SCHOOL BUD	SCHOOL EXP	SCHOOL ENC	SCHOOL BAL
120	BUS	200	6,076.14	2,759.09	1,194.63	8,198.56	1,179,442.76	842,370.75	142,466.36	337,072.01
124	CHEM	200	11,654.01	6,856.38	1,875.01	13,376.63	1,179,442.76	842,538.96	142,414.11	336,903.80
126	CLAS	200	16,310.25	7,336.22	3,614.56	9,669.72	1,179,442.76	842,779.21	142,297.14	336,663.45
127	CLIT	200	301.96	286.96	15.00	301.96	1,179,442.76	842,779.31	142,297.14	336,663.45
128	COL	200	34,304.29	31,461.66	11,553.03	25,593.89	1,179,442.76	842,831.42	142,179.92	336,611.34
130	ECON	200	508.92	324.12	285.80	407.92	1,179,442.76	842,866.67	142,154.42	336,576.09

```
.........1.........2.........3.........4.........5.........6.........7.........8
501 13200350294 DANCING PALM TREE          EAS0311000000000000000026900003950000000        MSG (MESSAGE)  CODE 19
```

FUND	FD NME	FD PER	FD BK BUD	FD BK EXP	FD BK ENC	FD BK BAL	SCHOOL BUD	SCHOOL EXP	SCHOOL ENC	SCHOOL BAL
132	EDUC	200	7,579.83	5,620.65	2,402.26	7,136.75	1,179,442.76	842,943.32	142,161.58	336,499.44
140	DFED	200	15,165.00	11,113.46	2,372.77	16,843.77	1,179,442.76	843,077.09	142,625.79	336,365.07
141	CFED	200	9,256.00	6,491.23	1,714.78	10,905.99	1,179,442.76	843,207.16	142,675.27	336,235.60
150	ENG	200	7,994.01	3,407.20	3,151.25	9,335.17	1,179,442.76	843,233.04	143,137.63	336,209.12
165	GSCI	200	30.78	30.78		30.78	1,179,442.76	843,233.64	143,137.63	336,209.12

Key:
Per = Percentage
FD = Fund
Bk = Book
EXP = Expenditure
ENC = Encumbrance
BAL = Balance
MSG = Message

*Percentage Fund may be overencumbered

cards). Our experience suggests that other libraries designing similar systems might anticipate the likelihood of errors from all five sources.
In fact, one conclusion was that we could have
benefited from the advice of an outside consultant.
The expertise of an individual who had experienced the pitfalls of implementing an automated
accounting system might have helped us to avoid
some of our mistakes, or at the very least, to
assure our staff that it would take time before the
system would be completely debugged. The advice of a consultant would have been particularly
useful during the design phases since our personnel were not experienced at designing an automated
accounting system.

SILO Subsystem

The SILO subsystem, like the accounting
subsystem, required modifications. As already
noted, the link between the accounting and SILO
subsystems is the IFT number. An incorrectly
keypunched IFT number generates the wrong book
card/pocket/label set or an error message.
Fortunately, the frequency of keypunch errors
was very low; however, such was the difficulty
of correcting an error when one occurred, that
a careful inspection of the IFT number was made
prior to machine processing. (111)

When an error message was reported on
the Book Update Report (See Figure 3.14), the
first step was to be sure that a keypunching error
had not been made. If no error were found, the
book along with the error message was returned
to the Order Department where a series of exception routines were triggered.

During May a log detailing errors returned
to the Order Department was maintained. The
analysis of errors provided the following profile:

Error		Frequency
1.	Error message, This document has not been expended either partially or fully."	200
2.	SILO subsystem keypuncher used a fund which varied from the fund inputed at the time of encumbrance.	36

Error		Frequency
3.	An invalid fund written on the original PR form.	18
4.	Information incomplete or missing from the original PR form.	7
5.	SILO keypuncher inputed an incorrect school code.	3
6.	Order Department personnel converted the Julian date incorrectly.	6
7.	No transaction number stamped on the PR form.	3
8.	Fuzzy or illegible transaction number on the PR form.	2
9.	PR form missing from the book which prevented initiation of the SILO routine.	7

Except for the problem of delayed invoices,
which was a design oversight, the errors identified
are due to operator miscues. Other than the incidence of keypunching incorrect fund designations,
thirty-six in all, the errors were judged to be
within acceptable limits. (83, 88, 99)

The inability to generate book card/pocket/
label sets until invoices had been cleared for payment became the bane of the Cataloging and Preservation Departments' existence. Hundreds of
books were delayed while SILO data were recycled
through the system. As discussed earlier, this
difficulty was overcome by introducing the sub-
routine which permitted book card/pocket/label
set production prior to invoice payment. (31, 80,
83)

The SILO delete procedure was used whenever a keypuncher inputed an incorrect IFT number.
When the incorrect IFT number generates an incorrect book card/pocket/label set, the correct
IFT number is submitted in the next computer run
in order to obtain the correct book card/pocket/
label set. Later, when the book for which the
wrong label set was printed initially is ready for
processing, the SILO input will generate an error
message reporting that the item has already been
expended. Although there are ways to correct
this problem by machine, this exception routine

is now handled manually. CaMP maintains a log book of erroneous IFT numbers retrieved so that when the diagnostic ". . . already expended" is received, the label set is produced manually and the invoice is corrected by hand. (70) One conclusion drawn from our experience has been that administrators should become wary when excessive machine manipulation is required to execute an exception routine. In such cases, the cheapest and most effective approach may be a manual routine.

Catalog Card Reproduction System

A variety of techniques were used to prepare master copy for catalog card reproduction. The Xerox 2400 was used to reproduce catalog card sets. Master copy was obtained from the following sources: 1) LC Title II depository cards, 2) National Union Catalog and other Library of Congress catalogs, and 3) copy supplied by a cataloger. (10) The following reproduction devices were used to prepare master copy: 1) Xerox model 4 camera system[2]; 2) the Polaroid CU-5 Land Camera[3]; and 3) typing of master cards (cards were typed only when entries from the National Union Catalog were short or when all other mechanical devices were overloaded.)

The preparation of master copy caused most headaches. Images produced from the Polaroid camera were judged to be of marginal quality only; consequently, the camera was used only as a backup to the Xerox camera process during peak periods of activity. (10) Unfortunately, there were many peak periods. Some participants soon began to object rather vocally about the poor quality of Polaroid produced copy and of the number of sets they were receiving. Assurances were given that the Polaroid camera was used as a backup system only, but this explanation was difficult to swallow when some shipments included as much as 25 per cent of the Polaroid type cards. (94) A further explanation was that the Xerox system was continuously overloaded.

It was not long before the majority of libraries requested that the Polaroid camera be withdrawn from service, but as late as March, no library had refused to accept the Polaroid-type cards. But it was not known if libraries were redoing the sets locally. (94) During the product acceptance study, we discovered that only one library had systematically redone the work. At the May Technical Advisory Group meeting, the members voted to discontinue production of master cards using the Polaroid camera. All master copy enlarged from the National Union Catalog hereafter would be produced by the Xerox camera system. (1) In addition, all master copy previously produced by the Polaroid camera was to be redone using the Xerox technique. (2)

Soon after the withdrawl of the Polaroid camera from service, the backlog of copy waiting to be enlarged from the National Union Catalog became critical. The Xerox process could not cope with the work load, and the Center did not have enough money to purchase a second camera. As a result, other enlargement techniques were investigated. It was finally decided to adapt a system based on a 35-millimeter camera similar to the one used at the University of Indiana.[4] Since the Center did not have the facilities for in-house processing of film, several commercial firms were contacted. After several months of negotiations with a number of firms, arrangements were completed to process prints on an overhead enlarger. In late February 1970, trial operations were initiated. The 35-millimeter camera is no substitute for the long-sought "catalogers camera," but the process does produce better quality copy than the Polaroid camera and at a slightly lower cost.

We believe that the attitudes of most librarians toward the acceptability of catalog card sets will gradually change. It was not too long ago that many librarians objected to catalog cards produced by the Xerox 914 machine. Now this is one of the most commonly used reproduction devices. Some librarians have successfully used Polaroid-type cards, why not other libraries? Hopefully, catalog card acceptability in the future will be based on

Figure 3.15

CATALOG CARD PRODUCTION IN 1969

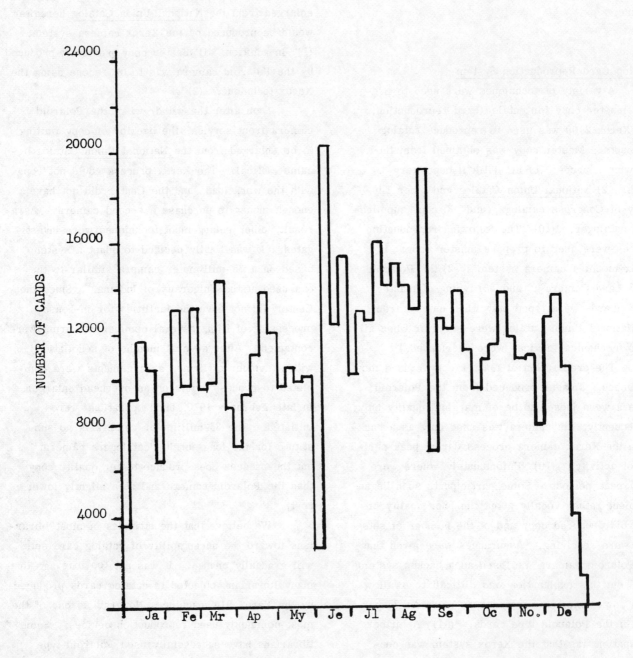

legibility rather than on card aesthetics.

The card reproduction unit also developed serious work backlogs. The unit could not keep up with the flow of books. Oftentimes books were ready for shipment as much as seven weeks before catalog card sets were finished. The backlogs were caused by several factors: 1) peak periods of activity, caused by fluctuations in activity from week to week and severe time schedules; 2) the requirement of the specifications to match cards with books prior to shipment, which is discussed in the next section; and 3) cumbersome procedures which had been designed to handle cards within the University of Colorado system only.

Analysis of the card reproduction procedures including card handling, typing of secondary entries, and preparation of cards for Xeroxing revealed that existing procedures needed to be overhauled. The revamped procedures were introduced during the later phases of the experiment. By the spring of 1970 the Head of CaMP could report that the average turnaround time of a catalog card set had been reduced to seven and one-half days. (119)

Extreme peak periods of activity was another major cause for the work arrearages. Work loads fluctuated from fewer than 4,000 cards to over 20,000 cards in one week. (See Figure 3.15) Some method had to be found to spread activity over a longer time frame. One suggestion was to initiate card reproduction before receipt of books. This idea led to the Advanced Card Production (ACP) experiment. In brief, a catalog card set is prepared shortly after an order for a title (published within the last two years) is placed with a vendor. The results of the first three months operations were promising. Based on an analysis of the first 750 titles received, errors were found for fewer than three percent of the items. As can be seen from the summary in Figure 3.16, the errors are attributable to a variety of sources ranging from vendor errors and errors in LC cataloging, to errors committed by personnel at the Center.

These initial findings prompted a continuation of the procedure.

The ACP project may enable the Center to modify drastically its processing workflow. It was found that Order Department personnel can effectively perform the inspections now performed by library assistants in the mass cataloging unit. Consequently, there seems to be no reason why books and card sets cannot be forwarded directly to CaMP to be SILO'd; thus cataloging, as it is traditionally viewed, will have been completely bypassed. (112)

One limitation of the ACP process is that some books ordered will not be received; thus, participants will have to absorb the extra cost of card set wastage. Based on the analysis of new titles not received during the experimental period, the wastage factor should approximate five to seven percent. No cost analysis has been performed as yet; it is assumed that the benefits of bypassing cataloging and eliminating the peak periods of activity will more than compensate for the wastage costs. When more experience is gained, a detailed analysis of this procedure will be undertaken.

Catalog Card Matching Subsystem

Commercial book processors usually ship books and catalog card sets together. This practice is welcomed by subscribers, for no other reason, because all check-in and book inspection procedures can be performed at once. For these reasons, CALBPC planned to emulate its commercial counterparts.

The cost of matching cards with books was included in the Phase I-II study, but the method used to extrapolate these costs was incorrect. We neglected to consider as the volume of work increased that the cost of matching would increase significantly. In addition, the cost of arranging books by location and title also increased as the number of volumes stored increased. Moreover, the completed catalog card sets also had to be arranged by destination (match the arrangement of the physical volumes) and alphabetized by title before they could be matched with books. In

Figure 3.16

ANALYSIS OF ERRORS FOUND IN CATALOG CARD SETS PRODUCED

AT THE TIME A BOOK IS ORDERED (750 titles)

Type of Error	Fre-quency	% of total	Source of Error					
			Vendor	Library of Congress	Biblio Searching Dept.	Order Dept.	Catalog Maint.	Requesting Library
Difference in date of publication (reprint)	7	26	X	X				
Difference in place of publication or publisher	4	16	X	X				
Open entry (set)	5	18			X			X
Different edition Received	2	7	X					
Wrong Title	2	7	X		X			
Cards Stamped with incorrect location	3	11				X		
Typists' errors	3	11					X	
PZ call no. (unacceptable to library)	1	4			X			X
Total	27	100						

other words, the cost of matching books with cards was much greater than had been anticipated.

By May, the card reproduction unit reported that over forty hours of clerical time were being expended in staging books; and that the matching process itself required thirty hours more than had been budgeted. (23, 78) And, as already mentioned, the time required to match books and cards contributed to the delay in delivery of books to users.

At the conclusion of the experiment, the Center proposed to discontinue the matching service. This recommendation was based on two factors. First, as the volume of business increased, the cost of card/book matching would become prohibitively expensive; and secondly, the present procedure added as much as six weeks to the processing time cycle. (84) Some librarians reacted negatively to this proposal. They did not believe books and cards could be shipped separately without degrading existing services. While there may be some justification to this view, existing evidence does not support it. The University of Colorado Library has shipped books and cards separately to its branch libraries for several years. Each branch librarian has the option of holding books until the cards arrive or putting them into circulation at once. The option selected depends mostly on the philosophy of each librarian. It was suggested that the same procedure would work for other libraries. Each library could maintain adequate control without generating an additional record since the original PR form is returned inside the book.

One valid objection to shipping card sets separately is that some sets will go astray; and, of course, this does happen on occasion. In order to ameliorate this problem, an automatic follow-up procedure was devised. Six weeks after a book is received, a library can request a new set of cards if the original card set has not arrived. The request will be honored without question. This follow-up routine has worked reasonably well, although there have been some problems. Occasionally books are misrouted by the Center or by the courier, or a mistake is made during the check-in procedure at the local library. In either case, requests for an additional card set may be generated even though the book does not belong to the library that received it. While these exceptions continue to be an irritant, by eliminating the book/card matching subsystem the overall delivery time has been reduced by as much as four to six weeks. From the point of view of a library user, this small change should be welcome indeed.

Shipping Subsystem

A courier truck which is used to deliver interlibrary loan materials was used also to deliver processed books from the Center to user libraries. The U.S. mail was used to deliver books to libraries that were not members of the courier circuit. Reusable tote boxes constructed of fiberboard were purchased to transport books in the courier truck. A full tote box weighs as much as fifty to sixty pounds. It wasn't long before the driver of the courier truck objected to the tote boxes. He complained that he had to carry the boxes a considerable distance at some libraries. (10) It was decided finally to fill the tote boxes half full and to gradually phase out these heavy containers in favor of reusable cardboard boxes. (55, 61) This new arrangement has proved successful.

The charge for transporting one box of books is equated with a single interlibrary loan transaction. The transportation costs per book are approximately two cents.

Each box of books contains a shipping document. A library is expected to check the contents of each box immediately upon receipt, and to notify the CALBPC Coordinator whenever a mistake is discovered. (55) However, some libraries have not found it possible to comply with this requirement. Consequently, when containers of books have been either mispacked or misrouted, the mistake may not be discovered for several weeks. In the meantime, the rightful owner may register a complaint, but the Center's records will show the books have been properly delivered. Misrouted books can only be traced, if at all, through tedious backtracking. As a result, the Center now encloses two shipping documents in each box, one of which must be returned to the Center signed accepting the shipment of books as listed. Otherwise the Center is not held responsible for items mishandled or misrouted. (120)

Notes

1. Mr. William Harper has prepared a detailed report of the accounting system documentation. The report is scheduled to be published by the Information Science and Automation Division of the American Library Association. For this reason we will limit our explanation to an overview of the system, its capabilities, and a review of the system modifications programmed.

2. Eugene Petriwsky and Joe Hewitt, "Producing card copy from book catalogs with the Xerox Model 4 camera," Library Resources and Technical Services 13:3 (Summer, 1969), p. 361-5.

3. Helen Custinoff, "The University of Vermont uses a Polaroid CU-5 to speed book processing," Library Resources and Technical Services 11:4 (Fall, 1967), p. 474-7.

4. Mary Helen Stanger, "The Cataloger's camera," Library Resources and Technical Services 11:4 (Fall, 1967), p. 474-7.

Chapter IV

THE CENTER AND ITS USERS

Up to now, the report has dwelled primarily on the impersonal aspects of book processing, mainly performance, techniques and procedures. But it is the human element of centralized book processing, or for that matter of any cooperative project, that bears most heavily on the ultimate success of cooperation. In this chapter, we will discuss the organizational aspects of the Center, communication among the users, the governing mechanisms of the Center, and the administration of the Center within the Technical Services Division of the University of Colorado. We will also review the external activities; that is, public relations activities which have been implemented in order to improve communications. We will also cover the question of compatibility among library systems and the need to dovetail systems of users with those of the central organization. The evolution of the classification, cataloging, and processing specifications used by the Center are treated in some detail because others contemplating cooperation will have to grapple with the same or similar problems. Finally, some of the by-products which have accrued to participants as a direct result of centralized book processing will be presented.

The Organizationsl Structure of CALBPC Through the Experimental Period, February 1 - September 30, 1969

The organizational structure of the Center as it existed throughout the experiment is charted in Figure 4.1. As can be seen, the Center was integrated into the Technical Services Division of the University of Colorado. There are both pros and cons to this organizational structure. On the plus side, it avoided the need to recruit and train a new staff and the cost of financing additional physical facilities. It also made control and monitoring of the processing system a great deal easier. On the minus side, the Center was closely associated with the University of Colorado, perhaps too closely. One or two participants viewed this arrangement suspiciously, in part because CU might receive favored treatment, and in part due to a natural antagonism often exhibited by small institutions toward large institutions. Also, the philosophy of "oneness" or integration of all procedures, so that they met the needs of all participants (including the University of Colorado) equally well, produced psychological obstacles for Center personnel. During the trying days of the experiment when operations were not going smoothly, many staff members were torn by a feeling of disloyalty to their employer. In the face of burgeoning backlogs, which had not existed prior to the experiment, they were being asked to defer CU processing in favor of other institutions. (97) It was an uncomfortable feeling.

The Organizational Structure of CALBPC After The Experiment, September 30, 1969 - February 28, 1970

By the time regular operations were begun it had become clear that the Center's governmental and organizational structure were in need of alteration. (46, 47)

The policy making body of the Center throughout the experimental period had been the Colorado Council of Librarians. All matters were decided on majority vote with each member casting one vote. Like all boards composed of mem-

Figure 4.1

ORGANIZATION CHART: CALBPC EXPERIMENTAL PERIOD
JANUARY 1969 – SEPTEMBER 1969

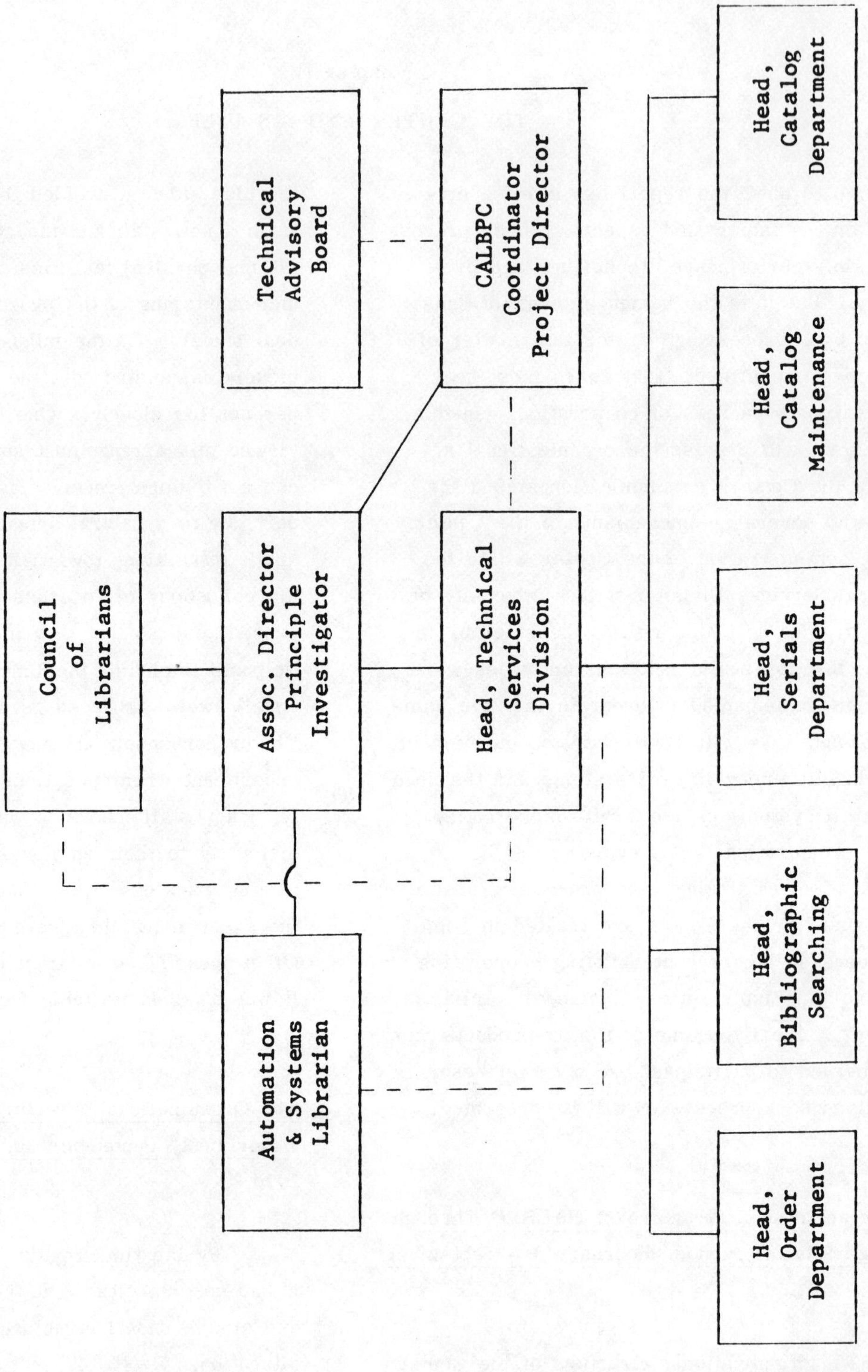

Figure 4.2

ORGANIZATION CHART: CALBPC OPERATIONS
OCTOBER 1969 - JUNE 30, 1970

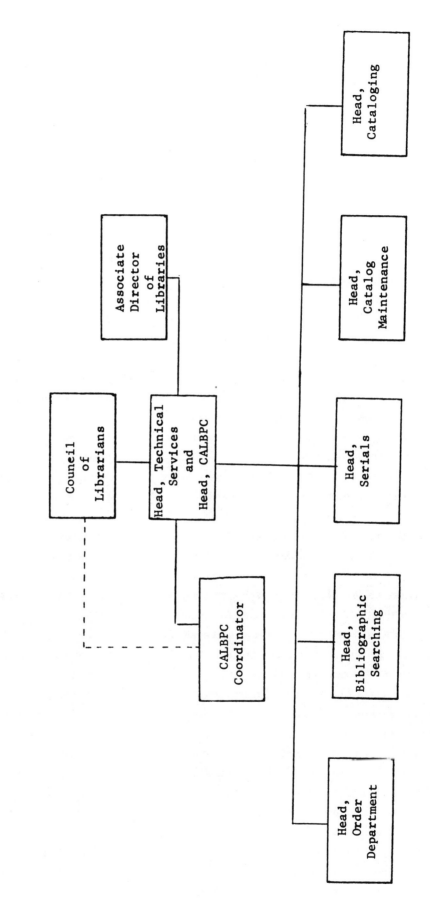

bers who are scattered wide geographically, it was difficult for the board to function effectively. With the conclusion of the experiment, the Board has been reconstituted to include only libraries which are using the services of the Center. Each member is still entitled to one vote. (114) Because it is still expensive to convene Board meetings, an Executive Committee empowered to act in behalf of the Board, subject to the Board's review, may be created.

At the end of the experiment the principal investigator was able to withdraw from the formal chain of command. This transferred the burden for managing the Center's affairs to the Assistant Director for Technical Services. However, this arrangement violates a basic tenet of administration, namely, that one should not have two bosses. In addition to the Center's activities, the Assistant Director is still responsible for technical services activities at the University which are not directly connected with book acquisitions and book processing, i.e., gift and exchange, serials check-in, catalog maintenance, etc.

The schizophrenic role of the Assistant Director has been fully aired by the Board. The short run solution was a pledge from the University of Colorado to members that no action would be taken unilaterally by the University on matters which affect other CALBPC members. The assistant Director for Technical Services will report directly to the CALBPC Board on CALBPC matters; but on questions which affect only the University of Colorado, he will work through the established Library chain of command. (114) Figure 4.2 shows the revised organizational structure. The long-range solution is a separately funded position to direct processing activities.

The organizational duelism within technical services actually permeates the entire division. The Center, as well as each participating library, must identify and categorize each technical services activity which will remain a local responsibility, i.e., filing catalog cards, checking in periodicals, etc., and separate them from those tasks which will be performed centrally, i.e.,

cataloging, card reproduction and so forth. This is an extremely critical issue. If, as is likely in Colorado, the size of processing staffs will be equated to book acquisition and processing costs, it is of paramount importance that libraries distinguish clearly between local and central operations. Otherwise, it will become increasingly difficult to finance local operations. The Center is presently beginning such a study, and it has been recommended that participants initiate similar studies.

Technical Advisory Group

To assist the Board of Directors, a Technical Advisory Group (TAG) was created to confer with the Coordinator, the principal investigator and the CALBPC supervisors on the technical aspects of processing operations. Although the Board might have provided similar guidance, in fact the directors had neither the time nor the expertise to deliberate over "nitty gritties" of cataloging. TAG was composed of a member or members from each library's technical processing division. The Group tackled problems such as the format of call numbers, format and location of tracings, and the use of abbreviations in subject headings. (3) It was TAG that recommended the discontinuance of the Polaroid camera. (2)

It was TAG's responsibility to negotiate problems and present recommendations to the CALBPC Board. TAG was not intended to serve as a decision making body but rather as an advisory group and a vehicle for communication. The future role of TAG is yet to be resolved, but there is clearly a need to retain some mechanism to discuss technical and procedural matters. (42)

Customer Relation Activities

Cooperation, at best, is not an easy undertaking. Even when participants are solidly behind the undertaking, the road will not be smooth, particularly if a cooperative venture causes basic changes in existing organization structures and/or procedures. Consequently, some librarians may not favor cooperation once it passes beyond the concept level.

The obstacles to cooperation are compounded when participants are widely scattered geographically. In such cases, communications may hold the key to success or failure. It is one matter when a book selector can amble into the Order Department of his own library to inquire about the status of a particular order; it is quite a different matter when that information file is located two hundred miles from his library. While the telephone and TWX can be used to retrieve status information, it is not so convenient, and the costs of supplying status information are considerably greater. (53, 54) Processing errors are also more difficult to resolve when libraries are dispersed. When an error can be corrected quickly, it is soon forgotten; but when the mistake is visible for several days, it becomes a constant reminder of an outside agency's misdeed.

As already discussed, the Board of Directors and the Technical Advisory Group provided the primary formal channels of communication. These bodies serve as the principal sounding boards for the administrative officials. But the person most responsible for customer relation activities is the Center's Coordinator. It is his responsibility to disseminate information, solve problems, and publicize the services of the Center.

Throughout the experiment the Coordinator prepared and distributed a monthly progress report to participating libraries and concerned state officials. The monthly report is now a newsletter in which policy changes, new programs, personnel changes and general news items are announced. (See Figure A4.1) The The newsletter is also being used to warn users of imminent problems and, if possible, how to avoid them. For instance, if a library were to concentrate its orders in the early fall or late spring, it could avoid the peak ordering periods

that are likely to occur during October, November and early spring.

The Center also distributes a variety of reports, either on a regular basis or on demand. These reports have already been mentioned in the section dealing with the accounting subsystem. How necessary they are, is not known; but there are suspicions that either their potential is not understood, or that some of the reports are not needed. The BAIS cumulative record is a listing of all books either on order or in process. It is a large report and requires several hours of computer time to be printed. Initially, a copy of this report was to be distributed periodically to each user, but now the BAIS record is produced by means of COM equipment (computer output of microfilm), and the record is retained at the Center and can be consulted on demand. (79)

It is still too early to judge what report configuration will prove most useful to users. The experimental period did not produce a heavy demand for information on the status of orders submitted. Most communications dealt with errors and accounting problems.

If we have given the impression that there were serious communication breakdowns, this was our intention. Especially in dealing with errors, there were times when people came close to "losing their cool." However, participants have worked hard to bridge communication gaps. The Coordinator made visits to twelve prospective member libraries during the summer of 1969 to acquaint them with CALBPC services. These included the eight that had originally formed the Center.

It is generally agreed that an intensive program of orientation and instruction on the capabilities and limitations of centralized processing should be offered to professional and key nonprofessional staff of all user libraries. The Board has agreed that future developmental activities will include allocations for such an educational program. This, in our opinion, represents a healthy step forward.

Handling of Customer Problems -- The Coordinator devoted considerable time screening
orders from participants, answering questions,
and responding to complaints. Initially, severe
restrictions were imposed on the types of materials user libraries could order through the
Center. Exclusions included out-of-print titles,
pamphlets, and classed-together series. It was
anticipated that a significant number of orders
received would fall outside of the specifications,
but experience showed that this did not happen.
Detailed records were kept of all orders returned
to requesters. Of the first 9,955 titles ordered,
only 35 were returned to participants as duplicates.
This total represents less than one percent of
the materials ordered. (32) (A duplicate included both orders cancelled by requesters and
titles found at the Center to be on order already
for the requesting library.) The returns for other
categories were also very low. Of the first
8,591 titles requested, 290 were returned for the
following reasons: 41 percent, title was a part
of a classed-together series; 28 percent, title
was part of a series that could have been on standing order at the local library; 13 percent, out-of-
print books; and the remaining 18 percent for
miscellaneous reasons such as price problems and
insufficient bibliographic information. On occasion
a title ordered was found upon receipt from the
vendor to fall outside of specifications. When
this occurred, the book was forwarded to the requesting library unprocessed. Figure A4.2 summarizes books returned between March and
November, 1969.

Finally, the Coordinator processed all
titles rejected by participants. This involved
not only making sure that errors were corrected but also using participant feedback to monitor
system effectiveness. Between May 1969 and
December 1969, one hundred-sixty books were
returned to the Center. Figure A4.3 categories the rejects. (32, 33, 102) (This number
does not represent the total number of errors,
only those returned to the Center for correction.)
The extremely low rejection rate observed

during the course of the experiment probably
reflects the thoroughness of local screening procedures. In part, local efforts can be reduced
once the categories of material which can be
ordered and processed through the Center are expanded. No doubt the restrictions imposed during
the experiment, regarding the types of material
users could order, limited the Center's usefulness.
At least this was a complaint frequently heard, and
one that seems to have been justified.

Processing Fees

The original processing fee structure implemented in July 1969 was based on the findings of
the Phase I-II study. The charges were categorized as follows:

    1) $1.85 -- added copies and/or added
        volumes.

    2) $2.35 -- titles for which Library of
        Congress copy is available.

    3) $3.95 -- titles for which original
        cataloging is performed.[1]

Subsequently, the schedule of charges was
expanded to include more specific information. A
revised fee schedule became effective October,
1969, and was as follows:

Category I ($1.85)

    1) Xerox camera copy or LC proof of
        an NUC entry used previously as a
        master card, i.e., used to create
        cards for a book previously cataloged.

    2) Added volumes to a multiple volume
        set, i.e., v.2, 3, 4, etc. of a set.

    3) Added copies of a single purchased
        volume, i.e., c.2, 3, etc.

Category II ($2.35)

    1) Exact Xerox camera copy with com-
        plete call number which has not been
        used as a master card before, in-
        cluding PZ classification numbers
        with a suggested literature number.

    2) University of Colorado main entry
        card, including all literature

classification numbers for titles
to which LC has assigned PZ num-
number.

Category III ($3.95)

1) LC proof without a call number or
with an incomplete call number.

2) Xerox camera copy without a call
number.

3) Variant copy of any other type.

4) No copy.

5) PZ call numbers not covered under
steps above. (51, 57)

In most cases, the person performing the
cataloging will determine the fee charged by the
Center; that is, if the work is performed by a professional cataloger, then the price charged will
usually be $3.95; if the work is performed by a
skilled nonprofessional, then the usual fee will
be $2.35. The cost analysis reported in Chapter
II suggests a revision of the fee schedule based
on the tasks actually performed in each of the
above categories.

Requests from users to perform additional
services have required an expanded schedule of
fees. Member libraries asked the Center to bind
paperback books as a regular service. The
charge for this work was arbitrarily set at
$1.25 per item, which is the amount charged by
one professional commercial vendor. (65) Users
also requested the Center to bind pamphlets. This
work is performed in-house and a charge of $1.15
is assessed. (65) The charge for pamphlet binding is not based on cost studies, but is the pre-
vailing charge for similar work performed by
commercial agencies. When time permits, the
appropriate cost studies will be conducted.

Additional charges have also been
established for the purchase of additional catalog
card sets. Upon making inquiries it was found
that some vendors charge 35 cents for a set of
unit cards; the Library of Congress was currently
charging 15 cents for the first card and 4 cents
for each additional card plus a 5 cent service
charge. Data from the Phase I-II study

established the cost of producing a card set, including reproduction costs, typing of call number
and added entries, revision of typing, and distribution costs to be 35 cents.[2] (64) An additional handling charge was added, so that the
total cost for an additional catalog card set is
40 cents--a very favorable rate indeed.

Charges were also established to defray the
cost of handling materials ordered but not cataloged, and for materials that are cataloged but not
ordered. The ordered but not cataloged category
includes titles which are not acceptable under the
existing specifications. In such cases, the requesting library is charged $1.85. The second cate-
gory, namely titles cataloged but not ordered, includes gift materials. The Center charges $1.85,
which includes the cost of one set of catalog
cards. The charge for cataloging gifts was
established arbitrarily at $1.85 to avoid further
complications of the fee schedule. However, the
cost of cataloging gifts was considered in the cost
presentations in Chapter II. A more precise
charge can be introduced in the coming months
based upon the updated cost analysis from the
study.

The above fees were assessed throughout
the 1969-70 fiscal year. The charges, however,
were calculated during the fall of 1968. Recent
increases in both labor and material costs, plus
the cost calculations of this study, suggest that
the fees will have to be revised at the beginning
of the 1970-71 fiscal year. The governing board
will be responsible for this decision.

The Evolution of Processing Specifications

Others contemplating cooperative centralized
processing should pay careful attention to the for-
mulation of processing specifications. It may be
a little easier for a commercial firm because
specifications are based on production costs and
the needs of the majority of users. Customers
have the option of buying standard products at a
moderate price or of paying a premium price for

customized service, which can be high on a per unit basis. A cooperative, nonprofit organization, on the other hand, must seek agreement among its users; otherwise products produced by the central agency will be modified later by customers. Consider the nonacceptance of the truncated titles discussed earlier in this study.

We have already described briefly in Chapter I some efforts to expand the specifications agreed upon during the Phase I-II study. Little did we realize that these initial efforts represented only a beginning. Once books actually begin to arrive at user libraries and were closely scrutinized by processing personnel, a steady stream of feedback regarding the specifications began to flow back to the Center. The issues discussed in the following paragraphs represent only some of the changes that were made. They are included in this report because the changes are typical of what others can expect to incur.

Format of Call Numbers -- The initial cataloging specifications contained an example of the agreed upon LC call number format. The example included in the specifications was DS/35/ W4/1966. (Each slash represents the beginning of a new horizontal line.) In the initial discussions, the only question was whether the alpha characters in the classification number should be printed on the same or a different line from the rest of the classification number.[3] It was agreed that the alpha and numerical symbols would be separated. Unfortunately, the original example did not illustrate a call number which included a double Cutter number. The Center's practice was to print a double Cutter number on the same horizontal line. But more than one library considered this to be in violation of specifications and returned books Cuttered in this manner for correction. (88, 89)

At a TAG meeting, the coordinator proposed that book numbers be expressed on one horizontal line of eight characters or less. Cutter lines which exceeded eight characters would be expressed in two horizontal lines. The break would

occur at the alpha character in the book number. The justifications for this recommendation were: 1) to conserve vertical space on spine labels since only up to eight lines could be printed on a label; 2) to reduce time, since computer costs are calculated on the number of vertical lines used, not the number of characters per line; and 3) this format does not affect shelving even though some member libraries have followed the custom of splitting the Cutter line for many years. On this last point, the University of Colorado's Denver Center Library had adopted the single Cutter line about two years ago and it has not reported any noticeable difficulties in shelving. The Council approved the change in call number format as proposed, after receiving a preliminary endorsement from TAG.

Location Symbols on Call Numbers -- The original specifications did not provide for the inclusion of location information as an element of the call number. In part, this was due to the fact that existing library practices were not uniform; that is, some printed this information at the top of the call number, while others printed it at the bottom. (100) Also, a requesting library might not know at the time of order where a particular book was to be shelved. (87) After considerable discussion, TAG concurred with the CALBPC supervisors that addition of location information in call numbers should continue to be a local activity.

Continuation Cards -- The University of Colorado and two other larger libraries do not file continuation cards under secondary entries. This is a very common practice among research libraries. Its intention is to effect economies in card reproduction and filing costs, and to conserve space in card catalogs. Some of the smaller CALBPC libraries argue that it was essential to continue to provide full information at all access points. However, one of the smaller libraries reported that it, too, only filed a continuation card behind the main entry. The cards for all secondary entries were stamped with directions referring readers to the main entry card for holdings information. Even though this library assured the others that this practice had not caused user dissatisfaction, the participating libraries could not reach agreement on this point. At present, the Center only provides a second card for the main entry. Those libraries requiring additional continuation cards must reproduce their own locally.

Abbreviations in Subject Headings -- Libraries often do not accept the forms of abbreviation the Library of Congress uses in the subdivisions of subject headings. The University of Colorado was no exception. A list of local exceptions has been in use for many years. At the beginning of the experiment, the abbreviations adopted at the University of Colorado were used on catalog card sets produced for user libraries. This practice was begun without realizing that each participant possessed its own list of local exceptions. Unfortunately, each differed from the other. (82, 93) It soon became apparent that standards for abbreviations would have to be adopted. After protracted discussions as to the merits of each library's list, it was proposed that the form of subject heading traced by the Library of Congress would be used without exception. Whenever abbreviations were encountered, these would be accepted. This policy was adopted, even though the Library of Congress itself is sometimes inconsistent in the use of abbreviations. This policy has increased typist productivity because a typist no longer has to be conscious of abbreviations that are exceptions. (1) One library, though it voted in favor of uniformity, has continued to spell out in full all abbreviations --even though this may mean redoing several catalog cards.

Title Input Keypunching Rules -- The fiasco of the truncated titles has already been recounted. It should be remembered that the original purpose in keypunching a truncated title

was to provide sufficient information for accounting purposes. The inclusion of a shortened title on the book card and the book pocket was considered an added bonus--a bogus bonus, as time proved. The results of the product acceptance study (See Figure 2.4) revealed that some libraries did not report their dissatisfaction with the product but manually changed each book pocket and book card locally. The Center was made aware of the difficulties from the complaints registered by two libraries. (88, 89)

The original keypunching instructions stated that the title was not to exceed twenty-eight characters. By and large, the rest was left up to the creativity and imagination of each keypuncher. This oversight was corrected unofficially midway through the experiment. The proposed specifications were discussed by TAG. However, the new specifications were not presented formally to the Council until October. (See Figure A4.5)

Standard Set of Catalog Cards -- The agreed upon standard catalog card set consisted of the following: shelf list, main entry, subject entries (as indicated by the LC tracings), added entries (as indicated by the LC tracings), Rocky Mountain Bibliographical Center notification card, National Union Catalog notification card, and a series added entry card when necessary. (25) Midway through the experiment, two libraries asked if additional cards could be provided. One library needed an extra card for security purposes and the other an extra card for filing in a branch catalog. The question was, would it be more expensive to offer customized service to these libraries, or simply increase the size of the standard set for all libraries. (49, 82) After some consideration, TAG agreed that the preferable alternative was to increase the standard set for all libraries rather than to make any exceptions.

Multiple Card Sets -- For different reasons, two libraries requested that the Center supply additional card sets with processed books. Although some procedural revisions were required,

the Center reported that this service could be offered. It was agreed by TAG that the cost of
each additional card set would be forty cents.
(43, 64, 82, 84)

We deliberately chose the term "evolutionary"
to introduce the topic of processing specifications,
to emphasize the impermanence of any one specification. The topics discussed above represent only
a part of the changes which were made in less
than six months, and the situation has by no means
stabilized. The following excerpts from the
minutes of a recent Board meeting illustrate what
can be expected for some time to come: (Names
have been changed.)

> The next item on the agenda was the
> November 19, 1969 draft of the CALBPC
> Specifications. Miss Smith noted that the
> acceptance of the Abel Approval Form
> as an order request was a change. Mrs.
> Jones explained that CALBPC had worked
> out procedures with Abel to use the form
> as a CALBPC order document. The forms
> are in the process of being revised. Mr.
> Swartz asked that any library wishing to
> order on Abel Forms, please consult
> with him in advance before sending in
> orders on these forms.

> Mr. Hendley expressed his objection to
> p. 4, **3.** (d) of the specifications in
> which it is stated that the CU rather
> than the LC form of series will be used.
> Mr. Swartz replied that the implication
> that CU form takes precedent over LC
> is due to poor wording of this statement
> in the specifications. He explained that
> the CU authority file follows LC; but
> when LC is in conflict with itself, i.e.,
> has traced a series in more than one
> form, the LC form adopted at CU will
> be used. If the CU form has not been
> set up according to LC, the LC form
> will be adopted when it is discovered.
> Mr. Swartz noted that the frequency of
> LC practice in tracing series varies.
> It is necessary for CU to adopt one
> form and stick with it. Mr. Hendley
> agreed and suggested that this state-
> ment in the specifications be rewritten,
> which Mr. Swartz agreed to do.

> Mr. Baker and Mr. Hendley pointed out
> that the treatment of fiction is not ac-
> ceptable to their institutions since they
> are using the PZ classification. While
> they attempt to avoid sending fiction
> orders to CALBPC, it is not always
> possible to screen them out. It was
> agreed that CALBPC would order fiction

> for these two institutions, but would
> return the books uncataloged and charge
> the minimum processing fee. The same
> arrangements apply to others on request.

> Mr. Miner brought up a problem with
> out-of-print titles where it is recom-
> mended that local libraries verify titles
> older than three years as to in-print
> status. He said that on many foreign
> titles there is no bibliographic tool which
> lists in-print books. Mrs. Davis noted
> that most foreign titles are still in
> print after three years, and that CALBPC
> can attempt to acquire them, relying on
> dealer reports for a determination of in-
> print status. Mr. Swartz suggested that
> this sentence be rewritten to apply to
> U.S. in-prints only, and this suggestion
> was approved. (114)

Even now other changes are under consideration. As services of the Center are diversi-
fied to accommodate other categories of materials,
new specifications will have to be written and some
existing specifications modified further. The
moral is that processing specifications had best
be kept in a sturdy loose-leaf binder. Readers
who are still not convinced should compare
specifications in Figure A4.4 which were the
original specifications with those in Figure A4.5,
which are a fairly recent version.

Approval Plan: A Study in Joint Processing

During the Phase I-II study, an investigation of the comprehensive approval plans of both
CU and CSU was undertaken to determine if
there was sufficient commonality in policy and
subject interest to justify coordinated processing
of books obtained on approval. Both libraries are
served by the same approval vendor who ships
books on a weekly cycle. The Phase I-II study
results showed a strong congruity of the two
approval plans based on a comparison of specifications, shelf list, and via a sample from
Choice.[4]

To test further the overlap between the two
plans, arrangements were made for Colorado State
University to send to the CALBPC office multiform slips representing all approval titles

Data Collector_____
Date_____

Figure 4.3

ABEL STUDY TABULATION SHEET, Part I
Characteristic and Processing of
Titles Purchased by Both C.U. and C.S.U. Currently
Sample 708

	C.S.U.	C.U.	Processed Alike	Processed Differently	Total Processed	% A	% D
1. Type of publication			701	7	708	99.01	0.99
(1) Mono	650	651	649			91.67	
(2) Serial	58	57	52			7.34	
2. Ordered from			639	69	608	90.25	9.75
(1) Vendor		59		59			8.33
(2) Direct		9		9			1.27
(3) Abel	708	639	639			90.25	
(4) Gift		1		1			0.15
3. Standing order?			48	9	57	84.21	15.79
(1) Yes	5	14	5	9		8.77	
(2) No	53	43	43			75.44	
4. Handling			56	1	57	98.24	1.76
(1) Classed separately	54	53	53			92.98	
(2) Classed together	4	4	3	1		5.26	1.76
5. Call Number					708	94.49	5.51
(1) Same	708	669	669			94.49	
(2) Different		39		39			5.51
6. Cataloging followed L.C.			670	38	708	94.64	5.36
(1) Yes	681	684	664	36		94.79	5.08
(2) No	27	24	6	2		0.85	0.28
7. Originally cataloged			672	36	708	94.92	5.08
(1) Yes	27	24	6	2		0.85	0.28
(2) No	681	684	666			94.07	
TOTAL							

accepted for a full month beginning with the last
week in May 1969, and a second four-week period during July. Due to time limitations, the data
analysis was conducted only on the first study.

Each multiform slip was attached to a data
collection sheet. (See Figure A4.6) The sample
was checked against the public catalog, order
file, Kardex, shelf list, LC depository card file
and Holding Unit file at the University of Colorado.
A similar search was conducted at Colorado State
University. Out of a sample size of 1,659 titles,
the following results were obtained:

1. 708 titles purchased and processed by
   both libraries.
2. 100 titles in process at either or both
   libraries.
3. 200 titles were reprints for which CU
   already owned the original edition
   (and consequently the necessary
   cataloging information was available).
4. 651 titles not selected by CU.

Therefore, Categories 1, 2 and 3 constitute
the overlap between the two approval plans; that
is, 1,008 titles or 61 percent. Six hundred and
fifty-one titles, or 39 percent, represent the degree of uniqueness between the two plans.

The data tabulation in Part I was performed
in two parts: 1) characteristics in processing of
titles, and 2) cycle time comparison.

Interpretation of the Data -- The results of
the first analysis show a 99 percent concurrence
on the type of publication included in the plan--
clearly monographic. The 10 percent difference
in the choice pattern and the 15 percent difference
in the standing order pattern is understandable because CSU has tried to limit its standing orders
and has relegated this function whenever possible
to the approval dealer. CU, on the other hand,
has elected to retain standing order relationships
which were enforced prior to the adoption of the
approval plan. (See Figure 4.3)

Both libraries depend on LC cataloging
information but there is sufficient variation in
Cuttering and the addition of internal location

symbols, and in the addition of secondary entries,
to produce a five percent variance in call number
and in cataloging format. The local modification
study as it pertains to CSU also revealed approximately the same degree of variation. Only
eight percent of the sample were titles that were
originally cataloged but even here there was 95
percent similarity.

The results of the Part I study supported
the belief that conjoint processing of titles was
feasible. Consequently, the data were then tabulated to compare processing time-lags. (See
Figure A4-7)

The duration of the processing cycle was
established by recording the date received and the
date shelf listed for each of the 708 titles ordered
by both institutions. No shelf list dates could be
found for 13 items, or one percent; consequently,
the actual sample size for the Part II study was
695.

The average processing lag-time for items
received on approval at CSU was 71 days, and for
CU, 85 days. Out of the 708 titles, 270, or 38
percent, were shipped to both libraries within two
weeks of each other. This would indicate that a
vendor could have arranged to ship copies of the
same titles to both institutions during the same
week. Thirty-two percent of the titles arrived
at CU first.

The analysis of lag-times show that CSU
processed its approval receipts on the average of
two weeks quicker than the same titles were
processed at CALBPC. Since the sample was
drawn midway during the experiment, it is likely
that the CALBPC processing times have been overstated. On the other hand, it is probable that no
significant advantage can be accrued to CSU by
sending approval plan books to the Center for
processing. Since there is such a high congruence
in the way books are cataloged at both libraries,
the most promising approach would be for CSU to
notify the Center on receipt of an approval title
at CSU. CALBPC would then prepare a bibliographical packet including a completed card set
and a book card/pocket/label set and forward the

packet to CSU. It is likely that this approach would significantly reduce CSU's present processing lag-time of 70 days.

Incompatibilities Among Library Systems

Cooperative undertakings such as the CALBPC project require careful consideration of existing differences among libraries. We talk so often about the theoretical commonalities that we tend to gloss over practical differences. The so-called differences may not be rooted in an intellectual substance, but based merely on tradition and local custom. Nevertheless they do exist and must be resolved. One contribution of this study is that it enabled us to gain a clearer understanding of these incompatibilities. If we can solve the problems outlined in the following paragraphs, most of the obstacles to cooperation will have been shattered.

Interface between Center and User Systems -- The CALBPC project focused primarily on the development of a centralized capability. To achieve this objective, existing procedures at each participating library were examined carefully as part of the Phase I-II study. However, no attempt was made to recommend improvements to local libraries. Each library director received the detailed flow charts and cost data for his library. The project team assumed rather naively that each library would initiate its own program of work improvement. This was not to be.

A cooperative program, which affects existing procedures and policies at local libraries, should not be created in a "systems" vacuum. By this is meant a centralized operation must be carefully interfaced with the procedures of local libraries; otherwise, expensive duplication of effort will result. This is probably a fundamental tenet for cooperative programs. A more detailed method for evaluating the effectiveness and compatability of processing systems of participants is presented in the next chapter.

Differences Due to Size -- Differences in the size of libraries produce striking contrasts in processing procedures. A small library can maintain an amazing array of records, files, and procedures that no large library would (or should) dare to emulate. A small library can maintain, as part of its order procedure, for example, a vendor file, requestor file, numerical file, and title file without experiencing prohibitive maintenance costs. As has already been discussed, small libraries often carry on the practive of filing continuation cards for secondary entries; whereas most larger libraries have discontinued this practice years ago. (1, 93)

These additional files are designed either to provide the library with greater control or to provide users with additional information. Whether or not the extra records enhance the responsiveness of a library to users is not known. From an operational viewpoint, the creation of a centralized system which does not allow for procedural variation due to differences in size will generate unnecessary duplication because its smaller libraries may tend to perpetuate the traditions of the past.

History and Tradition -- Long standing local traditions and policies also produce system incompatibilities. These differences are not easily erased, because of high change-over costs and human preference for the status quo. For example, if a processing center were to classify books according to the Library of Congress classification system only, those libraries on the Dewey scheme would be excluded from the benefits of centralization. Certainly a center such as CALBPC can classify books according to Dewey as well as LC, but the provision of this service would require establishing a series of subprocedures which would increase the further cost of processing. On the other hand, a decision to adopt the Library of Congress classification system might, though not inevitably, necessitate an expensive re-classification project. Many librarians still believe that the adoption of the Library of Congress classification system automatically signals reclassification. This assumption is specious since the decision to adopt LC and to reclassify are mutually exclusive. Several libraries which have adopted the Library of Congress system have avoided expense by not reclassifying their collections; still others have abandoned on-going reclassification projects because of prohibitive costs. Whatever one's philosophical position with regard to Dewey and LC, it is easy to see why traditional practice can act as a barrier to large-scale cooperation.

Another example, more specific, deals with the handling of monographic series. Here, even the Library of Congress is not always consistent. For example, R.C. Alston's works have been published in a series entitled, A Bibliography of the English Language From the Invention of Printing to the Year 1800. The numbers is this series have been classified both as separates and as a classed-together series. A library operating under a policy of strict adherence to Library of Congress classification would have changed when the Library of Congress changed, and some libraries would have reclassified the earlier Alston volumes. Other libraries very likely would have continued the former practice of classing these titles separately. The Phase I-II study findings identified the processing of monographic series as one area of significant incompatibility between the two largest CALBPC participants.[5] The present study reinforced the findings of the initial study. Unfortunately other long-standing traditions among the CALBPC libraries have created numerous similar incompatibilities.

Differences Due to Service Philosophies -- The philosophy of a librarian toward reader services may bear heavily on the performance of a system. A library which assigns top priority to service, over all other considerations, will exhibit a behavioral pattern far different from a library which assigns greater importance to the maintenance and condition of its internal procedures and records. A librarian who believes books ought to be made available for use as quickly as possible might be willing to circulate a title before the catalog cards are filed safely in the public catalog. In contrast, a librarian who attaches greater importance to the orderliness of his records may be inclined to hold a book in a work area or in an office until all records have been received, inspected and filed. In such cases both the user and cost of procedures are affected.

The design and implementation of cooperative systems must accommodate a spectrum of service philosophies in order to achieve maximum benefits from centralization and cooperation. This is not an easy assignment, but it must be tackled because most existing incompatibilities can be traced to fundamental differences in approaches to librarianship.

By-Products of CALBPC

In 1962 the recommendations of a study commissioned by the Council of Library Resources on how cooperation could further the goals of Colorado Academic Libraries included such items as a courier circuit to speed the flow of interlibrary loan materials, common circulation identification card to permit direct inter-institutional borrowing, centralized processing, and a TWX network.[6] The courier circuit was established in 1965. The courier extends from Ft. Collins, Greeley, through Boulder and Golden into Denver and back to Ft. Collins. The courier presently operates three days a week. The courier truck, as noted earlier, also transports materials from the Center to several user libraries.

The Center also served as the catalytic agent in a recent agreement on circulation standards. Initially, books processed by the Center included a book card to be used in manual circulation systems. But because the two largest libraries did not use the book cards, the question arose whether or not it would be cheaper overall for the Center to produce a machine-readable book card. A study conducted by the coordinator showed that it would be cheaper for the smaller libraries to type their own book cards as one step in their receiving routine than it was for the two largest libraries to keypunch a machine readable book card locally. (92) In 1969, a committee under the Chairmanship of Mr. Robert Braude prepared a set of standards relating to circulation ID cards and data elements to be included in a machine-readable circulation book card. These standards have been agreed to by the majority of academic libraries in Colorado.[7] No doubt this agreement was an outgrowth of CALBPC's capability to produce book cards in a machine-readable format, and CALBPC's political and economic viability. (58) TAG subsequently agreed to the recommended change and, beginning December 1, 1969, machine-readable book cards have been issued with each book. (92)

The presence of CALBPC has improved the chances for some form of coordinated ordering of basic materials. Coordinated ordering was discussed in greater detail on page 18. One developmental activity now contemplated by CALBPC is a follow-up study to the original duplication investigation. The objective will be to determine the percentage overlap and to identify the categories of titles which might be purchased in mass. These data will be used to construct a profile of basic materials.

In addition to coordinated ordering of basic materials, CALBPC could act as the clearing house for programs intended to acquire expensive, little used materials. Such a program has already been initiated by the two largest libraries. Materials purchased jointly are listed in the catalogs of both libraries. The materials themselves are located in the library that purchased them. As CALBPC grows, expansion of this cooperative type of acquisition program is a real possibility.

The most significant benefit, though still an intangible one in the opinion of the investigators, is that CALBPC has improved the climate for cooperation. Librarians are now able to talk about mutual problems in much greater specificity and candor than was previously possible. Colorado librarians are learning and profiting from the successes and failures and the trauma of an extensive cooperative project. It is one thing to talk about cooperative projects at a professional meeting, it is quite another matter to grapple with the problems on a day-to-day basis. These experiences, we believe, will enhance the prospects of future cooperation.

The presence of the Center has also helped librarians communicate to other education officials a clearer understanding of the limitations as well as the potential of centralized processing. For several years, academic officers of several institutions have made public pronouncements about the exchange of library resources without fully understanding the complexities of what is involved.

In a study completed recently on the feasibility of an educational complex which will involve close cooperation among the Community College of Denver, Metropolitan State College, and the Denver Center of the University of Colorado (the project is termed the Auraria Higher Education Complex), sharing of library facilities was recommended. The report urged the sharing of staff and book collections.[8] All agree that although the Auraria project is an exciting educational concept, the sharing of library resources and facilities cannot be administered easily. Here again, CALBPC has given concerned officials a clearer understanding of the complexities of library cooperation. CALBPC in the long run may contribute most to the establishment of cooperative programs which are not directly involved with centralized processing.

Notes

1. Dougherty, "Colorado Academic . . . ," p. 6-7.

2. Leonard, Centralized book processing, Appendix 3.5.8.

3. Ibid., p. 146.

4. Ibid., Chapter VI.

5. Ibid., p. 41.

6. Donald E. Oehlerts, A study to determine the
    feasibility of establishing a cooperative tech-
    nical processing program and direct trans-
    mission of interlibrary loans. (Denver,
    Colorado: Association of State Institutions
    of Higher Education in Colorado, 1962).

7. Robert M. Braude. "Automated Circulation
    Systems," Colorado Academic Library,
    5:4 (Autumn, 1969), p. 1-6.

8. Lamar Kelsey and Associates, Higher Education
    Center Auraria Area Denver, Colorado;
    feasibility study - planning report,
    December 10, 1968. (Author, 1968),
    p. 54-5.

Chapter V

SOME PROBLEMS TO BE ANTICIPATED BY OTHERS CONTEMPLATING CENTRALIZED PROGRAMS OF ACQUISITIONS AND CATALOGING

Much of what has been reported in this study is of relevance only to those who participated in the Colorado experiment. We do not pretend that the findings of the Colorado project can be extrapolated into all other processing environments. However, we believe that others contemplating centralization can profit from our mistakes. Even though the answers may not be different, the questions, at least, must be raised.

Finances

A large-scale processing center will require capitalization. Although we in academia may not be accustomed to thinking in terms of capitalization funding, it is difficult to establish an operation dependent solely on the resources of existing facilities. Furthermore, developmental funds are needed to prevent eventual stagnation.

A major capital investment will be required to finance staffing and equipment, and to acquire work space. The magnitude of initial capitalization costs should not be underestimated. The Arthur D. Little feasibility study of centralized processing for the State University of New York underscores this caveat. The Phase I costs, which include no production, are estimated to be $624,640. And as sobering as this cost estimate may seem, it still probably understates the actual costs.[1] Recently ANYLTS (Association of New York Libraries for Technical Services) reported the need for "an initial subsidy of $1,500,000."[2] ANYLTS estimates that the subsidy would decline proportionally each year until 1976 when revenues should offset expenditures.[3]

A related question is whether or not the operation should be located in an existing facility or established as a separate entity, building its resources from scratch. Either alternative possesses merits. Establishment within an existing library permits better utilization and exploitation of existing resources, expertise, bibliographical resources, physical space, etc. But there is the risk of creating a climate of divided loyalties, interinstitutional jealousies, and suspicion of favoritism. Moreover, it is unlikely that existing facilities will be sufficiently spacious to accommodate a greatly expanded workload.

Fiscal Regulations

The method by which academic institutions are funded frequently produces operational headaches. Some libraries cannot establish their processing commitments until after their funds have been appropriated, and this may not occur until late in the fiscal year. Until then, a library will not know exactly what to anticipate. Consequently, a center may only have a few weeks to recruit and train new staff members or, if circumstances warrant, to reduce its staff. Obviously more than a few weeks are required to gear for a larger operation. A few months is a much more reasonable lead time.

Based on our experiences, we believe that a way must be found to permit advance preparation for projected workloads. This might involve borrowing funds against anticipated revenues. If this is an accepted practice in industry, why should not it be adopted by non-profit organizations such as processing centers?

Another commonly encountered fiscal policy

is to require a library to encumber or expend all
of its book funds by the end of each fiscal year.
Failure to do so may mean reversion of the un-
used portion to the school's business office. Such
a regulation in the environment of centralized
processing can lead to gross waste and inefficiency
in spending. A center must be able to order materials throughout the year in order to avoid the
inefficiencies caused by peak periods of activity
and valleys of inactivity. These problems can
be avoided if a processing center is permitted to
carry over unspent book funds into the subsequent
fiscal period. The same principle should be applied to funds used to defray the cost of book
processing. That is, funds for book processing
should be available when the book is actually
purchased and acquired. Some college business
officers may resist this suggestion, for they may
have become accustomed to using reverted funds
to balance other college accounts at year end.
Nevertheless, the ability to carry over funds from
one fiscal period to another is central to centralized processing.

Product Diversity

CALBPC was intended to be a full service
processing center from the outset. The feasibility
study did not investigate the question of product
diversity. As work progressed it became clear
that in the long run the Center should offer a
variety of services to better serve different libraries. CALBPC both orders and catalogs
books because it can perform these functions
more efficiently than the member libraries. The
existing requirements at most schools that the
library submit orders for books through its business office generates much paperwork and occasionally results in a delay at the business office itself.[4] On the other hand, some user libraries are not governed by these fiscal regu-
lations. A private school may possess a quick
and efficient local ordering procedure. In such
cases the only advantage in ordering through

CALBPC would be to take advantage of large discount rates or to participate in a coordinated ordering plan.

The analysis of the approval plans currently
maintained by the University of Colorado and
Colorado State University also points to the need
for diversification of services. As discussed previously, the results of the study show clearly that
no real advantage will be accrued to a member library which sends the receipts of its approval plan
to CALBPC for processing, at least from the point
of view of speed. In this particular analysis the
data showed that CSU is processing its books on the
average of two weeks quicker than the Center
processed the identical books. Even though these
data were collected during the experimental period
when maximum peak loads existed, it is doubtful that
there is any significant advantage in CALBPC handling
approval books.

When physical handling of books proves to be
more efficient at a local library, a center can serve as
a distributor of bibliographic information, tapping the
resources of its data bank, computer capability, and
reprographic equipment. If a member were to notify
central when it has ordered a particular title or when an
approval book has been received, central would initiate
card reproduction procedures as well as generate a
book card/pocket/label set. The bibliographic information packet would then be forwarded to the requesting library. Or, a library could purchase bibliographic data
offered by an approval dealer.

Standardization of Processing Specifications

Libraries using a centralized processing
center will reflect the diversity of many years of
technological tradition. As a result, a center may
be asked to produce catalog cards in a variety of
formats accommodating local differences in subject
headings and secondary entries. Such a system
will embody great flexibility but it will cost more
to develop and more to maintain. More important,
it will act as a perpetuator of the past. The findings of the Colorado project do not support the
argument that local variation improves the quality

of service to users. It would appear that local idiosyncrasies are more a reflection of individual library staffs. The local practices identified by CALBPC did not seem to have a noticeable impact on service, one way or the other.

Processing specifications should be agreed upon by participants before operations commence; but provisions must be made to permit further modification on a continuing basis. It is unrealistic to expect users to anticipate all possible exceptions beforehand; it is equally unrealistic to presume all participants will be actively concerned about specifics until books actually appear at their libraries. A standard behavior pattern seems to be "out of sight, out of mind," to use an old cliché. It was for this reason that considerable discussion concerning the evolution of processing specifications has been included in this report. In retrospect, a great deal of time and energy might have been saved if more time had been devoted to the explication of specifications. The involvement of middle management personnel from participating libraries in formulating processing specifications is the best insurance for acceptance of products.

Interface of Procedures

The product acceptance study underscored the importance of tight system interface between users and the central operation. The existing differences among the CALBPC library systems could nullify much of the advantage of centralization. In order to evaluate the effectiveness of each library's system, each system was compared against a recommended standard system. (See Figure A5.1) The standard procedure, for the most part, was composed of the best features from the systems of the participants.

Three criteria were formulated to measure procedural efficacy:

1. Type A -- is this activity a result of a local institutional requirement that could not be avoided by the library,

i.e. a business office regulation.

2. Type B -- is this activity one that other libraries would normally perform if they were using the services of a commercial processor? It was assumed that there is a close relationship between the CALBPC recommended procedure and one that a library might use if it was purchasing services from a commercial firm.

3. Type C -- is this activity purely a local decision? An example might be the preparation of an additional order form so that the library can keep track of orders received, arranged by faculty.

Each local procedure was evaluated against the three criteria, Types A, B, and C, to arrive at the total score. For example, at one library all items costing $15 or more are set aside for special handling. The score for this step was one. The step was neither an institutional requirement nor was it a requirement of CALBPC, it was a local routine only. Another example, a library receives its order request forms in a variety of formats. For this step a three rating was assigned since the library is required to accept and handle the forms, a processing center requires a standard format, and this library has developed unique uses for other copies of the order forms. (See Figure A5.2)

A perfect score of twenty-six denotes an efficient procedure which is tightly interfaced with CALBPC's system. A summary of scores is shown in Figure 5.1. However, the scores cannot be evaluated against the ideal score of twenty-six in absolute terms. The investigators found so much local variation among libraries that it was not practical to make exact one to one comparisons for all steps. Consequently, some steps in the standard procedure have been combined, and they may not be in the same sequence as those of the participants. Nevertheless, one can use the figures to assess pretty accurately the present situation.

For example, library one scored twenty-five under Type B. This suggests that its basic procedures are in reasonably good shape. However,

FIGURE 5.1

COMPARISON OF LOCAL PROCESSING PROCEDURES
AGAINST AN IDEALIZED SYSTEM

Institution	Total Steps	Type A Score	Type B Score	Type C Score	Total Score
No. 1	35	4	25	28	57
No. 2	65	0	38	35	73
No. 3	76	3	52	55	110
No. 4	42	0	35	34	69
No. 5	41	1	31	29	61

this library has encumbered its procedures by adding a variety of local practices; consequently, under Type C twenty-eight was scored. A perfect score under Type C would have been zero. Library one's procedures are much more effective than those of library three which scored 110. Library three is guilty of maintaining an elaborate set of basic procedures, to which they have added a labyrinth of local practices which are basically unique to the system. This school should embark on a thorough reexamination of its present operations. The other schools can be evaluated in the same context as schools one and three.

Production Problems

Peak Load Activities -- Production delays caused by bottlenecks and peak periods of activity are not new to library technical processing. It is one matter to tolerate such delays in one's own operation; it is quite another matter to tolerate the same delays when they occur at an external agency. Commercial processors, we are sure, are familiar with this phenomenon.

Figures 5.2 and A5.3 illustrate clearly the peaks of activity which occurred during the experiment. The peak ordering period was February. Two peaks occurred in cataloging, one in June and the second in August. Needless to say, these extremes caused severe bottlenecks and delays.

Shortly after commencement of regular operations the Bibliographic Searching Department experienced an equally serious peak period of activity. (See Figure 5.3) A staff able to assimilate the influx of PR's during the first four months could not be expected to cope with the flood that hit during October and November. On the other hand, a staff able to handle the peak period of activity would have been excessive during the first four months.

One partial solution to this specific problem is to persuade users to order during the "off-season" periods. If orders were concentrated during late spring, summer and early fall, which are the periods of least activity, a Center could smooth out the extremes of production and service to users would be noticeably improved. (114) Since some users are subject to the vagaries of faculty ordering, it is doubtful that pleas to spread the work out will prove completely effective. Also, in Colorado, the smaller institutions habitually encumber all of their book funds by the end of the third quarter of the fiscal year, so that they can spend all of their allotted budget by the end of the year. Of course, the deposit system allows them to expend locally and spread their actual ordering throughout the year.

Fortunately, a center can take direct action to eliminate the effects of peak activity. During the experiment, it was observed that many processing peaks occur in a linear time sequence; that is, the peaks occur sequentually beginning with Bibliographic Searching, and appearing next in Order, Cataloging, and finally in the Catalog Maintenance Department. Therefore, CALBPC can create a

Figure 5.2

LAG TIME STUDY
TIME PERIODS COVERED BY SAMPLE I AND SAMPLE II

O Sample I
X Sample II
---- Percentage of Items Received at center
____ Percentage of Items Cataloged

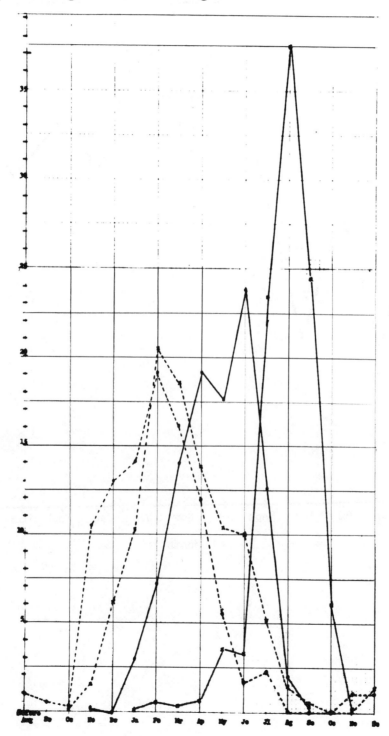

Figure 5.3

INPUT OF PRs INTO THE BIBLIOGRAPHIC SEARCHING DEPARTMENT
May 1969 – May 1970

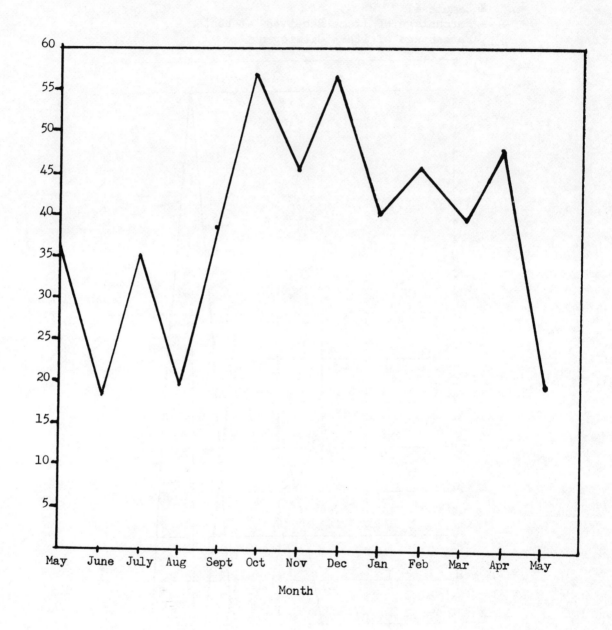

mobile personnel pool so that staff can be transferred to where they are needed. The "floater"
plan is particularly attractive since there are
great similarities among many technical processing activities. For example, bibliographic searching and mass cataloging of books with Library of
Congress copy require similar skills. So too
staff working in the Order Department can be
trained to work in the Catalog Maintenance Department. New job classifications will be established
whereby personnel will be employed to perform
work in two or more departments. This plan has
already been implemented on a trial basis. (50,
66)

Backlogs are also caused by factors which
are time independent. As discussed earlier, books
were often ready for distribution long before the
catalog card sets. The serious delays incurred by
this procedural imbalance caused the Center to
discontinue the card/book matching. The principle
to remember is that if X minutes are required to
perform procedure A, and 2X minutes to perform
procedure B, and if both must be completed during an identical time frame, then either the staffing pattern of procedure B must be twice that of
procedure A, or the work load for procedure B
will have to be spread out over a different time
frame. This latter alternative was used to solve
the problem cited above. By reproducing catalog
card sets for new books shortly after they were
ordered, the Catalog Maintenance Department was
able to expand the time frame for catalog card
preparation.

Holding Books for LC Copy -- The decision
on when to perform original cataloging will have
both an economical and service impact on user libraries. Since it is unlikely that the Library of
Congress will ever be able to distribute copy before all books are received locally, libraries and
processing centers must cope with the question of
how long to hold books for copy before initiating
original cataloging. It would be poor management
for a library to maintain a staff able to process
all books as soon as they arrive.

If the users of a center pay hard dollars for
services rendered, this policy decision is an important one. On the one hand, if books are released to original cataloging too soon, a library's
processing costs will be increased significantly; on
the other hand, if a library is overly parsimonious,
users will be inconvenienced. Obviously, a reasonable trade-off must be sought by policy and by
a rush procedure to invoke original cataloging by
special request.

The CALBPC policy is to wait six months
after a book is ordered before processing is
initiated, assuming of course, that Library of Congress copy is not available when the book is received. After six months, original cataloging is
initiated automatically. (114) Each centralized
processing center, or for that matter all libraries
dependent on LC cataloging, must formulate a similar
policy.

Errors and Quality Control -- Libraries traditionally have given short shift to the matter of
error analysis. There seems to be little recognition
that a vast difference exists in the importance of errors. At one extreme, there are errors which prevent a user from locating the information he is
seeking; that is, a service-damaging error; at the
other extreme, there are errors which might annoy
a reader but will not frustrate his efforts, such as
the misspelling of one word in the subtitle. Most
would agree that different weights could be attached
to such errors, but how often does library procedure
reflect these differences.

The question of quality control is particularly
germane to cooperative programs. If the members
of a cooperative activity really do not believe that
a certain number of errors are inevitable, they will
tacitly develop a local capability to detect errors committed by other members of the cooperative. With
regard to centralized processing, this could mean
that books cataloged centrally might be reexamined
by professionally trained personnel at the receiving
libraries.

It is perfectly reasonable for local libraries
to inspect products received from another agency.

Each library will want to ensure that the external agency maintains previously agreed upon quality control standards. But it is wasteful both for the external agency and the local library to perform exhaustive, duplicative inspections. Inspection programs should be coordinated and, above all, there must be recognition and acceptance that errors are inevitable. The only questions to resolve are how many errors, and how much money participants are willing to spend to eliminate errors.

Use of Specialists in Centralized Processing

One advantage of centralized processing is that it enables a group of libraries to concentrate its scarce human resources. The most obvious example is catalogers who possess specialized subject and language qualifications. A small library usually finds it difficult to secure the services of a cataloger who can satisfy all of its language requirements. Moreover, a small college library may only be able to afford the services of one or two catalogers. Certainly, it is more economical for one larger agency to employ the services of these specialized individuals.

But specialization can reach a point of diminishing returns. If only one or possibly two libraries acquire a particular category of specialized materials such as medical or agriculture titles, what are the advantages of locating a specialist at the central agency. The answer may be, none. If users of a processing center have agreed upon standard specifications, there should be no intellectual objection to locating a specialist at the library which actually requires the esoteric materials. The specialist would also serve the needs of other participants. Of course, in order for such an arrangement to function, member libraries must adhere closely to the agreed upon processing standards.

Categorization of Technical Service Activities not related directly to Book Acquisitions and Processing

A library using the services of a centralized processing agency must distinguish between technical services activities performed centrally and those which are still performed locally. Centralized processing does not eliminate the need to maintain a local technical services capabiiity. It is still necessary locally for a library to order, check-in serials, receive and acknowledge gifts, file in the card catalog, and conduct many other maintenance activities.

A library must prepare a job description for each position and divide the activities performed into two categories: activities which are performed centrally and activities which are performed locally. The results of this analysis will provide the foundation for two distinct technical service budgets. This analysis is important because, if fund appropriating agencies accept the premise of centralization on the grounds of economy, it is doubtful that they will view with favor continued staff growth at the local level without strong justification. Moreover, appropriators must be educated as to why centralized processing is most cost beneficial when closely coordinated with local operations as opposed to replacing them totally.

Notes

1. Arthur D. Little, Inc., A Plan for a library processing center for the State University of New York (New York: Author, 1967), p. 34.

2. ANYLTS Printout, 2:1 (March, 1970), p. 2.

3. Ibid.

4. Leonard, Centralized book processing, Chapter IV.

Chapter VI

SUMMARY OF CONCLUSIONS AND RECOMMENDATIONS

General

1. The concept of centralized acquisitions and cataloging for Colorado academic libraries is sound. The experimental operations supported the conclusion of the Phase I-II study that money would be saved, and the time required to acquire and catalog materials would be reduced. It is recommended that CALBPC as a total system be further refined and that it be continued and expanded as prescribed in the following specific recommendations.

2. The product acceptance study showed that the participants did accept the intellectual aspects of cataloging and classification. Most local changes involved the mechanical tasks associated with book preparation and maintenance of local control records. The results of the product acceptance investigation support the hypothesis that centralized processing is a viable concept.

3. Quality control programs must be established. The failure to recognize that errors are inevitable, adversely affected morale at participating libraries as well as the Center. From an operational viewpoint, this unrealistic attitude has already caused a proliferation of local inspection routines. It is recommended that the educational program (Recommendation five) include discussions of errors, error detection, and error prevention. The long range objective should be a realistic quality control program.

4. Communication breakdowns accounted for many problems. In part the geographical separation of the participants was partially to blame for the failures. Then, too, some staff members both at CALBPC and at the participating libraries do not clearly understand the role of CALBPC. They do not know how cooperation will

affect their jobs, their futures, or their status. It is recommended that greater emphasis be placed on disseminating information throughout the system and throughout each library, that the coordinator's role as a public relations officer be expanded, and that the effectiveness of the Board of Directors be improved by appointing an Executive Committee to act in behalf of the Board.

5. Most problems encountered in this project, which are spelled out in the other conclusions and recommendations, can be traced to human frailties rather than technological problems. Centralization, cooperation, and computerization have created a library environment that is completely alien to many librarians. It is recommended that an intensive continuing education program be sponsored by the CALBPC Board. The curriculum should include instruction on automation, communication, quality control, systems analysis, and the social role of libraries in an academic setting. The courses should be open to all professional and key nonprofessional staff members.

Cost and Performance

1. The analysis of costs indicates that the cost of acquiring and cataloging the average book has been reduced from $3.10 to $2.63. This reduction was achieved in spite of the inflationary cost increases which have occurred since the initial study. However, the cost of processing per volume is more than the Center now charges. It is recommended that the cost analysis of CALBPC operations be refined further, and that the CALBPC Board consider revising the present fee schedule.

2.   Cost savings based on unit costs are
not realistic because they are not readily visible to
fund appropriators. If resources could be real-
located rapidly from local libraries to a central
agency, unit cost savings might be a useful indi-
cator because budgetary patterns among the libraries would be affected. Unfortunately, this
has not occurred in the CALBPC project. Local
processing budgets have not decreased; however,
their growth has or will shortly level off. It is
recommended, therefore, that cost savings be expressed in terms of cost avoidance rather than
unit costs.

3.   The acquisition/cataloging time cycle
decreased thirteen days for the six participating
libraries as compared to the time lags observed
during the Phase I-II study. Overall performance
at four libraries improved; at the others, performance declined. One major contributant to the
delays was a decline in vendor performance from
62 days in the Phase I-II study to an average of
80 days. Also Library of Congress copy was
available for only 38 percent of the titles at the
time of their arrival. Consequently, books were
delayed until copy was received. The lag-time
data was gathered at a time when the Center
was beset with problems. (See Figure 5.2 for a
vivid picture of peak loads of activity which occurred during the study.) It is the consensus of
the CALBPC staff and Coordinator that performance
has improved significantly since normal operations
began. It is recommended that a follow-up lag-
time study be conducted to verify the reported
improvements.

4.   CALBPC had no discernible impact on
discounts received from vendors. In part this can
be attributed to the types of books ordered, the
volume of materials ordered, and the number of titles
for which multiple copies were purchased. It is recommended that as the volume and duplication rates increase,
efforts to effect more favorable discount rates be
renewed.

Services

1.   The current restrictions regarding the
types of material which can be ordered and processed through the Center have reduced the usefulness of CALBPC for some libraries. It is recommended that the Center accept orders for out-of-
print titles, microforms, and as soon as possible,
orders for non-print materials.

2.   The Center must begin now to diversify
its services. Handling of books is not always the
most effective approach to centralization. To serve
some libraries most effectively the Center should
also be a purveyor of bibliographic packets, i.e.,
a complete card set and a book card/pocket/label/
set. It is recommended that efforts to implement
new services be given a high priority.

3.   The analysis of approval plan congruence between CU and CSU showed that libraries receiving titles on approval will not benefit substantial-
ly by forwarding them to the Center. It is recommended that libraries receiving titles on approval
notify the Center on receipt, and that the Center
provide the requesting library with a bibliographic
packet.

4.   Both the Phase I-II project and the current project revealed considerable overlap among existing collections. Coordinated ordering of those titles
that the participants are most likely to purchase
independently would lower processing costs and improve service to users by reducing further the ac-
quisition/cataloging cycle. It is recommended that
further studies be conducted to identify the exact
degree of overlap, the subject areas, and the levels
of treatment duplicated. It is further recommended
that a study be undertaken to test the validity of the
objections to coordinated ordering which are bound
to be raised.

Systems and Procedures

1.   Each library must maintain a local
processing capability to handle specialized materials
such as local archives. Libraries must also

continue to perform technical processes activities that are not directly related to book acquisition and processing--such as serials handling, gift and exchange activities, and catalog maintenance. It is recommended that each participating library identify local processing tasks and the FTE requirement to perform each task.

2. The design of the automated accounting subsystem proved to be more complicated than had been anticipated. The types of error identified following implementation, e.g., design, user, hardware, etc., counsel a more intensive design program in all future automation projects. It is recommended that a panel of users evaluate all aspects of a designed system prior to actual programming. It is further recommended that the services of an outside expert be employed to review all plans with the user panel and system designers.

3. The CALBPC posture toward automation should be to strike an effective operational mix between automated and manual systems. Although it is technologically possible to automate most, if not all, of CALBPC's systems, it is not economically feasible at this time. It is recommended that the economic implications of each automation project be scrutinized for cost ramifications prior to design. This is particularly important since participants must pay hard dollars for services rendered.

4. The present interfacing of procedures between the participants and the Center are inefficient and cumbersome. The interfacing of the central with the local procedures so that CALBPC works as a total system is vital to success. It was found that very efficient ordering and receiving procedures could be articulated by selecting the best features of each participants' existing procedures. It is recommended that one phase of the education program (Recommendation 5) be devoted to procedural interface design.

5. There are more causes for the existing incompatibilities among the participating libraries than had been recognized at the outset of the project. Disparity among systems can be traced to differences in the size of libraries, history and tradition, and to service philosophies of individual libraries. It is recommended that future cooperative ventures compensate for existing incompatibilities; in the meantime, CALBPC and its Board should endeavor to ameliorate these incompatibilities. Again, the educational program will hold the key to success.

6. Some librarians placed too much emphasis on the aesthetics of catalog cards rather than on their content. The objections raised against Polaroid master copy were symptomatic of a more general preoccupation with the mechanical aspects of book processing rather than the intellectual quality of cataloging and classification. There was a time, not long ago, when many librarians rejected catalog cards reproduced by means of Xerography but these objections are largely a thing of the past. What is the relationship between aesthetics and quality of service? It is recommended that funds be obtained to investigate the correlation between product aesthetics and the quality of library service.

Future Developments

1. It is recommended that other types of libraries be encouraged to use the services of the Center. This would include not only those academic institutions not presently using the Center but public and school libraries as well. The Center's rich data base of cataloging copy can benefit all types of libraries.

2. It is recommended that the participants continue to assess themselves in order to finance a vigorous developmental program. It is further recommended that the CALBPC Board sponsor a study to determine the long-range costs and benefits of automation.

3. It is recommended that the CALBPC Board communicate the long-range facility requirements to the Colorado Commission on Higher Education to insure that adequate quarters will be made available to permit a continued, orderly expansion of the Center.

DOCUMENTS CITED

1. "Minutes of Advisory Board of the Colorado Academic Library Book Processing Center," June 2, 1969.

2. Sheldon to Morgan, May 29, 1969.

3. "Minutes of Advisory Board of the Colorado Academic Library Book Processing Center," June 2, 1969.

4. "Specification changes suggested by Mr. Petriwsky," February 27, 1969.

5. "Minutes of Advisory Board of the Colorado Academic Library Book Processing Center," December 20, 1968.

6. "Minutes of Advisory Board of the Colorado Academic Library Book Processing Center," November 26, 1968.

7. "Draft explanation of the PALMOPTW report," n.d.

8. "List of vendor codes," December 13, 1968.

9. Maier, Joan M. and Dougherty, Richard M. "The cost benefits of the Colorado Academic Book Processing Center: 1968-1980." (Boulder, Colorado: University of Colorado Libraries, 1968), 21p.

10. "Minutes of Advisory Board of the Colorado Academic Library Book Processing Center," March 24, 1969.

11. Harper to Petriwsky, September 25, 1969.

12. Sheldon to Petriwsky, September 30, 1969.

13. Dahl-Hansen to Dougherty and Rebuldela, December 16, 1968.

14. Dahl-Hansen to Maier, Harper, and Petriwsky, May 5, 1969.

15. Harper to Dahl-Hansen, May 5, 1969.

16. Petriwsky, Rebuldela and Dahl-Hansen to Dougherty, March 24, 1969.

17. Feyock to Dougherty, January 17, 1969.

18. Dahl-Hansen to Dougherty, January 13, 1969.

19. Feyock to Dougherty, December 18, 1968.

20. "Excerpt from University of Colorado Procedure Manual: Classification of Fiction at CU Libraries," March 6, 1967.

21. Maier to Dougherty, November 21, 1968.

22. Maucker to Sheldon, April 4, 1969.

23. Maier to Petriwsky and Sheldon, April 10, 1969.

24. "Organization chart of the University of Colorado Technical Services Division, the Processing Center and the Participating Libraries." n.d.

25. "Minutes of Advisory Board of the Colorado Academic Library Book Processing Center," December, 1968.

26. "Minutes of Advisory Board of the Colorado Academic Library Book Processing Center," October, 1968.

27. "Suggestions for changes in the CALBPC cataloging specifications," November 1, 1968.

28. "Minutes of Advisory Board of the Colorado Academic Library Book Processing Center," November, 1967.

29. Dahl-Hansen to CALBPC supervisors, May 5, 1969.

30. Dahl-Hansen to Maier and Dougherty, April 18, 1969.

31. "SILO Diagnostics," February 14, 1969.

32. "Tabulation of cancellations due to duplication," July 1, 1969.

33. "Tabulation of returned PRs," June 30, 1969.

34. "Tabulation of corrections made by Coordinator," April 24, 1969.

35. "Budgetary estimates of the CALBPC participants for fiscal 1970." (Collection of Worksheets, Memoranda, and Letters).

36. Wagener to Dougherty and Maier, October 9, 1969.

37. Maier to Dougherty, October 24, 1969.

38. Petriwsky to CALBPC supervisors, November 25, 1969.

39. Petriwsky to CALBPC supervisors, November 24, 1969.

40. Wagener to Dahl-Hansen, November 5, 1969.

41. Dahl-Hansen to Petriwsky and Wagener, October 28, 1969.

42. Dougherty to Wagener, October 31, 1969.

43. Sheldon to Petriwsky, October 27, 1969.

44. Petriwsky to Wagener, October 21, 1969.

45. Harper to Sheldon, October 17, 1969.

46. Dahl-Hansen to Petriwsky, October 16, 1969.

47. Dahl-Hansen to Petriwsky, October 16, 1969.

48. Petriwsky and Dahl-Hansen to Technical Services, October 15, 1969.

49. Sheldon to Petriwsky, October 15, 1969.

50. Petriwsky to Wagener, October 8, 1969.

51. Wagener to CALBPC supervisors, October 15, 1969.

52. Wagener to Dougherty, November 2ᴺ, 1969.

53. Wagener to Dahl-Hansen and Rebuldela, November 18, 1969.

54. Wagener to Rebuldela, November 12, 1969.

55. Wagener to CALBPC supervisors, November 7, 1969.

56. Wagener to Bachenberg, November 5, 1969.

57. "Processing fee schedule, draft version," n.d.

58. Wagener to Dougherty, Harper and Petriwsky, November 7, 1969.

59. Wagener to CALBPC supervisors, November 4, 1969, October 30, 1969.

60. Wagener to CALBPC supervisors, November 4, 1969, October 30, 1969.

61. Wagener to Sheldon, October 30, 1969.

62. Wagener to Dougherty and CALBPC supervisors, October 29, 1969.

63. Wagener to Sheldon, October 29, 1969.

64. Wagener to CALBPC supervisors, November 4, 1969, October 28, 1969.

65. Wagener to CALBPC supervisors, October 28, 1969.

66. Rebuldela to CALBPC supervisors, October 9, 1969.

67. "Minutes of the Supervisors of the Colorado Academic Library Book Processing Center," October 6, 1969.

68. Sheldon to Petriwsky, September 30, 1969.

69. "Title input specifications, a proposal," n.d.

70. Sheldon to Petriwsky, September 19, 1969.

71. "Three memos concerning the logic of the accounting subsystem expenditure routine," September 12, 1969.

72. Sheldon to Petriwsky, September 9, 1969.

73. Maier to Sheldon, August 28, 1969.

74. "Tabulation of Corrections made to truncated titles for one of the participating libraries," August 22, 1969.

75. Maier to Dahl-Hansen, August 1, 1969.

76. "Tabulation of corrections made to truncated titles for one of the participating libraries," August 11, 1969.

77. Dahl-Hansen to Rebuldela, Hewitt, Sheldon, Maier, Dougherty, and Harper, July 15, 1969.

78. "Minutes of the Supervisors of the Colorado Academic Library Book Processing Center," July 11, 1969.

79. Petriwsky and Maier to Harper and Maucker, July 1, 1969.

80. Harper to Petriwsky and Maier, July 1, 1969.

81. Maier and Petriwsky to Dougherty, June 10, 1969.

82. "Minutes of the Supervisors of the Colorado Academic Library Book Processing Center," June 2, 1969.

83. Petriwsky to Sheldon, May 28, 1969.

84. Maier to Council of Librarians and Other members of the governing Council of the Colorado Academic Libraries Book Processing Center, November 17, 1969.

85. "Flow chart of a standardized ordering and receiving procedure," n.d.

86. Maier to Council of Librarians, May 29, 1969.

87. Burns to Anderson, October 18, 1969.

88. Maier to Seager, June 6, 1969.

89. "Tabulation of errors returned by one of the participating libraries," May 27, 1969.

90. Maier to Directors of the CALBPC participating libraries, February 25, 1969.

91. "Analysis of discounts received from two jobbers," n.d.

92. Maier to Anderson, July 3, 1969

93. "Minutes of the Supervisors of the Colorado Academic Library Book Processing Center," June 2, 1969.

94. Maier to Petriwsky and Sheldon, May 27, 1969.

95. "Minutes of Meeting with the staff from Metropolitan State College," May 14, 1969.

96. "Minutes of the Supervisors of the Colorado Academic Library Book Processing Center," April 3, 1969.

97. "Minutes of the Supervisors of the Colorado Academic Library Book Processing Center," March 31, 1969.

98. "Minutes of the Supervisors of the Colorado Academic Library Book Processing Center," March 19, 1969.

99. "Minutes of the Supervisors of the Colorado Academic Library Book Processing Center," March 4, 1969.

100. "Minutes of meeting between Gene Petriwsky and Joan Maier concerning cataloging specifications," March 1, 1969.

101. Maier to Dougherty and Dahl-Hansen, September 25, 1968.

102. "Tabulation of titles returned to participants," n.d.

103. Maier, Joan M. and Dougherty, Richard M. "An accounting system for the Colorado Academic Libraries Book Processing Center: Proposal." (Boulder, Colorado: University of Colorado Libraries, 1968), 10p.

104. "Processing errors reported to the Center," various dates. (Collection of worksheets, memoranda, and letters).

105. "Title change method," March 11, 1969.

106. "Listing of report codes and their interpretations," n.d.

107. Maier to Dahl-Hansen, Harper, and Rebuldela, March 10, 1969.

108. "Sample of a FACS report and a shipping list," n.d.

109. Sheldon to Dougherty, March 13, 1970.

110. Petriwsky to Dougherty, March 15, 1970.

111. Sheldon to Dougherty, March 13, 1970.

112. Petriwsky to Dougherty, March 23, 1970.

113. Hewitt to Council of Librarians and other members of the governing Council of the Colorado Academic Libraries Book Processing Center, January 16, 1970.

114. Hewitt to Council of Librarians and Other Members of the Governing Council of the Colorado Academic Libraries Book Processing Center, February 11, 1970.

115. Dougherty, Richard M. "A Proposal to the National Science Foundation for continued support of Academic Libraries Cooperative Processing Center for all Colorado Colleges and Universities Phase III: Operational Experiment." (Boulder, Colorado: University of Colorado Libraries), 1968.

116. Maier to Dougherty and Dahl-Hansen, September 25, 1969.

117. Maier to Directors of the CALBPC participating libraries, October 18, 1968.

118. "Series of tables summarizing selected production statistics, such as volumes cataloged and shipped," various dates.

119. Sheldon to Petriwsky, May 13, 1970.

120. Hewitt to Dougherty, June 1, 1970.

121. Terry to Dougherty, January 9, 1969.

APPENDIX FIGURES

A2.1 - A2.44

(Chapter II)

Figure A2.1

BOOKS FROM
CATALOGING AREA
SHIPPING CENTERS

School	Month	Gift Volumes Shipped	Total
MSC	March thru July	-	
	August	25	
	September	218	
	October	301	
	November	5	
	December	-	549
CSM	March thru July	-	
	August	84	
	September	17	
	October	53	
	November	-	
	December	-	154
CSC	March thru June	-	
	July	18	
	August	33	
	September	31	
	October	51	
	November	27	
	December	-	160
ASC	March thru May	-	
	June	1	
	July	-	
	August	199	
	September	8	
	October	15	
	November	78	
	December	-	301
CSU	March thru July	-	
	August	310	
	September	284	
	October	620	
	November	261	
	December	12	1487
		GRAND TOTAL	2651

Figure A2.2

PROCESSING CENTER CATALOGING WORK LOAD
(Including Serials)
January - December 1969

	University of Colorado, Boulder Campus			Colorado Springs Campus	Denver Center Library	Member Libraries	University of Colorado Added		Total
	LC	No LC	Vols				Vols.	Cops.	
January	1418	843	1266	457	602		1750	544	6880
February	1031	757	557	335	428	189	1609	409	5315
March	1452	835	736	323	357	355	1854	309	6221
April	1891	643	1145	317	396	961	2033	378	7764
May	1502	675	1577	243	329	1127	2486	371	8310
June	1580	492	950	404	757	2465	1727	636	9011
July	2215	891	1088	237	779	2216	1760	393	9579
August	1725	738	757	290	342	2286	1544	521	8203
September	1730	1304	821	201	571	1241	1643	450	7961
October	1585	1050	935	295	309	478	1993	430	7075
November	1393	1092	1163	181	413	524	1466	543	6775
December	1296	936	499	241	444	758	1042	663	5879
TOTAL	18818	10256	11494	3524	5727	12600	20907	5647	88973

Figure A2. 3

PROCESSING CENTER CATALOGING WORK LOAD
(excluding serials)
January - December 1969

| | University of Colorado, Boulder Campus | | | Colorado Springs Campus | Denver Center Library | Member Libraries | University of Colorado Added | | Total |
	LC	No LC	Vols				Vols.	Cops.	
January	1356	743	474	457	536		1750	531	5847
February	986	668	285	236	383	189	1609	399	4755
March	1416	751	388	320	350	355	1854	308	5692
April	1835	526	702	314	391	961	2033	325	7087
May	1466	588	929	240	327	1127	2486	371	7534
June	1555	407	505	404	757	2465	1727	636	8456
July	2151	782	380	237	779	2216	1760	390	8695
August	1690	702	525	290	342	2286	1544	514	7893
September	1685	1250	459	192	562	1241	1643	443	7475
October	1531	860	371	275	305	478	1993	426	6239
November	1366	975	363	177	401	524	1466	539	5806
December	1270	886	361	241	425	758	1042	609	5592
TOTAL	18307	9138	5692	3383	5558	12600	20907	5486	81071

Figure A2.4

BOOK

BUYING PATTERNS BY PARTICIPANT

(SAMPLE 1)

Library	Domestic						Foreign						
	Current (1966+)		Retrospective (Earlier than 1966)		Domestic Total		Current (1966+)		Retrospective (Earlier than 1966)		Foreign Total		
	(No.)	(%)	(No.)	(%)	(%)		(No.)	(%)	(No.)	(%)	(%)		
ASC	59	71.1	22	26.5	97.6		1	1.2	1	1.2	2.4		
CSC	123	75.5	30	18.4	93.9		7	4.3	3	1.8	6.1		
CSM	34	85.0	3	7.5	92.5		2	5.0	1	2.5	7.5		
CSU	18	20.0	45	50.0	70.0		18	20.0	9	10.0	30.0		
CU	1092	59.0	415	22.4	81.4		196	10.6	149	8.0	18.4		
MSC	124	67.8	14	7.7	75.5		40	21.8	5	2.7	24.5		
Sub Total	1450	60.1	529	22.0	82.1		264	10.9	168	7.0	17.9		

Figure A2.5

BOOK
BUYING PATTERNS BY PARTICIPANT

(SAMPLE 2)

Library	Domestic					Foreign				
	Current (1966+)		Retrospective (Earlier than 1966)		Domestic Total	Current (1966+)		Retrospective (Earlier than 1966)		Foreign Total
	(No.)	(%)	(No.)	(%)	(%)	(No.)	(%)	(No.)	(%)	(%)
ASC	59	55.1	42	39.2	94.3	3	2.8	3	2.8	5.6
CSC	128	64.6	53	26.8	91.4	14	7.1	3	1.5	8.6
CSM	43	60.6	18	25.4	86.0	4	5.6	6	8.4	14.0
CSJ	39	15.6	72	28.8	44.4	81	32.4	58	23.2	55.6
CU	553	51.4	232	21.6	73.0	150	13.9	141	13.1	27.0
MSC	65	59.6	32	29.3	88.9	10	9.2	2	1.8	11.0
Sub Total	887	49.0	449	24.2	73.2	262	14.5	213	12.8	27.3

Figure A2.6

BOOK

BUYING PATTERNS BY PARTICIPANT

(SAMPLES 1 AND 2 COMBINED)

Library	Domestic						Foreign					
	Current (1966+)		Retrospective (Earlier than 1966)		Domestic Total		Current (1966+)		Retrospective (Earlier than 1966)		Foreign Total	
	(No.)	(%)	(No.)	(%)	(%)		(No.)	(%)	(No.)	(%)	(%)	
ASC	118	62.1	64	33.7	95.8		4	2.1	4	2.1	4.2	
CSC	251	69.5	83	22.9	92.4		21	5.8	6	1.7	7.5	
CSM	77	69.4	21	18.9	88.3		6	5.4	7	6.3	11.7	
CSU	57	16.8	117	34.4	51.2		99	29.1	67	19.7	48.8	
CU	1645	56.2	647	22.1	78.3		346	11.8	290	9.9	21.7	
MSC	180	64.7	46	15.7	80.4		50	17.1	7	2.4	19.5	
Sub Total	2337	55.4	978	23.2	78.6		526	12.5	381	9.0	21.5	

Figure A2.7

ANALYSIS OF TITLES ORDERED DURING THE EXPERIMENT BUT NOT RECEIVED

(1) TYPE OF VENDOR

TYPE OF VENDOR	ASC		CSC		CSM		CSU		MSC		CU		Totals	
	#	%	#	%	#	%	#	%	#	%	#	%	#	%
Domestic Jobber	91	92.8	262	90.3	39	92.9	210	72.2	132	94.9	783	43.5	1517	57.1
Domestic Publisher	7	7.2	16	5.6	2	4.8	10	3.4	2	1.4	97	5.4	134	5.0
Foreign Jobber			9	3.1	1	2.3	66	22.7	4	3.0	596	33.1	676	25.4
Foreign Publisher			2	.7			3	1.7	1	.7	37	2.1	45	1.7
Advertising			1	.3							286	15.9	287	10.8
	98	100.0	290	100.0	42	100.0	291	100.0	139	100.0	1799	100.0	2659	100.0

Figure A2.7 (Continued)

(2) CLAIMS INITIATED

	ASC		CSC		CSM		CSU		MSC		CU		Total	
	#	%	#	%	#	%	#	%	#	%	#	%	#	%
Yes	8	8.2	7	2.4	4	9.5	21	7.2	5	3.6	54	3.0	99	3.7
No	90	91.8	283	97.6	38	90.5	270	92.8	134	96.4	1745	97.0	2560	96.3
	98	100.0	290	100.0	42	100.0	291	100.0	129	100.0	1799	100.0	2659	100.0

(3) PUBLISHER'S REPORT RECEIVED

	ASC		CSC		CSM		CSU		MSC		CU		TOTAL (2659)	
	#	%	#	%	#	%	#	%	#	%	#	%	#	%
No Report	67	68.4	186	64.1	29	69.1	205	70.7	112	80.5	929	51.7	1528	57.4
Out of Print			7	2.5	1	2.3	44	15.1	3	2.2	582	29.3	583	21.9
Out of Stock	1	1.0	10	3.4			8	2.7	3	2.2	53	2.8	75	2.8
Back Order	29	29.6	68	23.5	8	19.2	14	4.8	16	11.5	109	6.1	244	9.1
Not Yet Published			15	5.2	3	7.1	10	3.3	5	3.6	122	6.7	155	5.8
Other	1	1.0	4	1.3	1	2.3	10	3.4			58	3.4	73	3.0
	98	100.0	290	100.0	42	100.0	291	100.0	139	100.0	1799	100.0	2659	100.0

Figure A2.7 (Continued)

(4) LIBRARY OF CONGRESS CATALOGING

	ASC		CSC		CSM		CSU		MSC		CU		Total	
	#	%	#	%	#	%	#	%	#	%	#	%	#	%
Exact	81	82.7	194	66.9	32	76.2	194	66.7	123	88.5	1120	62.3	1744	65.6
Different Edition	5	5.1	56	19.3	7	16.7	28	9.6	6	4.3	290	16.1	392	14.7
No Copy	12	12.2	40	13.8	3	7.1	69	23.7	10	7.2	389	21.6	523	19.7
	98	100.0	290	100.0	42	100.0	291	100.0	139	100.0	1799	100.0	2659	100.0

(5) VENDOR REASSIGNED

	ASC		CSC		CSM		CSU		MSC		CU		Total	
	#	%	#	%	#	%	#	%	#	%	#	%	#	%
Yes	11	11.2	55	19.0	5	11.9	32	11.0	29	20.9	191	10.6	323	12.2
No	87	88.8	235	81.0	37	88.1	259	89.0	110	79.1	16.8	80.4	2336	87.8
	98	100.0	290	100.0	42	100.0	291	100.0	139	100.0	179c	100.0	2659	100.0

Figure A2.7 (Continued)

(6)   TOTAL NUMBER OF BOOKS ORDERED NOT RECEIVED, ARRANGED BY DATE OF PUBLICATION

Year	ASC	CSC	CSM	CSU	MSC	CU	TOTAL
n.d.	6	9	–	13	1	169	198
1969	1	25	3	4	1	115	149
1968	30	61	22	50	35	193	391
1967	10	48	4	42	40	87	231
1966	8	32	5	22	22	45	134
1965	6	13	4	36	4	46	109
1964	7	17	1	19	7	61	112
1963	8	12	1	14	4	65	104
1962	5	10	–	6	5	78	104
1961	2	9	2	12	2	65	92
1960	7	6	–	6	2	78	99
Earlier than 1960	7	48	–	66	17	797	935
	98	230	42	291	139	1799	2659

(7)   TITLES NOT RECEIVED REPORTED OUT-OF-PRINT ARRANGED BY DATE OF PUBLICATION

Year	ASC Not Adv	CSC Adv	CSC Not Adv	CSM Not Adv	CSU Not Adv	MSC Not Adv	CU Adv.	CU Not Adv	Total Adver.	Total Not Adver.	Total OP
n.d	–	–	–	–	3	–	4	10	4	13	17
1969	–	–	–	–	–	–	–	2	–	2	2
1968	–	–	–	–	6	1	2	7	2	14	16
1967	–	–	–	–	2	–	–	6	–	8	8
1966	–	–	–	1	3	–	–	6	–	10	10
1965	–	–	–	–	5	–	5	6	5	11	16
1964	–	–	–	–	1	–	9	9	9	10	19
1963	–	–	–	–	1	–	6	12	6	13	19
1962	–	1	–	–	1	–	14	15	15	16	31
1961	–	–	1	–	2	–	13	16	13	19	32
1960	–	–	1	–	1	1	10	27	10	30	40
Earlier than 1960	–	–	4	–	19	1	188	161	188	185	373
	0	1	6	1	44	3	231	277	252	331	583

Figure A2.8

DISCOUNTS RECEIVED FROM FIVE JOBBERS, 1968 (FIRST ANALYSIS)[1]

Name of Firm	Dates of Invoices	Number of Items	Discount (in percent)												Weighted Average[2]
			Net	5	9	10	12	15	17	20	25	30	33	33.3	
Abel	1968	482	87			328				5		62			10.6
Stacey's	1968	303				303									10.0
Makely's	1968	308	40			228	40								9.0
Eastern	1968	215	39			114				15		47			13.2
E.B.S.	1968	520	5	4		2	280		73			156			18.0

Figure A2.9

DISCOUNTS RECEIVED FROM JOBBERS, 1969–70 (FOLLOW-UP STUDY)

Name of Firm	Dates of Invoices	Number of Items	Discount (in percent)												Weighted Average[2]
			Net	5	9	10	12	15	17	20	25	30	33	33.3	
Abel	July 9-Sept.23,1970	2700	706	66	3	1451		2		1		471			10.8
Stacey's	July 9-Feb.7,1970	1077	17	316		422	25	190		86	3		18		10.5
Makely's	July 9-March 1970	1144	358			522	264								7.3
Eastern	July 9-March 1970	859	212			357				57	4			229	14.5
E.B.S.	July 9-March 1970	2207	65	73		61	1038		381			589			17.0

1) Sample pulled from 1968 invoices

2) $\bar{X}_W = \dfrac{\sum X_i W_i}{\sum W_i}$

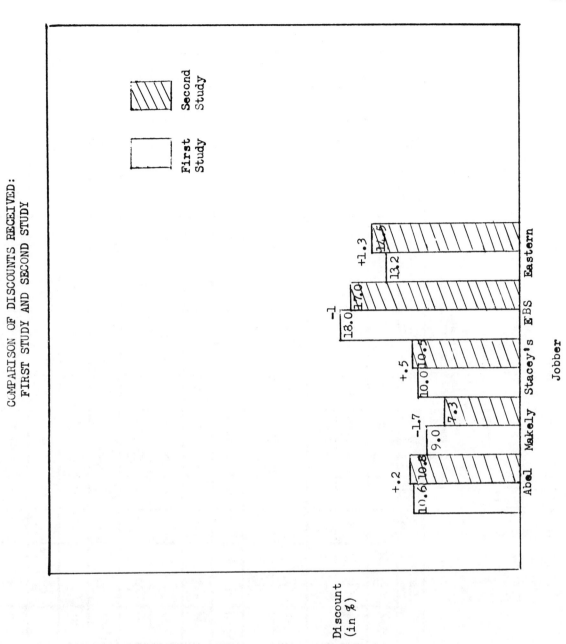

Figure A2.10

COMPARISON OF DISCOUNTS RECEIVED:
FIRST STUDY AND SECOND STUDY

Figure A2.11

ORDER-DELIVERY TIME LAGS
OF VENDORS FROM WHICH FIFTY OR MORE
TITLES WERE ORDERED (Feb.-Oct. 1969)

School No. 1 (C.U.)

Vendor Type Coded	No.	Ave. Days	Ordered	February Ave.	February No.	March Ave.	March No.	April Ave.	April No.	May Ave.	May No.	June Ave.	June No.	July Ave.	July No.	August Ave.	August No.	September Ave.	September No.	October Ave.	October No.
P	1	92	1465	5	22	6	27	12	34	65	99	30	19	103	254	84	92	98	227	93	342
J	2	104	742	4	8	30	14	43	20	68	131	90	108	122	165	124	141	103	57	142	47
P (1)	3	70	1445	1	9	5	29	7	46	48	110	12	17	82	346	77	124	75	339	60	261
P	4	31	62	3	3	17	4	29	2	48	3	15	1	31	8	27	4	22	8	3	2
J	5	79	1298	3	11	33	26	65	242	70	176	77	276	96	395	93	45	127	29	50	55
J (1)	6	26	15700	11	915	11	1333	16	1314	20	1097	31	1472	20	2816	29	1772	40	1196	31	2275
J	7	83	666	10	6	21	22	43	30	67	50	86	33	77	141	79	56	83	84	102	117
J	8	106	75	-	-	-	-	60	4	87	3	-	-	121	38	83	7	74	13	81	2
P	9	96	277	4	3	-	-	21	19	45	31	26	1	123	78	127	53	90	57	87	16
P	10	65	245	2	2	1	7	9	13	39	15	9	9	74	63	79	35	68	36	75	48
P	11	122	370	-	-	2	3	7	36	78	10	98	25	114	85	115	62	123	51	134	71
J	12	51	373	2	2	1	13	26	36	59	41	20	4	23	17	89	23	42	24	40	83
P	13	70	95	-	-	-	-	67	19	61	10	72	2	84	27	56	3	59	16	54	12
J	14	95	81	-	-	-	-	71	27	73	3	55	3	132	27	120	4	60	13	255	2

Figure A2.11 (Continued)

ORDER-DELIVERY TIME LAGS
OF VENDORS FROM WHICH FIFTY OR MORE
TITLES WERE ORDERED (Feb.–Oct. 1969) (Continued)

School No. 1 (C.U.)

Vendor	Time Ordered	Ave. Days Ordered	No. of Items Ordered	February Ave.	February No.	March Ave.	March No.	April Ave.	April No.	May Ave.	May No.	June Ave.	June No.	July Ave.	July No.	August Ave.	August No.	Sept. Ave.	Sept. No.	October Ave.	October No.
15	J	57	602	-	-	(1)	3	(2)	1	46	26	49	263	62	208	66	23	83	20	89	22
16	J	64	142	(5)	7	(3)	10	49	8	(9)	11	(8)	6	92	26	91	35	58	21	65	8
17	J	59	63	-	-	-	-	66	18	58	14	77	9	60	12	-	-	40	5	20	2
18	F	80	150	(3)	(1)	(7)	(2)	-	-	(21)	17	(2)	1	100	41	62	18	73	27	79	20
19	J	54	190	-	-	-	-	(23)	6	81	3	(22)	1	59	39	55	30	52	48	34	41
20	F	71	57	-	-	-	-	(8)	(1)	64	3	-	-	92	5	66	17	72	9	93	15
21	F	73	255	-	-	-	-	-	-	-	-	-	-	-	-	(4)	1	-	-	77	224
22	F	42	121	(19)	4	46	1	61	32	31	15	-	-	42	4	37	61	(3)	1	22	2
23	F	39	75	(4)	(1)	-	-	-	-	-	-	-	-	85	12	(3)	1	(1)	1	37	23
24	F	84	59	-	-	27	3	57	26	51	2	-	-	121	17	52	3	128	2	122	5
25	?	46	51	-	-	39	4	49	5	43	5	-	-	49	15	95	4	(1)	1	35	18
26	?	32	313	(8)	1	31	61	30	49	27	35	34	90	38	35	23	7	27	19	-	-

X̄ = 45 days

X̄ minus no. 6 = 77 days

Figure A2.11 (Continued)

ORDER-DELIVERY TIME LAGS
OF VENDORS FROM WHICH FIFTY OR MORE
TITLES WERE ORDERED (Feb.-Oct. 1969) (Continued)

School No. 2 (C.S.U.)

Vendor Code	Type Code	Ave. Days Delivered	No. of Items Purchased	February Ave.	February No.	March Ave.	March No.	April Ave.	April No.	May Ave.	May No.	June Ave.	June No.	July Ave.	July No.	August Ave.	August No.	Sept. Ave.	Sept. No.	October Ave.	October No.
2	J	141	197	-	-	39	3	52	9	94	16	96	21	132	54	154	65	195	8	228	17
1	F	131	155	-	-	-	-	-	-	85	12	-	-	126	117	142	4	150	9	213	8
5	J	84	174	-	-	25	2	60	22	57	32	83	66	102	42	138	4	189	1	194	5
7	J	120	93	-	-	-	-	77	6	88	20	107	9	106	38	154	3	172	9	241	5
16	J	147	77	-	-	-	-	61	7	63	9	99	2	132	19	170	10	186	24	203	1
3	F	116	278	-	-	-	-	-	-	90	8	-	-	110	208	119	38	150	18	210	2
9	F	125	123	-	-	-	-	-	-	88	11	-	-	122	30	146	67	64	15	-	-
11	J	127	52	-	-	-	-	-	-	83	1	108	14	125	28	132	3	-	-	188	6
6	J	66	260	-	-	-	-	43	1	72	1	66	2	53	137	74	96	108	9	118	4

$\bar{X} = 111$ days

Figure A2.11 (Continued)

ORDER-DELIVERY TIME LAGS
OF VENDORS FROM WHICH FIFTY OR MORE
TITLES WERE ORDERED (Feb.-Oct. 1969) (Continued)

School No. 3 (C.S.C.)

Vendor Type Code	Vendor Code	Ave. Days Delivered	No. of Items Ordered	February Ave.	February No.	March Ave.	March No.	April Ave.	April No.	May Ave.	May No.	June Ave.	June No.	July Ave.	July No.	August Ave.	August No.	Sept. Ave.	Sept. No.	October Ave.	October No.
F	1	130	57	-	-	-	-	-	-	86	2	-	-	122	37	114	6	148	7	214	3
J	2	108	394	-	-	34	16	41	21	72	78	81	72	127	94	143	72	166	20	186	17
J	5	87	1140	-	-	-	-	54	45	67	117	83	314	89	545	101	85	134	18	186	8
J	6	49	98	-	-	-	-	51	3	56	8	53	17	77	16	-	-	91	2	0	0
J	11	141	198	-	-	-	-	-	-	83	4	99	77	126	78	134	38	155	5	162	49
J	15	58	115	-	-	-	-	27	3	52	31	63	69	67	7	48	3	-	-	-	-

X̄ = 94 days

School No. 4 (A.S.C.)

Vendor Type Code	Vendor Code	Ave. Days Delivered	No. of Items Ordered	February Ave.	February No.	March Ave.	March No.	April Ave.	April No.	May Ave.	May No.	June Ave.	June No.	July Ave.	July No.	August Ave.	August No.	Sept. Ave.	Sept. No.	October Ave.	October No.
J	5	89	405					60	10	70	20	72	57	87	258	97	40	146	9	187	8
J	2	112	180			50	1	51	5	59	29	85	32	114	40	137	42	152	18	182	9
J	11	141	222					-	-	83	3	112	8	117	46	129	66	146	44	170	44

X̄ = 108 days

Figure A2.11 (Continued)

ORDER-DELIVERY TIME LAGS
OF VENDORS FROM WHICH FIFTY OR MORE
TITLES WERE ORDERED (Feb.-Oct. 1969) (Continued)

School No. 5 (M.S.C.)

Vendor Type	Code	Avg. Days	No. of Items Ordered	Feb. Avg.	Feb. No.	Mar. Avg.	Mar. No.	Apr. Avg.	Apr. No.	May Avg.	May No.	June Avg.	June No.	July Avg.	July No.	Aug. Avg.	Aug. No.	Sept. Avg.	Sept. No.	Oct. Avg.	Oct. No.
J	2	135	330	-	-	41	16	-	-	102	114	115	56	166	94	169	22	199	9	228	14
J	6	47	273	25	115	46	37	73	57	50	12	129	2	79	17	51	24	69	8	-	-
J	5	61	53	-	-	-	-	85	1	67	2	71	2	59	8	51	14	64	26	-	-

$\bar{X}$ = 92.3 days

School No. 6 (C.S.M.)

Vendor Type	Code	Avg. Days	No. of Items Ordered	Feb. Avg.	Feb. No.	Mar. Avg.	Mar. No.	Apr. Avg.	Apr. No.	May Avg.	May No.	June Avg.	June No.	July Avg.	July No.	Aug. Avg.	Aug. No.	Sept. Avg.	Sept. No.	Oct. Avg.	Oct. No.
J	2	61	228	-	-	-	-	45	2	35	42	34	92	71	37	91	31	137	10	158	9
J	11	151	54	-	-	-	-	-	-	-	-	99	1	124	9	122	6	144	11	163	19
J	5	78	287	-	-	-	-	-	-	71	3	56	24	74	199	85	49	116	7	184	4

$\bar{X}$ = 71 days

O = Represents those values received on standing order for which the I.T. number was assigned after receipt.

F = Foreign dealer
J = Domestic jobber
P = Domestic publisher

1) Receipt of books on an approval plan caused the overall average to be understated. Examine performance of dealer for other school for a more realistic index.

Figure A2.12

ORDER-DELIVERY TIME LAGS
OF VENDORS FROM WHICH FIFTY OR MORE
TITLES WERE ORDERED (June-Dec. 1969)

School No. 1 (C.U.)

Vendor Code	Type	Ave Days	No. of Items Ordered	June Ave.	June No.	July Ave.	July No.	August Ave.	August No.	September Ave.	September No.	October Ave.	October No.	November Ave.	November No.	December Ave.	December No.
1	P	98	1,452	㉒	15	104	241	84	88	99	215	93	332	105	360	99	201
2	J	116	596	90	108	122	165	124	141	103	57	142	47	118	54	126	24
3(1	P	67	1,446	⑫	17	82	337	113	74	74	329	57	251	66	135	48	264
4	P	27	62	⑮	1	31	8	③	3	⑦	6	③	2	32	31	33	11
5	J	86	885	77	276	96	395	93	45	127	29	50	55	55	55	103	30
6(1	J	29	13,016	31	1468	20	2803	29	1762	40	1191	31	2268	36	1401	29	2123
7	J	91	627	86	33	78	139	79	56	83	84	102	117	89	104	116	94
8	P	108	69	-	-	121	38	83	7	74	13	81	2	127	9	-	-
9	P	112	263	㉖	1	123	78	128	52	91	48	70	12	78	21	122	51
10	P	63	221	⑨	9	72	55	77	30	57	30	69	44	59	16	51	37
11	P	127	408	98	25	116	83	115	62	123	51	134	71	148	61	146	55
12(1	J	56	356	20	4	23	17	89	23	42	24	40	82	62	133	67	73
13	P	63	93	-	-	82	24	①	2	58	15	49	11	31	3	64	38
14	J																

Fewer than 50 items ordered

Figure A2.12 (Continued)

ORDER-DELIVERY TIME LAGS
OF VENDORS FROM WHICH FIFTY OR MORE
TITLES WERE ORDERED (June-Dec. 1969) (Continued)

School No. 1 (C.U.)

Vendor Code	Type Code	Ave. Days	No. of Items Ordered	June Ave.	June No.	July Ave.	July No.	August Ave.	August No.	September Ave.	September No.	October Ave.	October No.	November Ave.	November No.	December Ave.	December No.
15	J	59	580	49	263	62	208	66	23	83	20	89	22	70	36	114	8
16	J	72	132	(8)	6	92	26	92	32	58	20	65	8	39	30	133	10
17	J	Fewer than 50 items ordered															
18	F	88	153	(2)	1	100	41	62	18	73	27	79	20	116	21	93	25
19	J	Fewer than 50 items ordered															
20	F	73	53	-	-	92	5	66	17	72	9	93	15	-	-	33	7
21	F	60	369	-	-	-	-	(4)	1	-	-	77	224	41	35	31	109
22	F	36	95	-	-	42	4	37	60	(3)	1	22	2	31	1	34	27
23	F	39	75	-	-	85	12	(3)	1	(1)	1	37	23	29	37	-	-
24	F	Fewer than 50 items ordered															
25	?	Fewer than 50 items ordered															
26	?	35	167	34	90	38	35	23	7	27	19	-	-	40	11	63	5

X̄ = 49 days

minus no. 6 = 81 days

Figure A2.12 (Continued)

ORDER-DELIVERY TIME LAGS
OF VENDORS FROM WHICH FIFTY OR MORE
TITLES WERE ORDERED (June-Dec. 1969) (Continued)

School No. 2 (C.S.U.)

Vendor Type Code #	Ave. Days	No. of Items Ordered	June Ave.	June No.	July Ave.	July No.	August Ave.	August No.	September Ave.	September No.	October Ave.	October No.	November Ave.	November No.	December Ave.	December No.
J	2	153	171	96	21	132	54	154	65	195	8	228	17	259	4	282	2
F	1	135	143	-	-	126	117	142	4	150	9	213	8	199	5	-	-
J	5	97	118	83	66	102	42	138	4	189	1	194	5	-	-	-	-
J	7	139	69	107	9	106	38	154	3	172	9	241	5	246	3	314	2
J	16	174	71	99	2	132	19	170	10	186	24	203	1	247	5	201	10
F	3	117	271	-	-	110	208	119	38	150	18	210	2	237	1	260	4
F	9	128	113	-	-	122	30	146	67	64	15	-	-	-	-	-	-
J	11	128	51	108	14	125	28	132	3	-	-	188	6	-	-	-	-
J	6	69	263	88	2	53	137	74	96	108	9	118	4	113	10	208	5

$\bar{X}$ = 118 days

School No. 03 (C.S.C.)

Vendor Type Code #	Ave. Days	No. of Items Ordered	June Ave.	June No.	July Ave.	July No.	August Ave.	August No.	September Ave.	September No.	October Ave.	October No.	November Ave.	November No.	December Ave.	December No.
F	1	132	55	-	-	122	37	114	6	148	7	214	3	194	2	-	-
J	2	129	282	81	72	127	94	143	72	166	20	186	17	222	4	277	3
J	5	91	979	83	315	89	545	101	85	134	18	186	8	192	7	261	2

Figure A2.12 (Continued)

ORDER-DELIVERY TIME LAGS
OF VENDORS FROM WHICH FIFTY OR MORE
TITLES WERE ORDERED (June-Dec. 1969) (Continued)

School No. 03 (C.S.C.)

Vendor Type Code	Avg. Days	No. of Items Ordered	June		July		August		September		October		November		December	
			Avg.	No.	Avg.	No.	Avg.	No.	Avg.	No.	Avg.	No.	Avg.	No.	Avg.	No.
J	6	47	127	53	17	77	16	-	-	91	2	-	-	42	13	40	79
J	11	143	194	99	7	126	78	134	38	155	5	162	49	194	17	-	-
J	15	59	134	63	69	67	7	48	3	-	-	-	-	30	2	55	53

$\bar{\bar{X}}$ = 98 days

School No. 04 (A.S.C.)

J	5	90	375	72	57	87	258	97	40	146	9	187	8	220	3	-	-
J	2	125	144	85	32	114	40	137	42	152	18	182	9	193	3	-	-
J	11	141	220	112	8	117	46	129	66	146	44	170	44	196	12	-	-

$\bar{\bar{X}}$ = 112 days

School No. 05 (M.S.C.)

J	2	160	203	115	56	166	94	169	22	199	9	228	14	199	7	297	1
J	6	75	53	129	2	79	17	51	24	69	8	-	-	278	1	320	1
J	5	60	50	71	2	59	8	51	14	64	26	-	-	-	-	-	-

$\bar{\bar{X}}$ = 129 days

Figure A2.12 (Continued)

ORDER-DELIVERY TIME LAGS
OF VENDORS FROM WHICH FIFTY OR MORE
TITLES WERE ORDERED (June-Dec. 1969) (Continued)

School No. 06 (C.S.M.)

Vendor Type Code	Ave. days	No. of Items Ordered	June Ave	June No.	July Ave	July No.	August Ave	August No.	September Ave	September No.	October Ave	October No.	November Ave	November No.	December Ave	December No.
J 2	68	184	34	92	71	37	91	31	137	10	158	9	204	5	-	-
J 11	151	54	99	1	124	9	122	6	144	11	163	19	191	8	-	-
J 5	78	284	56	24	74	199	85	49	116	7	184	4	176	1	-	-

$\bar{X}$ = 82 days

F = Foreign dealer
J = Domestic jobber
P = Domestic publisher

1) Receipt of books on an approval plan causes the overall average to be understated. Remains performance of vendor for other school for a more realistic index.

Figure A2.13

DISCOUNTS RECEIVED FROM THREE SELECTED PUBLISHERS

Name of Firm			Discount in Percent								Weighted Mean
			Net	10	15	20	33	38	46		
Harper	Apr. 1969– Feb. 1970	114	3		58	4		49			24.7
Wiley	July 1969– Feb. 1970	113		113							10.0
Oxford U.P.	May 1969– March 1970	155	14	96		43	1		1		12.2

Figure A2.14

Item #_____
Data Collector_____
Date Tabulated_____

LAG TIMES (IN DAYS)

Lags	Date:	Source of Master Card:						
	Received at Center _____	a Proof Card	b Xerox Enlar.	c Polaroid Enlar.	d Typed from NUC	e Typed from C.U.m.e.	f Original Cat.	g C.U. m.e.
1)								
	Initially stored							
2)								
	Identified for use							
3)								
	Pulled from C.U. Catalog							
4)								
	Enlarged or Typed							
5)								
	Matched to book							
6)								
	Stored in Master File							
7)								

Lags		
8)	Order Packed _____	
9)	Encumbered _____	
10)	Book received _____	
11)	Expended _____	
12)	Shelved in holding _____	
13)	Released from holding _____	
14)	Cataloged _____	
15)	SILO'd _____	
16)	Shipped _____	
17)	Received at local lib. _____	
18)	Shelflist filed _____	

Figure A2.14 (Continued)

Item # _____
Data Collector _____
Date Tabulated _____

ORDERING PATTERNS

| Library | Domestic | | Foreign | | Total |
	Current (1966+)	Retrospective (before 1966)	Current	Retro	
ASC					
CSC					
CSM					
CSU					
CU					
MSC					
Total					

Figure A2.14 (Continued)
LOCAL MODIFICATION OF CALBPC PROCESSING

Data Collector _____
Date Tabulated _____

	ASC		CSC		CSM		CSU		CU		MSC		**Total**	
	Yes	No	Yes	No	Yes	No	Yes	No	Yes	No	Yes	No	Yes	No
1. Call Number:														
1.1 Classification														
1.2 Cutter														
1.3 Additions														
1.4 Location info.														
2. Book:														
2.1 Pocket position changed (If so, specify where)														
2.2 Pocket removed														
2.3 Circulation card removed														
2.4 Title on pocket and card														
2.5 Plastic jacketed														
2.6 Spine label replaced														
2.7 Blurb pasted in														
2.8 Property stamping (# of times)														
2.9 Other marks inside book														
2.10 Other changes (specify)														

Figure A2.14 (Continued)

LOCAL MODIFICATION OF CALBPC PROCESSING   Data Collector_____

                                               Date Tabulated_____

	ASC		CSC		CSM		SCU		CU		MSC		Total	
	Yes	No	Yes	No	Yes	No	Yes	No	Yes	No	Yes	No	Yes	No
3. Catalog Cards:														
3.1 Main entry														
3.2 Subject headings altered														
3.3 Subject headings increased (# of)														
3.4 Subject headings decreased (# of)														
3.5 Added entries altered														
3.6 Added entries increased														
3.7 Added entries decreased														
3.8 If continuation card set:														
3.9.1 Cards increased														
3.9.2 Cards decreased														
3.10 Info. stamped on body of card														
3.11 Info. typed on body of card														
3.12 Other changes (specify)														
3.13.1 Info. added to S.L. (specify)														
3.13.2 No. of characters (specify)														
4.0 Other Records Maintained:														
4.1 Kardex														
4.2 Receipt file														
4.3 Faculty request file														
4.4 Other (specify)														

Figure A2.15

MASTER FILE STUDY

Task Chart

	a	b	c	d	e	f	g	h	i
DATA TO COLLECT	Date Order Received	Date Proof Filed	Date Main Entry Filed	Date Proof Found	Date Main Entry Found	Date NUC Entry Found	Date Proof Pulled for Cataloging	Date Main Entry Pulled	Date Camera Copy Made
SOURCE DOCUMENTS	PR	Proof	M.E. (date positioned on verso)	yellow slip code	PR (call number box)	PR or yellow slip code	yellow slip code	Yellow slip code	Camera Copy (date positioned on verso)
DEPARTMENT PERFORMING TASK	Order	CAMP	CAMP	Bib.	Bib.	Bib.	Bib.	Bib.	CAMP
MARKING METHOD SUGGESTED	stamp	Edge Color or T.M.	T.M. or stamp	stamp	penciled on	penciled (if PR, left of LC box)	stamp	stamp	T.M. or stamp

T.M. = Tick-o-meter, an automatic stamping and counting machine

Yellow Slip Code = Date code mimeographed on verso of yellow order slip (Temp. shelf list slip)

Continue

Figure A2.15 (Continued)

MASTER FILE STUDY

Task Chart

	j	l	m	n	o	p	q
DATA TO COLLECT	Date Camera Copy Pulled	Date Proof Refiled	Date Main Entry Refiled	Date Camera Copy Filed In Proof File	Date Book Shelved in Bib. (Holding)	Date Book Released From Holding	Date NUC-MC card ready to mail
SOURCE DOCUMENTS	yellow slip code	Proof	M.E. (date positioned on verso)	Camera Copy (date positioned on verso)	yellow slip code	yellow slip code	NUC-MC
DEPARTMENT PERFORMING TASK	Order and Bib.	CAMP	CAMP	CAMP	Bib. (Holding)	Bib.	CALBPC
MARKING METHOD SUGGESTED	stamp	T.M. or stamp	T.M. or stamp	T.M. or stamp	stamp	stamp	stamp

T.M. = Tick-o-meter, an automatic stamping and counting machine

Yellow Slip Code = Date code mimeographed on verso of yellow order slip (temp. shelf list slip)

Figure A2.16

LAG TIME DATA TABULATION SHEET

CU	CSU	CSC	ACS	MSC	CSM	1 Date PR Recd.	2 Date IFT Assigned	3 Date Book Recd.	Date Cataloged B	Recd. Local Library A	Shelf List Filed C	Silo Called D	Total Type A	Total Type B	Total Type C	Total Type D	LC Copy Available Before Order recd.	LC Copy Available when book recd.

Figure A2.17

ACQUISITION/PROCESSING TIME LAG STUDY

Name of Institution	Sample I	Sample II	PR received and IPT assigned	IPT assigned and date received from vendor	Book received and date book released from cataloging	Total(1) days PR received and book cataloged	Book received and date book shelf-listed	Total(2) PR received and date book shelf-listed	Book received and date book siloed	Total(3) PR received and date book siloed	Book received at CAL&PC and date book received at local library	Total(4) PR received and date book received at local library	Average totals 1-4	Average Sample I Sample II
University of Colorado	936	682	20 (936)(a) 35 (682)	35 (936) 46 (682)	28 (880) 36 (652)	83 (880) 126 (652)	46 (56) 62 (30)	114 (56) 138 (30)					98 132	115
Colorado State University	36	102	24 (36) 31 (102)	75 (36) 95 (102)					36 (31) 76 (102)	150 (31) 213 (102)	62 (33)	163 (33)	156 213	184
Colorado State College	84	117	24 (84) 27 (117)	76 (84) 97 (117)					58 (5) 61 (117)	170 (5) 187 (117)	64 (79)	170 (79)	170 187	178
Adams State College	22	51	29 (22) 29 (51)	79 (22) 101 (51)			73 (1)	196 (1)	47 (4) 53 (51)	180 (4) 187 (51)	86 (17)	199 (17)	192 187	190
Metropolitan State College	55	51	43 (55) 31 (51)	75 (55) 133 (51)					48 (55) 73 (51)	159 (55) 237 (51)			159 237	198
Colorado School of Mines	15	35	35 (15) 34 (35)	71 (15) 85 (35)					25 (1) 43 (35)	131 (1) 162 (35)	63 (14)	156 (14)	144 162	153

a) number in parentheses indicate number of items in sub-category

Figure A2.18

SOURCE OF CATALOGING COPY

Source of Copy	Study One		Study Two	
	Average # of Items	%	Average # of Items	%
LC depository card	719	65.5	517	54.7
Xerox enlargement from NUC	163	14.8	201	21.3
Polaroid enlargement from NUC	30	2.7	4	0.4
Typed copy from NUC	2	0.2	51	5.4
Typed copy University of Colorado main entry card	74	6.6	35	3.7
Original cataloging (typed)	90	8.2	113	12.0
Xerox of University of Colorado main entry	22	2.0	24	2.5
Totals	1100	100.0	945	100.0

Figure A2.19

CATALOGING CHARACTERISTICS
(By Institution and Cataloging Difficulty)

Items in the Sample

	A.S.C.	C.S.C.	C.S.M.	C.S.U.	C.U.	M.S.C.	Total
Mass Cataloging	60	117	61	133	1478	129	1978
Original Cataloging	31	54	26	136	1169	44	1460
Total	91	171	87	269	2647	173	3438

Read Horizontally

	A.S.C.	C.S.C.	C.S.M.	C.S.U.	C.U.	M.S.C.	Total %
Mass Cataloging	3.03	5.92	3.08	6.72	74.72	6.52	100.00
Original Cataloging	2.12	3.70	1.78	9.32	80.07	3.01	100.00
Total	2.65	4.97	2.54	7.82	76.99	5.03	100.00

Read Vertically

	A.S.C.	C.S.C.	C.S.M.	C.S.U.	C.U.	M.S.C.	Total
Mass Cataloging	65.93	68.42	70.11	49.44	55.84	74.56	57.53
Original Cataloging	34.07	31.58	29.89	50.56	44.16	25.44	42.47
Total Percentage	100.00	100.00	100.00	100.00	100.00	100.00	100.00

Figure A2.20

CATALOGING CHARACTERISTICS
(By Institution and by Language)

Vertical Percentages

	A.S.C.	C.S.C.	C.S.M.	C.S.U.	C.U.	M.S.C.	Total
English	90.11	99.42	95.40	52.42	72.65	95.95	74.61
Western Europe	9.89		3.45	44.98	19.08	3.47	18.73
Scandinavian				0.74	0.91		0.76
Eastern Europe		0.58	1.15	1.12	6.01	0.58	4.80
Oriental (incl. N.E.)				0.74	0.91		0.76
Other					0.45		0.35
Total	100.00	100.00	100.00	100.00	100.00	100.00	100.00

CATALOGING CHARACTERISTICS
(By Institution and by Language)

Items in the Sample

	A.S.C.	C.S.C.	C.S.M.	C.S.U.	C.U.	M.S.C.	Total
English	82	170	83	141	1923	166	2565
Western Europe	9		3	121	505	6	644
Scandinavian				2	24		26
Eastern Europe		1	1	3	159	1	165
Oriental (inc. N.E.)				2	24		26
Other					12		12
Total	91	171	87	269	2647	173	3438

Figure A2.21

LIBRARY OF CONGRESS CLASSIFICATION

A   General Works. Polygraphy

B   Philosophy. Religion

C   Auxiliary Sciences of History

D   Universal History

E   American History

F   American History

G   Geography. Anthropology

H   Social Sciences

HF   Business

J   Political Science

K   Law

L   Education

M   Music

N   Fine Arts

P   Language and Literature

Q   Science

R   Medicine

S   Agriculture

T   Technology

U   Military Science

V   Naval Science

Z   Bibliography. Library Science

Figure A2.21 (continued)

CATALOGING CHARACTERISTICS SUMMARY
(By Library of Congress Classification and by Cataloging Difficulty)
Items in the Sample

	A	B	C	D	EF	G	H	HJ	J	K	MISC CLS	L	M	N	P	Q	R	S	T	U	V	Z	Total
Mass Cat.	16	139	20	193	101	39	240	55	51	14	8	89	99	72	461	198	32	5	83	14	2	47	1978
Orig. Cat.	2	72	11	85	38	19	188	83	20	10	95	15	116	37	420	84	20	6	107	2		30	1460
Total	18	211	31	278	139	58	428	138	71	24	103	104	215	109	881	282	52	11	190	16	2	77	3438

CATALOGING CHARACTERISTICS SUMMARY
(By Library of Congress Classification and by Cataloging Difficulty)
Horizontal Percentages

	A	B	C	D	EF	G	H	HJ	J	K	MISC CLS	L	M	N	P	Q	R	S	T	U	V	Z	Total %
Mass Cat.	0.81	7.03	1.01	9.76	5.11	1.97	12.13	2.78	2.58	0.71	0.40	4.50	5.0	3.64	23.31	10.01	1.62	0.25	4.20	0.71	0.10	2.38	100.00
Orig. Cat.	0.14	4.93	0.75	5.82	2.60	1.30	12.88	5.68	1.37	0.68	6.51	1.03	7.9	2.53	28.77	5.75	1.37	0.41	7.33	0.14		2.05	100.00
Total	0.52	6.14	0.90	8.09	4.04	1.69	12.45	4.01	2.07	0.70	3.00	3.03	6.2	3.17	25.63	8.20	1.51	0.32	5.53	0.47	0.06	2.24	100.00

CATALOGING CHARACTERISTICS SUMMARY
(By Library of Congress Classification and by Cataloging Difficulty)
Vertical Percentages

	A	B	C	D	EF	G	H	HJ	J	K	MISC CLS	L	M	N	P	Q	R	S	T	U	V	Z	Total
Mass Cat.	88.89	65.88	64.52	69.42	72.66	67.24	56.07	39.85	71.83	58.33	7.77	85.58	46.06	66.06	52.33	70.21	61.54	45.45	43.68	87.50	100.00	61.04	57.53
Orig. Cat.	11.11	34.12	35.48	30.58	27.34	32.76	43.93	60.15	28.17	41.67	92.23	14.42	53.9	33.94	47.67	29.79	38.46	54.55	56.32	12.50		38.96	42.47
Total	100.00	100.00	100.00	100.00	100.00	100.00	100.00	100.00	100.00	100.00	100.00	100.00	100.00	100.00	100.00	100.00	100.00	100.00	100.00	100.00	100.00	100.00	100.00

Figure A2.22

CATALOGING CHARACTERISTICS
(By Library of Congress Classification and by Language)
Items in the Sample

Language:	A	B	C	D	LF	G	H	HF	J	K	KLM	L	M	N	P	Q	R	S	T	U	V	Z	Total
English	7	152	26	167	126	55	400	138	57	24	55	95	118	89	522	233	48	8	181	11	2	62	2565
Western European	6	49	5	67	12		21		9		47	6	89	14	247	44	4	1	8	4		11	644
Scandin.	2			1					1		1	1	2		7	10			1				26
Eastern European	2	5		32	1	2	6		3			2	6	5	96	1		1				3	165
Oriental (inc.N.E.)	1	1		11		1	1							1	6	1				1		1	26
Other		5													3	3		1					12
Total	18	211	31	278	139	58	428	138	71	24	103	104	215	109	881	282	52	11	190	16	2	77	3438

Figure A2.23

CATALOGING CHARACTERISTICS
(By Library of Congress Classification and by Language)
Horizontal Percentages

Language:	A	B	C	D	E.F	G	H	HF	J	K	Kf-Ris	L	M	N	P	Q	R	S	T	U	V	Z	Total %
English	0.27	5.89	1.01	6.51	4.91	2.14	15.59	5.38	2.22	0.94	2.14	3.70	4.60	3.47	20.35	8.69	1.87	0.31	7.06	0.43	0.08	2.42	100.00
Western European	0.93	7.61	0.78	10.40	1.86		3.26		1.40		7.30	0.93	13.82	2.17	38.35	6.83	0.62	0.16	1.24	0.62		1.71	100.00
Scandin.	7.69			3.85					3.85		3.85	3.85	7.69		26.92	38.46			3.85				100.00
Eastern European	1.21	3.03		19.39	0.61	1.21	3.64		1.82			1.21	3.64	3.03	58.18	0.61		0.61				1.82	100.00
Oriental (inc. N.E.)	3.85	3.85		42.31		3.85	3.85		3.85					3.85	23.08	3.85				3.85		3.85	100.00
Other		41.67													25.00	25.00		8.33					100.00
Overall %	0.52	6.14	0.90	8.09	4.04	1.69	12.45	4.01	2.07	0.70	3.00	3.03	6.24	3.17	25.63	8.20	1.51	0.32	5.53	0.47	0.06	2.24	100.00

Figure A2.24

CATALOGING CHARACTERISTICS
(By Library of Congress Classification and by Language)
Vertical Percentages

Language:	A	B	C	D	E-F	G	H	HF	J	K	Multi-ple	L	LM	N	P	Q	R	S	T	U	V	Z	Overall
English	38.89	71.56	83.87	60.07	90.65	94.83	93.46	100.00	80.28	100.00	53.40	91.35	54.88	81.65	59.25	79.08	92.31	72.73	95.26	68.75	100.00	80.52	74.70
Western European	33.33	23.22	16.13	24.10	8.63		4.91		12.68		45.63	5.77	41.40	12.84	28.04	15.60	7.69	9.09	4.21	25.00		14.29	21.64
Scandin.	11.11			0.36					1.41		0.97	0.96	0.93		0.79	3.55			0.53				0.76
Eastern European	11.11	2.37		11.51	0.72	3.45	1.40		4.23			1.92	2.79	4.59	10.90	0.35						3.90	4.79
Oriental (inc.N.E.)	5.56	0.47		3.96		1.72	0.23		1.41					0.92	0.68	0.35		0.09		6.25		1.30	0.76
Other		2.37													0.34	1.06		9.09					0.35
Total	100.00	100.00	100.00	100.00	100.00	100.00	100.00	100.00	100.00	100.00	100.00	100.00	100.00	100.00	100.00	100.00	100.00	100.00	100.00	100.00	100.00	100.00	100.00

Figure A2.25

CATALOGING CHARACTERISTICS
(By Library of Congress Classification and by Institution)
Items in the Sample

Library	A	B	C	D	EF	G	H	HF	J	K	Micro-film	L	M	N	P	Q	R	S	T	U	V	Z	Total
A.S.C.		9	1	3	3	1	5	3	1	6		7	2	9	19	13	4	1	4			1	91
C.S.C.		7	1	21	16	7	17		5	5		14	2	9	21	22	8		2	2		12	171
C.S.M.		4	2	2	2	6	12	1	1	1		1	2	2	12	22	1		13	1		2	87
C.S.U.	2	15	4	60	11	3	21		10			7	5	4	95	12	8	1	5	4		2	269
C.U.	16	158	22	173	97	37	348	131	53	9	103	68	200	80	692	192	29	7	162	9	2	59	2647
M.S.C.		18	2	19	10	4	25	3	1	3		7	4	5	42	21	2	2	4			1	173
Total	18	211	31	278	139	58	428	138	71	24	103	104	125	109	881	282	52	11	190	16	2	77	3438

Figure A2.26

CATALOGING CHARACTERISTICS
(By Library of Congress Classification and by Institution)
Horizontal Percentages

Library	A	B	C	D	EF	G	H	HF	J	K	Misc. LC	L	M	N	P	Q	R	S	T	U	V	Z	Total
A.S.C.		9.89		3.30	3.30	1.10	5.49	3.30	1.10	6.59		7.69	2.20	9.89	20.88	14.29	4.40	1.10	4.40			1.10	100.00
C.S.C.		4.09	0.58	12.28	9.36	4.09	9.94		2.92	2.92		8.19	1.17	5.26	12.28	12.87	4.68		1.17	1.17		7.02	100.00
C.S.M.		4.60	2.30	2.30	2.30	6.90	13.79	1.15	1.15	1.15		1.15	2.30	2.30	13.79	25.29	1.15		14.94	1.15		2.30	100.00
C.S.U.	0.74	5.58	1.49	22.30	4.09	1.12	7.81		3.72			2.60	1.86	1.49	35.32	4.46	2.97	0.37	1.86	1.49		0.74	100.00
C.U.	0.60	5.97	0.83	6.54	3.66	1.40	13.15	4.95	2.00	0.34	3.89	2.59	7.56	3.02	26.14	7.25	1.10	0.26	6.12	0.34	0.08	2.23	100.00
M.S.C.		10.40	1.16	10.98	5.78	2.31	14.45	1.73	0.98	1.73		4.05	2.31	2.89	22.28	12.14	1.16	1.16	2.31			0.58	100.00
Total	0.52	6.14	0.90	8.09	4.04	1.69	12.45	4.01	2.07	0.70	3.00	3.03	6.25	3.17	25.63	8.20	1.51	0.32	5.53	0.47	0.06	2.24	100.00

Figure A2.27

CATALOGING CHARACTERISTICS
(By Library of Congress Classification and by Institution)
Vertical Percentages

Library	A	B	C	D	LJ	G	H	HT	J	K	Micro-film	L	M	N	P	Q	R	S	T	U	V	Z	Overall
A.S.C.		4.27		1.08	2.16	1.72	1.17	2.17	1.41	25.00		6.73	0.93	8.26	2.16	4.61	7.69	9.09	2.11			1.30	2.66
C.S.C.		3.32	3.23	7.55	11.51	12.07	3.97		7.04	20.83		13.46	0.93	8.26	2.38	7.80	15.38		1.05	12.50		15.58	4.97
C.S.M.		1.90	6.45	0.72	1.44	10.34	2.80	0.72	1.41	4.17		0.96	0.93	1.83	1.36	7.80	1.92		6.84	6.25		2.60	2.53
C.S.U.	11.11	7.11	12.90	21.58	7.91	5.17	4.91		14.08			6.73	2.33	3.67	10.78	4.26	15.38	9.09	2.63	25.00		2.60	7.82
C.U.	88.89	74.88	70.97	62.23	69.78	63.79	81.31	94.93	74.65	37.50	100.00	65.38	93.02	73.39	78.55	68.09	55.77	63.64	85.26	56.25	100.00	76.62	76.99
M.S.C.		8.53	6.45	6.83	7.19	6.90	5.84	2.17	1.41	12.50		6.73	1.86	4.59	4.77	7.45	3.85	18.18	2.11			1.30	5.03
Total	100.00	100.00	100.00	100.00	100.00	100.00	100.00	100.00	100.00	100.00	100.00	100.00	100.00	100.00	100.00	100.00	100.00	100.00	100.00	100.00	100.00	100.00	100.00

Figure A2.28

FREQUENCY COMPUTATION FOR C.A.L.B.P.C.

Acquisitions

* "Orders from Members" includes purchases plus books received for processing only.	vp = volumes processed NA = Not applicable to specifications AF = Another function used

Activity Description	Frequency Percentage Formula
1. Open, sort and distribute incoming mail.	$\dfrac{\text{Orders from Members}}{\text{Volumes Processed}}$
2. Review book order requests; review selection media.	NA
3. Select titles to be ordered.	NA
4. Type library order request card.	NA
5.1 Search and verify bibliographic information	$\dfrac{\text{*Orders from Members}}{vp}$
5.2 Return non-specification orders to member libraries.	$\dfrac{\text{purchase requests returned unfilled}}{vp}$
6. Assign vendor.	$\dfrac{\text{Valid Purchase Requests}}{vp}$
7. Prepare multiple order record.	Same as #6
8. Type purchase requisition, etc.	NA
9. Mail requests.	Same as #6
10. Burst forms.	NA
11. File forms in appropriate files.	Same as #6
12.1 Keypunch encumbrances.	Same as #6
12.2 Verify encumbrances.	Same as #6
13.1 Unpack books; check against packing list or invoice. Check outstanding order file.	$\dfrac{\text{Orders received from vendor}}{vp}$
13.2 Unpack "processing-only" books.	$\dfrac{\text{processing only volumes received}}{vp}$
14. Check in serials on Kardex.	$\dfrac{\text{added volumes}}{\text{volumes processed}}$
15. Collate books	Same as #13.1
16. Book return procedure (incorrect shipment, defective copy, approval books.	$\dfrac{\text{volumes returned}}{\text{volumes processed}}$
17. Book accessioning routine.	NA
18. Write sourcing information.	NA.
19. Prepare gift record form.	Same as 13.1
20. Book distribution routine	1

Figure A2.28 (Continued)

FREQUENCY COMPUTATION FOR C.A.L.B.P.C.

ACQUISITIONS

Activity Description	Frequency Percentage Formula
21. Prepare receiving report.	NA
22. Prepare invoices for payment.	Same as 13.1
23.1 Keypunch expenditures.	Same as #13.1
23.2 Verifying expenditures.	Same as #13.1
24. Clear in-process file.	Same as #5
25. File forms, etc., in completed records or discard.	Same as #5
26. Requestor notification routine.	NA
27. Periodic accessions list routine.	NA
28. Vendor status routine.	$\dfrac{\text{reports processed}}{\text{volumes processed}}$
29. Claims routine.	$\dfrac{\text{claims sent}}{\text{volumes processed}}$
30. Cancellations routine.	$\dfrac{\text{orders cancelled}}{\text{volumes processed}}$
31. Out-of-print order routine.	$\dfrac{\text{out-of-print titles purchased}}{\text{volumes processed}}$
32. Process inquiries.	$\dfrac{\text{requests handled}}{\text{volumes processed}}$
33. General typing - correspondence, etc. (specify).	NA
34. General revision (specify).	NA
35.1 Sorting tab cards.	1
35.2 Prepare a computer run.	1
35.3 Check in computer run.	1
35.4 Keypunch title changes.	$\dfrac{\text{titles changed}}{\text{vp}}$
36. Bi-monthly accounting reports to members.	AF

Figure A2.28 (Continued)

FREQUENCY COMPUTATION FOR C.A.L.B.P.C.

CATALOGING

Activity Description	Frequency Percentage Formula
37. Sort books, assign and distribute.	1
38. Search for LC copy; verify bibliographic information.	$\dfrac{\text{titles in holding}}{vp}$
39.1 Advanced card production: C.U. instruction slips.	$\dfrac{\text{master cards found on first search of C.U. order}}{vp}$
39.2 Advanced card production: member library instruction slips.	$\dfrac{\text{master cards found on first search of member library order}}{vp}$
40. Receive and arrange LC cards.	NA
41.1 Receive and arrange LC proof slips or proof sheets.	$\dfrac{\text{Proof and materials handled}}{vp}$
41.2 Stamp date and destination code on verso of master cards.	$\dfrac{\text{cards entering master file initially}}{vp}$
42. File LC copy. (cards or proof)	$\dfrac{\text{cards filed}}{vp}$
43. Match LC cards or proof copy and books.	$\dfrac{\text{volumes mass cataloged}}{vp}$
44. Added copies/added volumes routine.	$\dfrac{\text{added copies + added volumes}}{\text{volumes processed}}$
45. Catalog and classify with LC cards/copy.	Same as #43.
46. Original cataloging and classifying.	$\dfrac{\text{titles originally cataloged}}{\text{volumes processed}}$
47. Shelf listing (for 44, 45 and 46).	NA
48. Type complete card sets.	NA
49. Type master card.	$\dfrac{\text{titles originally cataloged}}{vp}$
50. Revise master card.	Same as #49.
51. Type modification on a card or proof slip.	Same as #43
52.1 Reproduce card sets (other than typing). Sort cards into sets.	$\dfrac{\text{titles cataloged + "added" copies}}{vp}$
52.2 Sort card sets by member or departmental library and stamp location code on each card.	Same as 52.1
53. Type call number, added entries.	Same as #52.1
54. Revise typing on card sets.	Same as #52.1
55. Prepare authority cards.	$\dfrac{\text{authority cards typed}}{\text{volumes processed}}$
56. Prepare cross-reference cards.	$\dfrac{\text{cross-reference cards typed}}{\text{volumes processed}}$
57. Prepare circulation card.	NA
58. Prepare book pocket.	NA

Figure A2.28 (Continued)

FREQUENCY COMPUTATION FOR C.A.L.B.P.C.

CATALOGING

Activity Description	Frequency Percentage Formula
59. Apply date due slip and spine label.	1
60.1 Match label sets and invoices to books.	1
60.2 Burst label sets and affix pockets.	1
60.3 Inspect pockets and remove flags.	1
61. Affix biographical and review material in book.	NA
62. Stamp property marks.	NA
63. Affix plastic jacket to book.	NA
64. Paper back books — in house binding routine.	0 or $\dfrac{\text{paperbacks bound in house}}{\text{volumes processed}}$
65. Revise completed books before forwarding.	1
66. Sort and alphabetize shelf list and all catalog cards.	NA
67. File shelf list and all catalog cards.	NA
68. Revise filing of shelf list and all catalog cards.	NA
69. Route card sets to departmental or member libraries.	1
70. Paperback books — bindery routine (preparation).	$\dfrac{\text{paperbacks commercially bound}}{\text{volumes processed}}$
71. Paperback books — bindery routine (receiving).	Same as #70
72. Catalog maintenance (other than filing).	NA
73. General typing (specify).	NA
74. General revision (specify).	NA
75. General filing (specify).	NA
76. Other cataloging activities not listed above (specify).	NA
77.1 Distribution of books to pre-keypunch staging area.	1
77.2 Keypunch SILO cards.	1
77.3 SILO error	$\dfrac{\text{Errors re-cycled}}{\text{vp}}$
78. Arrange books by library	1
79. Invoice/shipping list production.	AF
80. Billing.	NA

Figure A2.28 (Continued)

FREQUENCY COMPUTATION FOR C.A.L.B.P.C.

CATALOGING

Activity Description	Frequency Percentage Formula
81.1 Pack member-library books.	$\dfrac{\text{member library volumes}}{vp}$
81.2 Inspect shipments and mail out.	Same as #81.1
82. Union catalog (arrange and file).	AF
83. Bibliographic Center notification	AF

Figure A2.29

FREQUENCY STATISTICS COMPILATION

Acquisitions

Key:
1.0 = Frequency
Volumes Processed = 81071
N.A. = Not Available
A.F. = Another Function Used

T.S. Report = C.U. Technical Services Reports

Activity No.	Statistics Utilized	Source	Statistics on CALBPC Specification Books
1.	Purchase Requests / Volumes Processed	T.S. Report	42857
2.	N.A.		
3.	N.A.		
4.	N.A.		
5.1	Purchase Requests / vp	T.S. Report	42857
5.2	purchase requests returned unfilled / vp	A2.31 Figures A2.32	646-110=536
6	Valid purchase requests / vp		42857-536=42321
7.	Valid purchase requests / vp		42321
8.	N.A.		
9.	Valid purchase requests / vp		42321
10.	N.A.		
11.	Valid purchase requests / vp		42321
12.1	Valid purchase requests / vp		42321
12.2	Valid purchase requests / vp		42321
13.1	Orders received from vendor / vp	T.S. Report	81071-8737=72334
13.2	"Processing only" volumes received / vp	T.S. Report	8737
14.	added volumes / volumes processed	Figure A2.3	20907
15.	orders received from vendor / vp		72334
16.	volumes returned to vendor / volumes processed	Leonard, p. 134	0.61%
17.	N.A.		
18.	N.A.		

Figure A2.29 (Continued)

FREQUENCY STATISTICS COMPILATION

<u>Acquisitions</u>

Activity No.	Statistics Utilized	Source	Statistics on CALBPC Specification Books
19.	N.A.		
20.	1.0		
21.	N.A.		
22.	<u>Orders received from vendor</u> volumes processed		72334
23.1	<u>Orders received from vendor</u> vp		72334
23.2	<u>Orders received from vendor</u> vp		72334
24.	1.0		
25.	1.0		
26.	N.A.		
27.	N.A.		
28.	<u>reports processed</u> volumes processed	Leonard p. 135	15.76%
29.	<u>claims sent</u> volumes processed	Figure A2.7	3.72%
30.	<u>orders cancelled</u> volumes processed	Figure A2.7	583 (repeated o.p.)
31.	N.A.		
32.	<u>requests handled</u> volumes processed	Leonard, p. 324	1.5%
33.	N.A.		
34.	N.A.		
35.1	1.0		
35.2	1.0		
35.3	1.0		
35.4	<u>titles changed</u> vp	data from bookkeeping	0.6%
36.	A.F.		

Figure A2.29 (Continued)

FREQUENCY STATISTICS COMPILATION

Cataloging

Activity No.	Statistics Utilized	Source	Statistics on CALBPC Specification Books
37.	1.0		
38.	titles in holding / vp	Figure 2.18	14.7+19.7=34.4%
39.1	LC copy found on first search of CU order / vp	Figure 2.18	62.3%
39.2	LC copy found on first search of member library order / vp	Figure 2.18	76.2%
40.	N.A.		
41.1	proof and master cards handled / vp	T.S. Report	244587
41.2	cards entering master file initially / vp	T.S. Report	177425
42.	cards filed / vp		177425
43.	volumes mass cataloged / vp	Figure A2.3	18307
44.	added copies + added volumes / volumes processed	Figure A2.3	81071-18307-9138=53626
45.	volumes mass cataloged / vp		18307
46.	titles originally cataloged / volumes processed		9138
47.	N.A.		
48.	N.A.		
49.	titles originally cataloged / vp		9138
50.	titles originally cataloged / vp		9138
51.	volumes mass cataloged / vp		18307
52.1	titles cataloged + "added" copies / vp	Figure A2.3	81071-5692-20907=54472
52.2	titles cataloged + "added" copies / vp		81071-5692-20907=54472
53.	titles cataloged + "added" copies / vp		81071-5692-20907=54472
54.	titles cataloged + "added" copies / vp		81071-5692-20907=54472
55.	authority cards typed / volumes processed	Leonard, p. 326	1.0%

Figure A2.29 (Continued)

FREQUENCY STATISTICS COMPILATION

<u>Cataloging</u>

Activity No.	Statistics Utilized	Source	Statistics on CALBPC Specification Books
56.	<u>cross-reference cards typed</u> volumes processed	Leonard, p. 326	3.1%
57.	A.F.		
58.	1.0		
59.	1.0		
60.1	1.0		
60.2	1.0		
60.3	1.0		
61.	N.A.		
62.	N.A.		
63.	N.A.		
64.	0 or <u>paperbacks bound in house</u> volumes processed	Figure 2.10	6.25%
65.	1.0		
66.	N.A.		
67.	N.A.		
68.	N.A.		
69.	1.0		
70.	<u>paperbacks commercially bound</u> volumes processed	Figure 2.10	7.94%
71.	<u>paperbacks commercially bound</u> volumes processed	Figure 2.10	7.94%
72.	N.A.		
73.	N.A.		
74.	N.A.		
75.	N.A.		
76.	N.A.		

Figure A2.29 (Continued)

FREQUENCY STATISTICS COMPILATION

Cataloging

Activity No.	Statistics Utilized	Source	Statistics on CALBPC Specification Books
77.1	1.0		
77.2	1.0		
77.3	errors re-cycled / vp	SILC Statistics Unpublished	10.85%
78.	1.0		
79.	A.F.		
80.	A.F.		
81.1	member library volumes shipped / vp	Figure A2.33	11816
81.2	member library volumes shipped / vp	Figure A2.33	11816
82.	N.A.		
83.	A.F.		

Figure A2.30

FREQUENCY CALCULATIONS

Key:
Volumes Processed = 81071
N.A. = Not Applicable
A.F. = Another Function Used

Acquisitions

Activity Description Number	Activity Description	Preliminary Calculation	Frequency Quotient n/81701 vols.	Frequency
1.	Open, sort and distribute incoming mail.	42857	42857	.529
2.	Review book order requests; review selection media.			N.A.
3.	Select titles to be ordered.			N.A.
4.	Type library order request card.			N.A.
5.1	Search and verify bibliographic information.	42857	42857	.529
5.2	Return non-specification orders to member libraries	646 - 110 = 536 returned sent back to center	536	.007
6.	Assign vendor.	42857 - 536 = 42321 purchase requests non-specificaton PR's	42321	.522
7.	Prepare multiple order record.		42321	.522
8.	Type purchase requisition, etc.			N.A.
9.	Mail requests.		42321	.522
10.	Burst forms.			N.A.
11.	File forms in appropriate files.		42321	.522
12.1	Keypunch encumbrances.		42321	.522
12.2	Verify encumbrances.		42321	.522
13.1	Unpack books; check against packing list or invoice. Check outstanding order file.	81071 - 8737 = 72334 vols.processed gifts searched	72334	.892
13.2	Unpack "processing-only" books.		8737	.108

Figure A2.30 (Continued)

FREQUENCY CALCULATIONS

Acquisitions

Activity Description Number	Activity Description	Preliminary Calculation	Frequency Quotient n/81701 vols.	Frequency
14.	Check in serials on Kardex.		20907	.258
15.	Collate books.		72334	.892
16.	Book return procedure (incorrect shipment, defective copy, approval books.)	Leonard, Centralized book processing, p. 135		.006
17.	Book accessioning routine.			N.A.
18.	Write sourcing information.			N.A.
19.	Prepare gift record form.			N.A.
20.	Book distribution routine.			1.000
21.	Prepare receiving report.			N.A.
22.	Prepare invoices for payment.		72334	.892
23.1	Keypunch expenditures.		72334	.892
23.2	Verifying expenditures.		72334	.892
24.	Clear in-process file.			1.000
25.	File forms, etc., in completed records or discard.			1.000
26.	Requestor notification routine.			N.A.
27.	Periodic accessions list routine.			N.A.
28.	Vendor status routine	Leonard, Centralized book processing, p. 134		.158

Figure A2.30 (Continued)

FREQUENCY CALCULATIONS

Acquisitions

Activity Description Number	Activity Description	Preliminary Calculation	Frequency Quotient n/81701 vols	Frequency
29.	Claims routine.	Figure		.037
30.	Cancellations routine.	583 reported o.p.	583	.007
31.	Out-of-print order routine.			N.A.
32.	Process inquiries.			
33.	General typing – correspondence, etc. (specify).	Leonard, Centralized book processing, p. 324		.015
34.	General revision (specify).			N.A.
35.1	Sorting tab cards.			N.A.
35.2	Prepare a computer run.			1.000
35.3	Check in computer run.			1.000
35.4	Keypunch title changes.	Data from bookkeeping		.006
36.	Bi-monthly accounting reports to members.			A.F.

Figure A2.30 (Continued)

FREQUENCY CALCULATIONS
Cataloging

Activity Description Number	Activity Description	Preliminary Calculation	Frequency Quotient n/81701 vols.	Frequency
37.	Sort books, assign and distribute.			1.000
38.	Search for LC copy; verify bibliographic information.	Figure 2.18		.334
39.1	Advanced card production: C.U. instruction slips.	Figure 2.18		.623
39.2	Advanced card production: member library instruction slips.	Figure 2.18		.762
40.	Receive and arrange LC cards.			N.A.
41.1	Receive and arrange LC proof slips or proof sheets.		244587	3.017
41.2	Stamp date and destination code on verso of master cards.		177425	2.188
42.	File LC copy. (cards or proof)		177425	2.188
43.	Match LC cards or proof copy and books.		18307	.226
44.	Added copies/added volumes routine.	81071 − 18308 − 9138 = vols.processed mass cataloged originally cat	53626	.661
45.	Catalog and classify with LC cards/copy.		18307	.226
46.	Original cataloging and classifying.		9138	.113
47.	Shelf listing (for 44, 45 and 46).			N.A.
48.	Type complete card sets.			N.A.
49.	Type master card.		9138	.113
50.	Revise master card.		9138	.113

Figure A2.30 (Continued)

FREQUENCY CALCULATIONS

Cataloging

Activity Description Number	Activity Description	Preliminary Calculation	Frequency Quotient n/31701 vols.	Frequency
51.	Type modification on a card or proof slip.		18307	.226
52.1	Reproduce card sets (other than typing). Sort cards into sets.	81071 − 5692 added vols. of new titles = 20907 added vols. of new titles vols. processed	54472	.672
52.2	Sort card sets by member or departmental library & stamp location code on each card.		54472	.672
53.	Type call number, added entries.		54472	.672
54.	Revise typing on card sets.		54472	.672
55.	Prepare authority cards.	Leonard, Centralized book processing, p. 326		.010
56.	Prepare cross-reference cards.	Leonard, Centralized book processing, p. 326		.031
57.	Prepare circulation card.			A.F.
58.	Prepare book pocket.			1.000
59.	Apply date due slip and spine label.			1.000
60.1	Match label sets and invoices to books.			1.000
60.2	Burst label sets and affix pockets.			1.000
60.3	Inspect pockets and remove flags.			1.000
61.	Affix biographical and review material in book.			N.A.
62.	Stamp property marks.			N.A.
63.	Affix plastic jacket to book.			N.A.

Figure A2.30 (Continued)

FREQUENCY CALCULATIONS

Cataloging

Activity Description Number	Activity Description	Preliminary Calculation	Frequency Quotient n/81701 vols.	Frequency
64.	Paper back books -- in house binding routine.	Figure 2.10		.062
65.	Revise completed books before forwarding.			1.000
66.	Sort and alphabetize shelf list and all catalog cards.			N.A.
67.	File shelf list and all catalog cards.			N.A.
68.	Revise filing of shelf list and all catalog cards.			N.A.
69.	Route card sets to departmental or member libraries.			1.000
70.	Paperback books -- bindery routine (preparation).	Figure 2.10		.079
71.	Paperback books -- bindery routine (receiving).	Figure 2.10		.079
72.	Catalog maintenance (other than filing).			N.A.
73.	General typing (specify).			N.A.
74.	General revision (specify).			N.A.
75.	General filing (specify).			N.A.
76.	Other cataloging activities not listed above (specify).			N.A.
77.1	Distribution of books to pre-keypunch staging area.			1.000
77.2	Keypunch SILO cards.			1.000
77.3	SILO error	SILO statistics Figure--unpublished		.108

Figure A2.30 (Continued)

FREQUENCY CALCULATIONS

Cataloging Activity Description Number	Activity Description	Preliminary Calculation	Frequency Quotient n/81701 vols.	Frequency
78.	Arrange books by library.			1.000
79.	Invoice/shipping list production.			A.F.
80.	Billing.			A.F.
81.1	Pack member-library books.		11816	.146
81.2	Inspect shipments and mail out.		11816	.146
82.	Union catalog (arrange and file).			N.A.
83.	Bibliographic Center notification.			A.F.

Figure A2.31

PURCHASE REQUESTS RETURNED UNFILLED
(By Institution)

Institution	Series Classed Together	Set	Out of Print	Traced Numbered Series on Standing Order	Other	Total
CSU	80	6	17	46	51	224
ASC	31	4	29	22	23	109
CSM	8	1	—	35	5	49
CSC	75	5	21	112	29	242
MSC	17	1	2	1	1	22
Totals	211	17	93	216	109	646

Figure A2.32

ORDERS RESUBMITTED

(By Institution)

School	Series Classed Together	Set	In-Print	Traced Numbered Series on Standing Order	Other	Total
ASC	1	3	12	–	2	18
CSC	–	1	1	42	2	46
CSM	–	–	–	5	1	6
CSU	–	2	7	29	2	40
MSC	–	–	–	–	–	–
Total	1	6	20	76	7	110

Figure A2.33

SHIPPING

(By Institution)

School	Volumes	Boxes	(Gifts)[*]
ASC	1470	57	301
CSC	2946	101	160
CSU	3355	104	1487
CSM	875	29	154
MSC	3152	91	549
TOTAL	11816	382	2651

*Included in the volume count

Figure A2.34

GROSS OPERATING SALARIES

	Job Class 2 Clerk 2	Job Class 3 Clerk 3	Job Class 4 LA I	Job Class 5 LA II	Job Class 6 LA III	Job Class 7 Asst. Libr.	Job Class 8 Assoc. Libr.	Job Class 9 Senior Libr.
	C.A.M.P.	C.A.M.P.	C.A.M.P.	Order/Bookkeeping	C.A.M.P./CALBPC	Cataloging	C.A.M.P.	Order/Bookkeeping
1)	228	375	415	530	585 / 505	348*	821	925
2)	340	395	455	Bibliographic 395	CAMP/CALBPC 455	354*	Bibliographic limit 867	
3)	CAMP/CALBPC 340	375	455	Cataloging 455	Order/Bookkeeping 455	654	Cataloging 917	
4)	Order Bookkeeping 355	395		395	505 (CIK4)	667	338*	
5)	355	395		505	505	687	825	
6)	340	375		530	Bibliographic 455	348*	878	
7)	355	395		530	530	344*		
8)	340				455			
9)	CAMP/CALBPC 340				530			
10)	340				455			
11)	340				555			
12)	355				Cataloging 615			
13)	355							
14)	340							
15)	Order Bookkeeping 415							
16)	455							
17)	340							
18)	355							

*Part-time

Figure A2.34 (Continued)

GROSS OPERATING SALARIES CONTINUED

	Job Class 2 Clerk 2	Job Class 3 Clerk 3	Job Class 4 LA I	Job Class 5 LA II	Job Class 6 LA II	Job Class 7 Asst. Libr.	Job Class 8 Assoc. Libr.	Job Class 9 Senior Libr.
19)	340							
20) Bibliographic	340							
Total	6968	2705	1325	2810	6605	3401	4646	925

weighted student wpm = $1.57

Figure A2.35

PROCESSING CENTER PERSONNEL

Job Class	Order/Bookkeeping	Bibliography	Cataloging	Catalog Maintenance	
Class 2 Clerk 2	$340.00 340.00 355.00 415.00 455.00	$340.00		CAMP: CALBPC 340.00 340.00 340.00 355.00 355.00	$228.00 340.00 340.00 340.00 340.00 340.00 355.00 355.00 355.00
Class 3 Clerk 3	375.00 395.00 395.00			395.00	375.00 395.00 395.00
Class 4 Library Assistant 1					415.00 455.00 455.00
Class 5 Library Assistant 2	530.00	395.00 455.00	$395.00 505.00 530.00		
Class 6 Library Assistant 3	455.00 505.00 505.00	455.00 455.00 455.00 530.00 530.00 555.00	615.00	455.00	505.00 585.00
Class 7 Assistant Librarian			344.00 348.00 348.00 354.00 654.00 667.00 687.00		
Class 8 Associate Librarian		867.00	338.00 825.00 878.00 917.00		821.00
Class 9 Senior Librarian	925.00				

Figure A2.36

STUDENT PERSONNEL
Job Class 1

Department		Number of Students per Wage Rate Category				Number of Hours per Week
		1.50	1.60	1.75	1.90	
CAMP	Regular	8	11	1	1	497.85
	Work Study	1	6			89.20
CATALOGING	Regular	1				62.31
ORDER	Regular	4	6			388.37
	Work Study	1				20.94
BIBLIOGRAPHY	Regular	2	2			230.22
	Work Study	1				28.43
TOTAL		22	26	1	1	1317.32

One Man Year in Hours
(52 X 5 X 8)   2080

Total Estimated Hours
Worked in One Year (1317.32 x 52)   68501

Number of F.T.E. Man Years
in Student Help (6850 ÷ 2080)   33

Figure A2.37

STUDENT WAGE PER MINUTE
Job Class 1

Number of Students	%	Wage Rate	Pro-rated
22	44	1.50	.066
26	52	1.60	0.83
1	2	1.75	.04
1	2	1.90	.04
Total 50	100		Weighted hourly wage 1.57

wpm = .0262

Figure A2.38

WAGES PER MINUTE

Job Class Position Title	1 Student	2 Clerk 2	3 Clerk 3	4 Library Assistant 1	5 Library Assistant 2	6 Library Assistant 3	7 Assistant Librarian	8 Associate Librarian	9 Senior Librarian	Average Wage Rate
Slots	33(F.T.E.)	20	7	3	6	13	5	5.5	1	
Gross Operating Salaries		$ 6968	$ 2705	$ 1325	$ 2810	$ 6605	$ 3401	$ 4646	$11,100	
Average Wage per slot (X)		$ 348	$ 386	$ 442	$ 468	$ 508	$ 680	$ 845	$ 925	
Average Annual Salary (12X)		$ 4176	$ 4632	$ 5304	$ 5616	$ 6096	$ 8160	$10,140	$11,100	
Wage per Minute *	$.0262	$.0364	$.0404	$.0462	$.0490	$.0531	$.0711	$.0884	$.0968	$.0574

* The wage per minute = $\dfrac{\text{Average annual salary}}{\text{One man year in minute (113720)}}$

Figure A2.39

SUPPLIES COST (5)

Supply Item	Cost per M	Total Cost	Quantity	Unit Cost
Purchase Request Card	4.50			.0045
Order Pack	3.60			.0036
Card Sheets (6 cards per sheet)	31.10/M			.0052 (per card) or .036 per set
Catalog Card Sets (7 cards per set)				
Catalog Cards (Single)	5.00			.0050
Date Due Slips	2.60			.0026
Card/Pocket/Label Forms	35.85			.0359
Tab Cards (incl. 5 plates)		519.78	302M	.0002
Labeling Adhesive		132.86	*	.0016
Self-Carboning Paper		50.00	60M	.0008
Rubber Stamps		73.24	(pro-rated over 11816 vols. shipped to M.L.'s	.0062
Postage		38.31	(pro-rated)	.0032
Processing Flags		42.18	2750	.0153
Total Unit Cost				.1153

*Pro-rated over the total volumes processed: 81,071.

Figure A2.40

EQUIPMENT RENTAL AND CONTRACTUAL SERVICES (O_r)

Photocopying

Card Production:

  Card Sheets 99267

   @ 6¢ per sheet (set) $ 5,956.02

Order Packs:

  Order Placed 42321

   @ 6¢ per pack   2,539.26

Equipment Rental

Postage Meter

  Prorated 25 %

  for Technical Services $1,750.00

  Maintenance   168.00   1,918.00

Desks (2) ($15.00/mo. x 2 x 12)   360.00

Chairs (2) Secretarial ($3.00/mo. x 2 x 12)   72.00

Typewriters:

  IBM ($33.60/mo. x 12) $ 403.20

  Olympia Typewriters (8)

   ($ 2.50 x 8 x 12)   240.00   643.20

Speaker - Phone   67.50

Code-a-Phone   150.00

Tichometer   480.00

Equipment Repair

Calculator   7.50

Xerox Camera   36.42

Rapid-print Numbering Machine 64.60

Polaroid Camera   15.77   124.29

Data Processing

Computer Fees $14,506.10

Keypunch Equipment   1,486.20

             $15,992.30

  Prorated 40% for operational 6,396.92   6,396.92

           Total $13,807.19

Figure A2.40 (Continued)

DEPRECIATION (O_d)

Equipment Purchases (O_p)

Tichometer Attachments		$ 643.00
Book Trucks (7)		448.35
Hand Truck		24.50
Tote-Boxes		730.50
Typewriter Tables (2)		44.00
	Total	$ 1,890.35
Pro-rated over 10 years	Depreciation	$ 189.04

Figure A2.41

WEIGHTED AVERAGE WAGE PER MINUTE (h_a)

Category of Worker	Average Wage Rate (g)	Slots	Per Cent of Slots per Category	h_a Weighted Wage Rate
1	.0262	33 F.T.E.	35	.009170
2	.0364	20	21	.007644
3	.0404	7	8	.003232
4	.0462	3	3	.001386
5	.0490	6	7	.003430
6	.0531	13	14	.007434
7	.0711	5	5	.003555
8	.0884	5.5	6	.005304
9	.0968	1	1	.000968
Total		93.5	100.0	.042123

Figure A2.42
LABOR (L)
Unit Cost Calculation for Technical Processing Activities
(Frequencies Not Used)
Acquisitions

Library C.A.L.B.P.C.
KEY:

AF = Another function incorporated this activity at the center.
NA = Not applicable (not performed at the center).
( ) = Simulated data
P = Performed in parallel for C.U. non-specification items
u = Performed for C.U. books only

m = Performed at most libraries for CALBPC orders
+ = Standardizing factor (1.4771)
d = Data taken from the diary
f_1 = student
f_2 = Clerk 2
f_3 = Clerk 3
f_4 = Library Assistant 1

f_5 = Library Assistant 2
f_6 = Library Assistant 3
f_7 = Assistant Librarian
f_8 = Associate Librarian
f_9 = Senior Librarian

Code / Activity Description		a Observed Mean Time	b Personal Rating Factor	c Standard Time	d Frequency	e Proportioned Time	f Category of Worker	g Wage/Minute	h Cost of Activity
1. Open, sort and distribute incoming mail.	P	.249	1.07	0.393			2	.0364	.0143
2. Review book order requests; review selection media.	P	u,m							
3. Select titles to be ordered.	P	u,m							
4. Type library order request card.	P	u,m							
5.1 Search and verify bibliographic information.	P	3.489	1.10	5.669			6	.0531	.3010
5.2 Return non-specification orders to member libraries.	P	(.300)	1.00	0.443			7	.0711	.0315
6. Assign vendor.	P	.063	1.10	0.099			8	.0884	.0088
7. Prepare multiple order record.	P	.580	1.10	0.942			5	.049	.0462
8. Type purchase requisition, etc.	P	NA u							
9. Mail requests.	P	.112	1.05	0.174			2	.0364	.0063
10. Burst forms.	P	NA							
11. File forms in Appropriate files.	P	.324	1.15	0.549			5	.0498	.0269

Figure A2.42 (Continued)

Acquisitions

Code / Activity Description	P	a Observed Mean Time	b Personal Rating Factor	c Standard Time	d Frequency	e Proportioned Time	f Category of Worker	g Category Wage/Minute	h Cost of Activity
12.1 Keypunch encumbrances.	P	.160	1.15	0.272			3	.0404	.0110
12.2 Verify encumbrances.	P	.121	1.05	0.188			3	.0404	.0076
15.1 Unpack books; check against packing list or invoice. Check outstanding order file.	P	5.200	1.08	8.295			2	.0364	.3019
13.2 Unpack "processing-only" books.	P	(.812)	1.08	1.295			2	.0364	.0471
14. Check in serials on Kardex.	P	.483	1.10	0.784			4	.0462	.0362
15. Collate books.	P	.311	1.20	0.551			2	.0364	.0200
16. Book return procedure (incorrect shipment, defective copy, approval books).	P	6.924	1.08	11.046			6	.0531	.5865
17. Book accessioning routine.		NA							
18. Write sourcing information.		NA							
19. Prepare gift record form.	P	u							
20. Book distribution routine.	P	.191	1.07	3.01			2	.0364	.0110
21. Prepare receiving report.		NA							
22. Prepare vendor invoices for payment.	P	.334	1.08	5.33			6	.0531	.0283
23.1 Keypunch expenditures.	P	.143	1.10	0.232			3	.0404	.0094
23.2 Verifying expenditures.	P	.086	1.05	0.133			3	.0404	.0054

Figure A2.42 (Continued)

Acquisitions

Code	Activity Description	P	a Observed Mean Time	b Personal Rating Factor	c Standard Time	d Frequency	e Proportioned Time	f Category of Worker	g Wage/ Minute	h Cost of Activity
24.	Clear in-process file.	P	.302	1.05	0.468			1	.0262	.0123
25.	File forms, etc., in completed records or discard.	P	.369	1.10	0.600			1	.0262	.0157
26.	Requestor notification routine.	P	u,m							
27.	Periodic accessions list routine.									
28.	Vendor status routine.	P	.985	1.15	1.669			3	.0404	.0674
29.	Claims routine.	P	3.264	1.10	5.303			3	.0404	.2142
30.	Cancellations routine.	P	1.864	1.15	3.167			3	.0404	.1279
31.	Out-of-print order routine.	P	u,m							
32.	Process inquiries.	P	10.208d	1.10	16.587			6	.0531	.8808
33.	General typing – correspondence, etc. (specify).		NA							
34.	General revision (specify).		NA							
35.1	Sorting tab cards.	P	.013	1.05	0.021			2	.0364	.0008
35.2	Prepare a computer run.	P	.005	1.05	0.007			3	.0404	.0003
35.3	Check in computer run.	P	.066	1.10	0.103			3	.0404	.0044
35.4	Keypunch title changes.	P	2.255	1.00	3.331			3	.0404	.1346
36.	Bi-monthly accounting reports to members.	AF								

Figure A2.42 (Continued)

LABOR (L)

Unit Cost Calculation for Technical Processing Activities
Cataloging

Code / Activity Description	P	a — Observed Mean Time	b — Personal Rating Factor	c — Standard Time	d — Frequency	e — Proportioned Time	f — Category of Worker	g — Category Wage/Minute	h — Cost of Activity
37. Sort books: assign and distribute.	P	4.894	1.05	7.591			6	.0531	.4031
38. Search for LC copy; verify bibliographic information.	P	.895	1.10	1.453			6	.0531	.0772
39.1 Advanced card production: C. U. instruction slips.	P	.436	1.10	0.709			2	.0364	.0258
39.2 Advanced card production: member library instruction slips.	P	.952	1.10	1.547			6	.0531	.0821
40. Receive and arrange LC cards.		NA							
41.1 Receive and arrange LC proof slips or proof sheets.	P	.171d	1.10	0.278			1	.0262	.0073
41.2 Stamp date and destination code on verso of master cards.	P	.010	1.10	0.162			2	.0364	.0059
42. File LC copy. (cards or proof)	P	.244	1.15	0.415			1	.0262	.0109
43. Match LC cards or proof copy and books.	P	.290	1.15	0.493			2	.0364	.0179
44. Added copies/added volumes routine.	P	.373	1.09	0.601			5	.0498	.0294
45. Catalog and classify with LC cards/copy.	P	1.510	1.05	2.343			6	.0531	.1244
46. Original cataloging and classifying.	P	14.081d	1.10	22.879			8	.0384	2.0225
47. Shelf Listing (for 44, 45, and 46).	P	u,m							

Figure A2.42 (Continued)

Cataloging

Code	Activity Description	P	a Observed Mean Time	b Personal Rating Factor	c Standard Time	d Frequency	e Proportioned Time	f Category of Worker	g Wage/Minute	h Cost of Activity
48.	Type complete card sets.	P	NA							
49.	Type master card.	P	1.304	1.18	2.273			2	.0364	.0827
50.	Revise master card.	P	.270	1.10	0.439			4	.0462	.0203
51.	Type modification on a card or proof slip.	P	.155	1.10	0.251			2	.0364	.0091
52.1	Reproduce cards sets (other than typing). Sort cards into sets.	P	1.489	1.10	2.419			3	.0404	.0977
52.2	Sort card sets by member or departmental library & stamp location code on each card.	P	.959	1.10	1.558			2	.0364	.0567
53.	Type call number, added entries.	P	.821	1.05	1.273			2	.0364	.0463
54.	Revise typing on card sets.	P	.479	1.10	0.778			4	.0462	.0359
55.	Prepare authority cards.	P	1.168	1.00	1.725			2	.0364	.0628
56.	Prepare cross-reference cards.	P	1.648	1.10	2.678			2	.0364	.0975
57.	Prepare circulation card.		AF							
58.	Prepare book pocket.									
59.	Apply date due slip and spine label.	P	.546	1.15	0.928			1	.0262	.0243
60.1	Match label sets and invoices to books.	P	.427	1.05	0.662			2	.0364	.0241
60.2	Burst label sets and affix pockets.	P	.704	1.15	1.196			1	.0262	.0313

Figure A2.42 (Continued)

Cataloging

Code	Activity Description	P	a Observed Mean Time	b Personal Rating Factor	c Standard Time	d Frequency	e Proportioned Time	f Category of Worker	g Wage/Minute	h Cost of Activity
60.2	Inspect pockets and remove flags.	P	.279	1.10	0.453			1	.0262	.0119
61.	Affix biographical and review material in book.		NA							
62.	Stamp property marks.	P	u,m							
63.	Affix plastic jacket to book.		NA							
64.	Paperback books — in house binding routine.	P	2.618	1.00	3.867			3	.0404	.1562
65.	Revise completed books before forwarding.	P	.127	1.15	0.216			3	.0404	.0087
66.	Sort and alphabetize shelf list and all catalog cards.	P	NA u,m							
67.	File shelf list and all catalog cards.	P	NA u,m							
68.	Revise filing of shelf list and all catalog cards.	P	NA u,m							
69.	Route card sets to departmental or member libraries.	P	.437u	1.05	0.678			2	.0364	.0247
70.	Paperback books — bindery routine (preparation).	P	2.724	1.05	4.224			3	.0404	.1706
71.	Paperback books — bindery routine (receiving).	P	.685	1.10	1.114			3	.0404	.0450
72.	Catalog maintenance (Other than filing).	P	NA u,m							
73.	General typing (specify).		NA							
74.	General revision (specify).		NA u,m							

Figure A2.42 (Continued)

Cataloging

Code	Activity Description	P	a Observed Mean Time	b Personal Rating Factor	c Standard Time	d Frequency	e Proportioned Time	f Category of Worker	g Wage/Minute	h Cost of Activity
75.	General filing (specify).		NA u,m							
76.	Other cataloging activities not listed above (specify).		NA u,m							
77.1	Distribution of books to pre-keypunch staging area.	P	.056	1.05	0.087			4	.0462	.0040
77.2	Keypunch SILO cards.	P	.419	1.10	0.681			3	.0404	.0275
77.3	SILO error routine.	P	.974	1.05	1.511			2,4,7	.0512*	.0774
78.	Arrange books by library.	P	.240	1.10	0.390			1	.0262	.0102
79.	Invoice/shipping list production.									
80.	Billing.									
81.1	Pack member library books.		.205	1.10	0.334			4	.0462	.0154
81.2	Inspect shipments and mail out.		.433	1.10	0.703			2	.0364	.0256
82.	Union catalog (arrange and file).		NA							
83.	Bibliographic Center notification		AF							

* Average of the three wage rates

Figure A2.43

UNIT COST CALCULATION FOR CERTAIN EXCEPTION ACTIVITIES WITH FREQUENCY
(Class 2)

Code	Activity Description	Standard Time	Cost of Activity Without Frequency	Frequency	Category of worker	Wage/ Minute	Cost of Activity Without Frequency
16.	Book return procedure.	11.046	.5865	.006	6	.0531	.0035
28.	Vendor status routine.	1.669	.0674	.158	3	.0404	.0107
29.	Claims routine.	5.303	.2142	.037	3	.0404	.0079
30.	Cancellations routine.	3.167	.1279	.007	3	.0404	.0009
32.	Process inquiries.	16.587	.8808	.015	6	.0531	.0132
55.	Prepare authority cards.	1.725	.0628	.010	2	.0364	.0006
56.	Prepare cross-reference cards.	2.678	.0975	.031	2	.0364	.0030
	Total	42.175	2.0371				.0398

Recommended Prorated Fee = $.0398

Figure A2.44

LABOR (L)

Unit Costs for Technical Processing Activities:
A Comparison

Acquisitions

Library ___C.A.L.B.P.C.___

KEY:

AF = Another functions incorporated this activity at the center
NA = Not applicable (not performed at the center)
( ) = Simulated data
--- = Inconsequential
Note: These figures were calculated using frequency data

Reasons for Increase or Decrease in Cost --

a = Performed at C.U. for non-specification items
b = Parts of activity performed locally
c = Simplified by specifications
d = Complicated by the need to serve additional libraries
e = Simplified in Phase III manual procedures or converted to machine function
f = Additional to originally planned system

Activity Description / Code	C.U. 1967 [1]	CALBPC (Simulated) 1967 [2]	CALBPC Phase III 1969 [3]	At least a 5¢ increase or decrease between column 1 and 3	At least a 5¢ increase or decrease between column 2 and 3
1. Open, sort and distribute incoming mail.	.018	.014	.008		
2. Review book order requests; review selection media.	NA	NA	NA		
3. Select titles to be ordered.	NA	NA	NA		
4. Type library order request card.	AF	NA	NA		
5.1 Search and verify bibliographic information.	.195	.020	.159		
5.2 Return non-specification orders to member libraries.					
6. Assign vendor.	.057	.008	.005	-c	
7. Prepare multiple order record.	.033	.034	.024		
8. Type purchase requisition, etc.	.001	NA	NA		
9. Mail requests.	---	.006	.003		
10. Burst forms.	NA	NA	NA		
11. File forms in Appropriate files.	.060	.020	.014	-a	-e

[1]Leonard, p. 322-327.
[2]Ibid, p. 134-138.
[3]See Figure

Figure A2.44 (Continued)

Acquisitions

Code	Activity Description	C.U. 1967	CALBPC (Simulated) 1967	CALBPC Phase III 1969	At least a 5% increase or decrease between column 1 and 3	At least a 5% increase or decrease between column 2 and 3
12.1	Keypunch encumbrances.	.026	.026	.010		
12.2	Verify encumbrances.					
13.1	Unpack books; check against packing list or invoice. Check outstanding order file.	.199	.299	.269	+d	
13.2	Unpack "processing-only" books.		.001	.001		
14.	Check in serials on Kardex.	.022	.001	.009		
15.	Collate books.	NA	.020	.018		
16.	Book return procedure (incorrect shipment, defective copy, approval books).	.001	.002	.004		
17.	Book accessioniong routine.	NA	NA	NA		
18.	Write sourcing information.	NA	NA	NA		
19.	Prepare gift record form.	.010	NA	NA		
20.	Book distribution routine.	.042	.011	.011		
21.	Prepare receiving report.	NA	NA	NA		
22.	Prepare vendor invoices for payment.	.016	.458	.025		
23.1	Keypunch expenditures.			.008		-b,e
23.2	Verifying expenditures.	.005		.005		

Figure A2.44 (Continued)

Acquisitions

Code	Activity Description	C.U. 1967	CALBPC (Simulated) 1967	CALBPC Phase III 1969	At least 5% increase or decrease between column 1 and 3	At least 5% increase or decrease between column 2 and 3
24.	Clear in-process file.	.017	.169	.012		
25.	File forms, etc., in completed records or discard.	.038	.216	.016		-b
26.	Requestor notification routine.	.005	NA	NA		
27.	Periodic accessions list routine.	NA	.002	NA		
28.	Vendor status routine.	.006	.010	.011		
29.	Claims routine.	.003	.007	.008		
30.	Cancellations routine.	.012	.004	.001		
31.	Out-of-print order routine.	---	NA	NA		
32.	Process inquiries.	.009	NA	.013		
33.	General typing – correspondence, etc. (specify).	.027	NA	NA		
34.	General revision (specify).	.306	NA	NA	-a	
35.1	Sorting tab cards.					
35.2	Prepare a computer run.	.047	NA	.001		
35.3	Check in computer run.			---		
35.4	Keypunch title changes.			.004		
36.	Bi-monthly accounting reports to members.	---	.038	.001		
	Sub-totals	1.155	1.365	0.640	AF	+	-

Figure A2.44 (Continued)

Code / Activity Description	C.U. 1967	CALBPC (Simulated) 1967	CALBPC Phase III 1969	At least a 5% increase or decrease between Column 1 and 3	At least a 5% increase or decrease between Column 2 and 3
37. Sort books, assign and distribute.	.273	NA	.403	+d	+f
38. Search for LC copy; verify bibliographic information.	.103	.039	.027	-c	
39.1 Advanced card production: C. U. instruction slips.	NA	NA	.016	+f	
39.2 Advanced card production: member library instruction slips.			.063	+f	+f
40. Receive and arrange IC cards.	NA	NA	NA		
41.1 Receive and arrange LC proof slips or proof sheets.	.003		.022		
41.2 Stamp date and destination code on verso of master cards.		.010	.013		
42. File LC copy. (cards or proof)	.004		.024		
43. Match LC cards or proof copy and books.	.092	.004	.004	-a,c	
44. Added copies/added volumes routine.	.212	.037	.019	-a	
45. Catalog and classify with LC cards/copy.	.106	.055	.028	-a,c	
46. Original cataloging and classifying.	.455	.174	.228	-a,c	+d
47. Shelf Listing (for 44, 45, and 46).	.152	NA	NA	-a	

Figure A2.44 (Continued)

Cataloging

Code	Activity Description	C.U. 1967	CALBPC (Simulated) 1967	CALBPC Phase II 1969	At least a 5¢ increase or decrease between column 1 and 3	At least a 5¢ increase or decrease between column 2 and 3
48.	Type complete card sets.	NA	NA	NA		
49.	Type master card.	.070	.008	.009	-a	
50.	Revise master card.	.003	.001	.002		
51.	Type modification on a card or proof slip.	.009	.001	.002		
52.1	Reproduce cards sets (other than typing). Sort cards into sets.	.248	.081	.066	-e	
52.2	Sort card sets by member or departmental library & stamp location code on each card.			.038		
53.	Type call number, added entries.	.023	.217	.031		-e
54.	Revise typing on card sets.	.060	.006	.024		
55.	Prepare authority cards.	.001	.062	.001		-a,b
56.	Prepare cross-reference cards.	.006	.096	.003		-a,b
57.	Prepare circulation card.	NA	.013	AF		
58.	Prepare book pocket.	NA	.016	AF		
59.	Apply date due slip and spine label.	.100	.025	.024	-e	
60.1	Match label sets and invoices to books.			.024		
60.2	Burst label sets and affix pockets.	.001	.007	.031		

Figure A2.44 (Continued)

Cataloging

Code	Activity Description	C.U. 1967	CALBPC (Simulated) 1967	CALBPC Phase III 1969	At least a 5% increase or decrease between column 1 and 3	At least a 5% increase or decrease between column 2 and 3
60.3	Inspect pockets and remove flags.			.012		
61.	Affix biographical and review material in book.	NA	NA	NA		
62.	Stamp property marks.	.009	NA	NA		
63.	Affix plastic jacket to book.	NA	NA	NA		
64.	Paperback books -- in house binding routine.	.002	NA	.010		
65.	Revise completed books before forwarding.	.006	.016	.009		
66.	Sort and alphabetize shelf list and all catalog cards.	.250	NA	NA	-a,b	
67.	File shelf list and all catalog cards.	.032	NA	NA		
68.	Revise filing of shelf list and all catalog cards.	.114	NA	NA	-a,b	
69.	Route card sets to departmental or member libraries.	.014	NA	.025		
70.	Paperback books -- bindery routine (preparation).	.012	.009	.014		
71.	Paperback books -- bindery routine (receiving).	.004	.003	---		
72.	Catalog maintenance (Other than filing).	.001	NA	NA		
73.	General typing (specify).	AF	NA	NA		
74.	General revision (specify).	.002	NA	NA		

Figure A2.44 (Continued)

Cataloging

Code / Activity Description	C.U. 1967	CALBPC (Simulated) 1967	CALBPC Phase III 1969	At least a 5% increase or decrease between column 1 and 3	At least a 5% increase or decrease between column 2 and 3
75. General filing (specify).	--	NA	NA		
76. Other cataloging activities not listed above (specify).	.029	NA	NA		
77.1 Distribution of books to pre-keypunch staging area.	NA		.004		
77.2 Keypunch SILO cards.	NA	.012	.028		
77.3 SILO error routine.	NA		.008		
78. Arrange books by library.	NA	.015	.010		
79. Invoice/shipping list production.	NA	.002	AF		
80. Billing.	NA	.002	AF		
81.1 Pack member library books.	NA				
81.2 Inspect shipments and mail out.	NA	.015	.002		
82. Union catalog (arrange and file).	NA	.041	.004		
83. Bibliographic Center notification	NA	.014	AF		
Sub-totals	2.413	0.981	1.237	-	
Acquisitions	1.155	1.365	0.640	-	+
Cataloging	2.413	.981	1.237	-	-
2L	3.568	2.346	1.877	-	+

APPENDIX FIGURE

A3.1

(Chapter III)

Figure A3.1

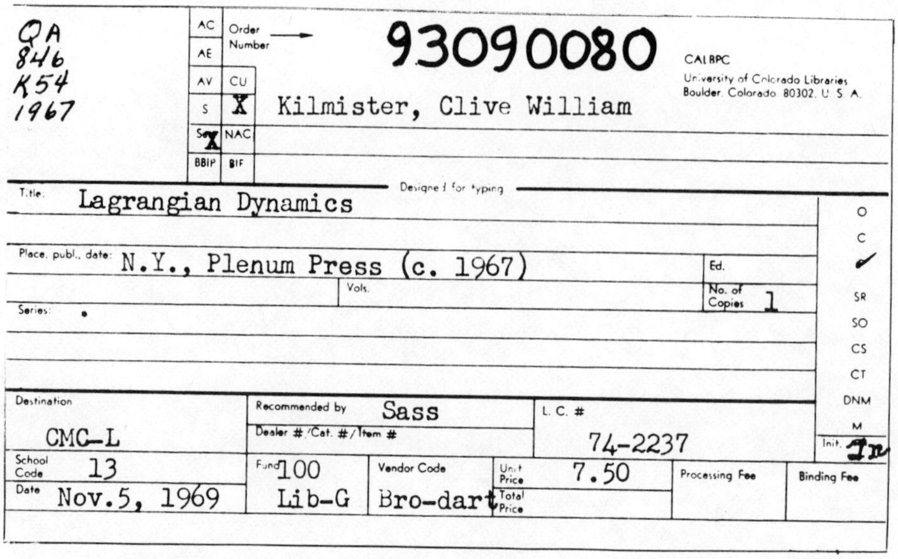

QA 846 K54 1967

AC | AE | AV | S | X | BBIP — CU | X | NAC | BIF

Order Number → 93090080

CALBPC
University of Colorado Libraries
Boulder, Colorado 80302, U. S. A.

Kilmister, Clive William

Title: Lagrangian Dynamics

Designed for typing

Place, publ., date: N.Y., Plenum Press (c. 1967)

Ed.

Vols.

No. of Copies 1

Series:

O C ✓ SR SO CS CT DNM M

Destination CMC-L

Recommended by Sass

L. C. # 74-2237

Dealer #/Cat. #/Item #

Init. Jn

School Code 13

Fund 100 Lib-G

Vendor Code Bro-dart

Unit Price 7.50

Total Price

Processing Fee

Binding Fee

Date Nov.5, 1969

Order Card
(Revised, July 1969, to Facilitate Keypunching)

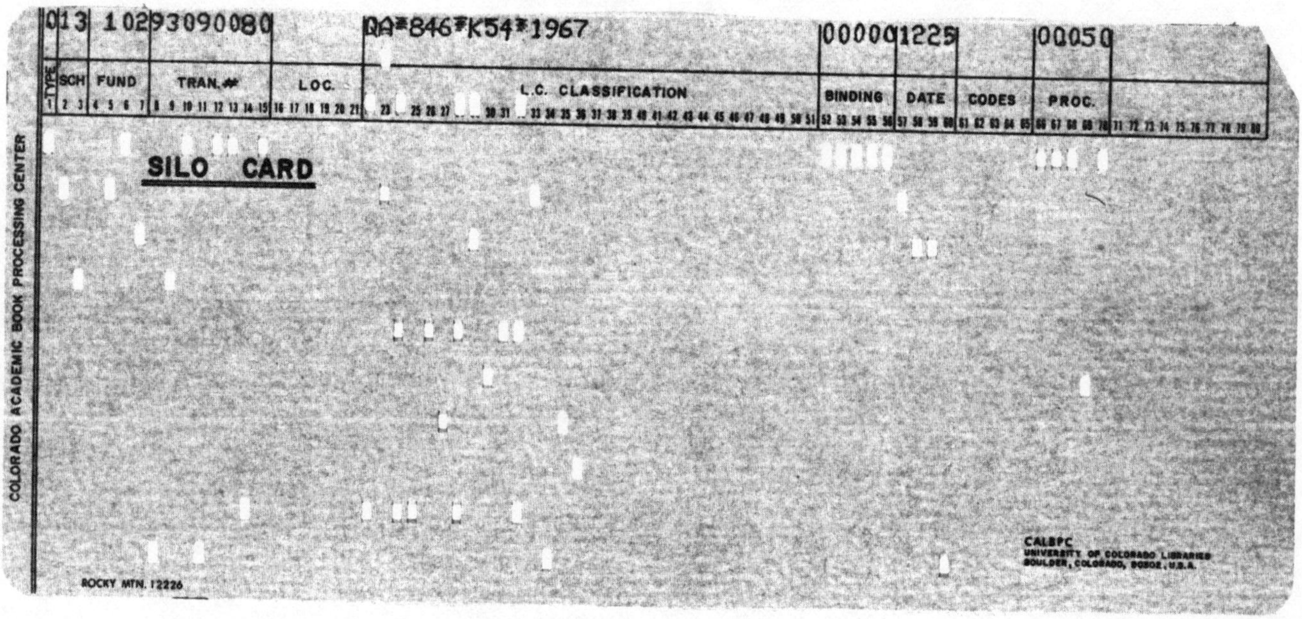

013 102 93090080 QA*846*K54*1967 00000 1225 00050

TYPE SCH FUND TRAN.# LOC. L.C. CLASSIFICATION BINDING DATE CODES PROC.

SILO CARD

COLORADO ACADEMIC BOOK PROCESSING CENTER

CALBPC
UNIVERSITY OF COLORADO LIBRARIES
BOULDER, COLORADO, 80302, U.S.A.

ROCKY MTN. 12226

Silo Card
(To call up Label Set and Invoice)

APPENDIX FIGURES

A4.1 - A4.7

(Chapter IV)

Figure A4.1

CALBPC NEWSLETTER

no. 1
November 4, 1969

To: The Council of Librarians and Technical Advisory Committee
From: Mrs. Violet Wagener, CALBPC Coordinator

This Newsletter is being inaugurated to provide CALBPC libraries a closer
contact with the CALBPC system operations. It will not replace Council
decision and policy making, but it will include system interpretation of
Council decision and policy making, and announcements of general interest.

ORDERS -
PR CARD

The system is trying to standardize on the letters used to designate each
library and has decided to use NUC symbols because they are the least likely
to change. Therefore, please use your NUC symbol in the destination box on
the PR card.

Harriet Rebuldela, Searching Supervisor, reports that the percentage of correctly filled out PR's is increasing rapidly and that the revised PR card is
working out very well in the work flow. Abby Dahl-Hansen, Order Supervisor,
is developing a tape slide explanation of filling out the card. This is being
done in her spare time and when finished should be a helpful tool for you to
use with your staff.

There are actually 14 items on the card which you should fill in: (The date
box is not for member library use.)

author	
title	
imprint data	Examples:
series note	be sure to indicate if you have information
inclusive volumes	v. 1-3, v. 1-4, v.2 only
edition	
number of copies	
LC card number	
destination	your NUC symbol
school code	05, 11, 09, etc., your school code
recommended by	your dept. or faculty member
fund	400, 550, etc.
unit price	list price which will be encumbered
total price	unit price times number of copies

After several telephone calls to you concerning variant imprints I have
inferred that you wish to accept them when author, title, language, and
year (or later edition) are as specified on your PR. Therefore, we will
accept these books routinely, and not hold them up to telephone you.

PROCESSING
FEE

To make input routine and for clear understanding by the System staff, it
has been necessary to spell out explicitly what is included in each of the
processing fee categories. We think the following schedule covers all the
variations now, but we may have to add further interpretation in a later
Newsletter. Do not hesitate to call me if you have a question about a fee
charge.

$ 1.85

1. Titles for which the Center has a master catalog card used to
   create cards for a book previously cataloged for CALBPC.
   (Because of the call number pattern specified in CALBPC

**ROOM 9 NORLIN LIBRARY UNIV. OF COLO.
BOULDER COLORADO 80302 TEL. 443-2211 x 7641**

Specifications, rev. Dec. 1968, p.2, as well as location symbols
on face of CU main entries, many titles for which CU has a master
catalog card cannot be included in this price category)

2. Added volumes to a multiple volume set, i.e., v.2, v.3, etc.
3. Added copies on a single purchase request, i.e., copy 2, copy 3, etc.
4. Items which are purchased by the Center for a member library but
   which cannot be cataloged under the agreements of the Specifications
   will be charged the initial processing fee of $1.85 until some future
   cost study changes this amount.

$2.35

1. Exact LC proof with a complete call number and which has not been
   used as a master card.
2. Exact Xerox camera copy with complete call number which has not been
   used as a master card before, including PZ classification numbers with
   a partial suggested literature number in brackets.
3. CU main entry card, including literature classification numbers for
   titles to which LC has assigned PZ number, and for which CU has
   assigned a literature classification number.

#3.95

1. LC proof without a call number or with an incomplete call number.
2. Xerox camera copy without a call number.
3. Variant copy of any other type.
     (Note that variant copy is distinct from modified copy.
      The former involves a change of content, the latter, a
      correction of typing error)
4. PZ call numbers not covered under steps above.
5. No copy
     (Note that a decision must be made on length of time
      books will be held for LC copy)

CIRCULATION
SYSTEM, BOOK CARDS

Our label, pocket and book card supplier did not meet specifications on the
order to be delivered in October. Paul Sheldon, Supervisor of CaMP (Catalog
Maintenance and Preservation) and Bill Harper, Systems Analyst did frantic
reorganization and programming in order to maintain the flow of books processed.

Simultaneously, while changes were being made, it was propititous to program
for the Hollerith or punched circulation card. Joan Maier received Council
approval through an individual poll to launch this system. The card was
specified by the Action Committee for Automated Circulation Systems in Colorado
Libraries, Bob Braude, chairman. Information about the system was given at the
CLA convention and in the current issue of Colorado Academic Libraries. About
November 15 the manual book card will be replaced by the Hollerith circulation
card. Eventually these cards will be preprinted with an appropriate "mountain
libraries motif", but it will be necessary for you to affix your stamp. A
sample is attached to this newsletter.

CALBPC'ers
MEETINGS

The System is having a number of aches and pains during this shakedown period
and your patience is much appreciated. One of our most difficult problems is
interpreting specifications to cover many variations, and then to articulate a
routine procedure so that we do not waste time on exceptions, questions and

value judgments. We hold a weekly meeting of CALBPC'ers, Tuesdays at
9:00 a.m. to solve as many of these problems as we can within the limits of
our authority. You are welcome to attend one of these meetings if you are in
Boulder and give us prior notification.

EXTRA CARD   You may indicate your request for one or more _extra_ catalog card sets by
SETS   writing in the narrow margin below the PR processing fee box, "1 extra card
                set," 2 extra card sets," etc.

The fee for these sets will be 45 cents a set based on the following data,
and subject to further research.

From feasibility study, Library 8. See Centralized Book Processing,
Appendix 3.5.8. This is the book published from the project's Phase I
and II report which you have.

		Cost
Activity 52, Reproduce card sets (other than typing)		.248
Sort cards into sets		
" 53, Type call number, added entries		.023
" 54, Revise typing on card sets		.060
" 69, Route card sets		.014
Estimated keypunch cost for additional fee input and cataloger time to transfer extra card set indication		.055
10% cost of living increase since study & rounding off		.05
		.45

The fee will be added to the processing fee for the individual title and
will be included here in the invoice and BAIS report. Since the total sum
will be unique, i.e., $2.30, $2.80, $4.40 you will be able to identify it
easily.

BINDING   Catalogers decide if new monographs are to be bound. They then send the items
                in need of binding to the Binding Unit of CaMP with notes about peculiarities,
                if any, that will affect the binding instructions to the commercial binder. The
                fees are: for buckram, $2.35; Permabind/vinabind, $1.25. Now a third cate-
                gory has been added. Pamphlet binding will be done for a fee of $1.15. Some
                pamphlets were bound for you during the research project, phase III, at no cost.
                We set the $1.15 fee arbitrarily because we have not been able to do the timing
                and supply checking to compute labor and supply costs. The fee may be adjusted
                later.

THIS IS A PREPRINTED FORMAT SUGGESTED
FOR DISCUSSION BY COUNCIL MEMBERS AT
NEXT COUNCIL MEETING.

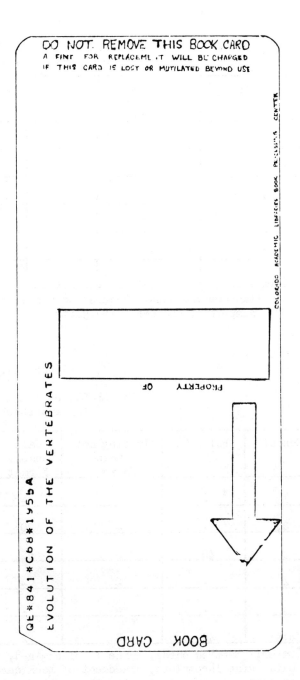

Figure A4.2

BOOKS PURCHASED BUT SHIPPED UNPROCESSED
March 1969 – November 1969

Institution	Series Classed Together	Music	Document	Miscellaneous[*]	Total
1	-	-	-	-	-
2	20	1	-	1	22
3	9	3	-	1	13
4	5	-	-	3	8
5	20	-	2	3	25
Totals	54	4	2	8	68

[*]Miscellaneous includes: Request to cancel received too late, art folios, juvenile title, pamphlets, and defective gifts.

Figure A4.3

BOOKS REJECTED BY MEMBER LIBRARIES
(By Institution)

School	Polaroid	Tracing not on Main Entry	Call Number Format	Wrong Card Sets	Wrong Title	Other[*]	Total
1	-	-	-	-	-	4	4
2	-	-	20	4	12	17	53
3	40	8	52	-	-	-	70
4	-	-	-	-	-	-	-
5	-	-	-	2	1	-	3
Total	40	8	72	6	13	21	160

[*]Other: Smeared cards, spine label damaged, title incomplete, wrong call number, cataloging incomplete, placement of back card and pocket wrong, wrong school code on card set, subject heading in black instead of red, and call number differing between book and cards.

Figure A4.4

ORIGINAL SPECIFICATION SHEET
COLORADO ACADEMIC LIBRARIES BOOK PROCESSING CENTER

Order Request Card -- Two part order request, similar to CU's, to facilitate searching. Second copy remains at requesting library. See sample attached.

Multiple-Order Record -- Participating libraries will be notified whenever a basic title is ordered centrally.

Orders Placement Procedure -- One copy of multiform will be sent to vendor. IBM encumbrance card punched for each title.

Library Accounting Procedure -- Each participating library will receive a monthly statement of its account. The statement will include: 1) encumbrances, 2) expenditure, and 3) free balance.

Receiving-Payment Procedure -- Checks from member libraries will be recorded on IBM cards and forwarded to the business office for payment. Expenditure data will be punched and collated against encumbrance cards. Invoices and accounting slips will be forwarded for payment.

Classification -- Library of Congress.

Cuttering -- Library of Congress.

Author and Subject Heading Authority -- Library of Congress for both author and subject.

Authority and Cross-Reference Cards -- Believe this can be better accomplished at the local library.

Catalog Card Reproduction and Processing -- Xerox reproduction using die cut stock; cards photo reproduced six-up; power cut to size. May use perforated stock four-up.

Subject headings will be in red. Pattern of capitalization follows tracings on Library of Congress card. Call number will be formulated the same on everything. Example: DS
35
W4
1966.

Sourcing Information -- Local operation.

Accessing Procedure -- No accessioning.   (Copy numbers will be used to distinguish multiple copies ordered by one library).

Book Pocket -- Pocket with IBM label (call number, title) pasted inside front board. Hinged if flyleaf contains a map.

Spine Label -- An IBM printed label applied with plastic glue: coating.

Date Due Slip -- Yes, located inside front flyleaf opposite pocket.

Circulation Card -- One circulation card. Call number and title.

Property Stamp -- None.

Plastic Jacketing -- None.

Biographical-Review Information -- None. Book jackets will be forwarded with book.

Paperback Books -- Cataloged and forwarded to University bindery when a paperback is received instead of hardback, or when requested by a Library. Prebounds will be ordered from a dealer when so requested. (University bindery does a binding equivalent to "permabound" in quality.)

Periodic Accessions List -- Special lists produced by computer as by-products will be one goal, but development of such a system will take some time.

Figure A4.5

DRAFT SPECIFICATIONS
COLORADO ACADEMIC LIBRARIES BOOK PROCESSING CENTER

ORDER FORMS--(See p. 1 & 4, Dec. Specs.)

Orders must be submitted on:
1. The official CALBPC Purchase Request Card (PR). CALBPC Member libraries will be provided with a sufficient supply of the PR's and self carbon slips to meet anticipated purchase levels. The carbon slip will be retained by the requestor library. All Purchase Request Cards should be typed.

2. A copy of the multiforms provided as a by-product of the Abel Approval Program. A clean, unmarked copy of this form should be submitted.

ORDER PLACEMENT PROCEDURE -- (See p. 1, Dec. Specs.)

One copy of the CALBPC order pack will be sent to the vendor. An IBM encumbrance card will be punched for each title.

LIBRARY ACCOUNTING PROCEDURE--(See p. 1, Dec. Specs.)

Each participating library will receive a periodic statement of account, including (1) encumbrances, (2) expenditures, and (3) free balance. Each library will also receive a title by title listing of each title in the system. The document will show which titles are on order, which have been paid for, and which have been cataloged.

RECEIVING-PAYMENT PROCEDURE--(See p.1, Dec. Specs.)

Checks from member libraries will be recorded on punched cards for CALBPC accounting routines, then forwarded to the business office for deposit to the proper account number. Encumbrances will be punched at the time an order is placed; expenditures will be punched when the item is received. Invoices will be forwarded to the CU Finance Office, where warrants will be issued to the proper vendor.

TITLES--(See minutes of Oct. 1, 1969 Denver meeting)

1. The title will reflect the first three or four words of the title as it appears on the purchase request and will be updated from LC cataloging.

2. Ellipses will be used to indicate partial titles. A colon, semi-colon, or a period will serve as a natural stopping point. Initial articles will be omitted to achieve a more meaningful title. Words will not be fragmented, will not be deleted within the body of the title, and will not be included if they are enclosed in parentheses.

3. The following selected general words will be abbreviated to achieve more meaningful titles:
Information   --   info
Introduction   --   intro
International   --   int'l

SETS--(See p. 3, Dec. Specs.)

Orders for monographs issued simultaneously in multiple physical volumes will be accepted by the center if all volumes are in print and available at the time the order is placed; in other words, the Center is not equipped to handle standing orders. Orders for specific volumes of a set should read vol. 1 only; vol. 1-4 inclusive. The basic processing fee will be charged for each physical volume after the first volume; the initial volume will be charged according to the process fee schedule.

OUT-OF-PRINT TITLES--(See Feb. Supplement)

CALBPC will not place orders for out-of-print titles. To avoid duplication of effort in the search procedure it is recommended to the local library that titles less than three years old not be verified as to in-print status. Conversely, titles older than three years must be verified as to in-print status. For example, in 1969 titles with imprints, 1966-- date, need not be verified as to in-print status, whereas titles 1965 or older must be verified as to in-print status.

ORDERS CALBPC WILL NOT PLACE--(See Feb. Supplement)

Out-of-print titles, titles which are members of series classed together, volumes of sets which may have already been cataloged locally, music scores, pamphlets, periodicals, non-book formatted material and juvenile fiction. However, should the Center receive a title which falls into one of the above categories, the volume will be returned to the member library. The basic processing fee will be charged for all such acquisitions.

PAMPHLETS--(See Feb. Supplement)

It is recommended that titles less than fifty pages

222

in length and costing less than one dollar not be ordered through CALBPC unless the requesting library has a special reason for doing so and clips an explanation to the purchase request cards for such titles.

PRICE NOT KNOWN--(See Feb. Supplement)

Member libraries may submit orders without prices at their own risk. The amount of $3.50 per volume will be encumbered.

PAPERBACK BOOKS--(See p.3, Dec. Specs; Feb. Supplement)

Each purchase request card for a paperbound title should bear the designation "pa" in front of the price within the price box. Indicate the binding cost separately or in the price box, i.e., pa*3.95+1.25. Permabind is the style of binding normally provided by US jobbers and the current unit price is $1.25 for the service. However, CALBPC will order only US imprints from a paperbound book jobber; foreign titles will be ordered through normal channels. Titles which arrive in an unbound state will be bound as the Norlin library normally binds them, i.e., cloth or buckram via a commercial bindery, or pamphlet casings if the book is less than 3/8" thick.

*(cost of book + 1.25)

CATALOGING--(See p.2,3, Dec. Specs.; Feb. Supplement)

1. The Processing Center will accept Library of Congress classification, descriptive cataloging and analysis without modification.

2. Mistakes on proof cards originating at LC: Obvious mistakes will be corrected in the Cataloging Department.

3. Serials, Monographic:
   (a) Classed Separately. These will be handled in the same way as monographs.

   The form of the series used by LC and the LC classification will be used. No change will be instituted for inconsistencies in the main entry selected for titles belonging to this type of serials.

   A series entry will be provided with a card set if the CU library uses this entry in the tracings. If the form of the LC series tracing differs from the established CU form, the CU form of entry will be followed. If a series tracing is indicated on the LC card copy and there is no series authority file card for it at the CU Library, the LC entry will be used.

   (b) Classed Together. Orders for serials classed together by the Library of Congress will not be accepted because of potential local duplication.

   (c) However, CALBPC will accept any title for ORIGINAL CATALOGING, upon request.

   Foreign Language cataloging available:
   Slavic Languages   Italian
   Greek and Hebrew   Spanish
     (transliterated)   German
   Latin   Portuguese   French
   Chinese   Japanese   Korean

4. Fiction: Fiction will be accepted and classified according to the new LC rules published in the LC Information Bulletin, v. 27, no. 42, October 17, 1968, p. 631:
   ... a literature class number will be provided hence-forth for all titles that the Library of Congress classifies in PZ3 and will be printed in the lower left-corner of the card below the PZ3 or PZ4 call number used at the Library of Congress.
   CU will assign the Cutter numbers. CALBPC will not use PZ classifications. Libraries which do not use LC for fiction should not send their orders to CALBPC; however, CALBPC will not return fiction orders to member libraries for confirmation.

5. Call numbers:

   (a) Class number format samples--The Cutter line of the call number will be expressed on one horizontal line for eight characters or less. A Cutter line of more than eight characters will be expressed in two horizontal lines, the split occuring at the alpha character of the title. This format will be followed on the cards, in the book, and on the spine.

		Rare Books Room	
HB	PR	Engine	
4867	6005	Q	PQ
1952	Q 4L6	76	2603
S42	1950	R4413	A7 1 5

PQ	PS	PG
2603	3537	3376
A7 1 513	A426	Q 37
	Z72488	I 713

   (b) Location Symbols--No location symbols will be appended to the call number for libraries other than those on the CU main campus.

   (c) Volume designations on book spines of foreign language titles: The vernacular will be used where appropriate. For instance, sets in the German language will be designated by Bd. for Band instead of v. for volume.

6. Shelf List: In the case of multiple volumes, holdings on shelf list cards will be summarized. For example:
   v. 2-16
   v. 7
   v. 9-12

7. Corporate entries: When there is a change in the form of the name of a corporate body, the latest form used by LC will be the one adopted.

CLASSIFICATION--(See p.1, Dec. Specs.)

Library of Congress.

CUTTERING--(See p.1, Dec. Specs.)

Library of Congress.

AUTHOR AND SUBJECT HEADING AUTHORITY--(See p.1, Dec. Specs.)

Library of Congress for both author and subject.

TITLE ADDED ENTRIES

CALBPC will follow LC practice for tracing titles.

CATALOG CARD REPRODUCTION AND PROCESSING --(See p.1, Dec. Specs.)

Xerox reproduction using die cut stock; cards photo reproduced six-up; power cut to size. Subject headings typed in red. Pattern of capitalization follows tracing on Library of Congress card. The standard card set consists of the following:
   shelf list
   main entry
   subject entries (as indicated by the LC tracings)
   added entries ("   " " " "   )*
   extra card
   Bibliographic Center notification card (to be sent direct from CALBPC)
   National Union Catalog notification card (to be sent direct from CALBPC)
Additional card sets will be provided on request for an additional fee.

*For series added entry specifications see paragraph three of 3(a) under Cataloging.

REPORTING HOLDINGS--The Center will report titles processed to the National Union Catalog and to the Rocky Mountain Bibliographic Center. Official NUC symbols for CALBPC participants are used for Internal identification as well as for NUC and Bib. Ctr. reporting.

BOOK POCKET--Pocket with call number and title pasted inside front board will be provided. Hinged if flyleaf contains a map.

SPINE LABEL--A printed label applied with plastic glue; coating.

DATE DUE SLIP--Yes, located inside front flyleaf opposite pocket.

CIRCULATION CARD--One machine readable circulation card which will include call number and title.

PROPERTY STAMP--None.

PLASTIC JACKETING--None.

BIOGRAPHICAL-REVIEW INFORMATION--None. Book jackets will be forwarded with book.

SOURCING INFORMATION--Local operation.

ACCESSIONING PROCEDURE--No accessioning. (Copy numbers will be used to distinguish multiple copies ordered by one library.)

SHIPPING

1. Methods:

   (a) Subscribers to the Courier Service will receive their in reusable tote boxes which must be returned to CALBPC on the next delivery.

   (b) Libraries not subscribing to the Courier Service will receive their books in cardboard boxes via US mail, library rate. The libraries will be charged for postage.

   (c) NOTE: Exception for libraries with their own pick-up service; Pick-up must be made within one week of a telephoned message from CALBPC that a shipment is ready. CALBPC will ship in reusable tote boxes IF they can be returned to CALBPC within one week of pick-up.

2. Content: One copy of a shipping document will be enclosed in a box. Catalog cards may be included but do not necessarily match books in the shipment. Occasionally books or messages will be sent in a manila envelope with regular book shipments and directed to the attention of a professional librarian.

3. Receipt procedure: The boxes should be opened the day they are received and the shipment verified against the shipping document. Any error in shipment should be reported to the CALBPC Coordinator immediately. Reusable tote boxes should be readied for return to CALBPC on the next delivery date.

Figure A4.6

ITEM # 641

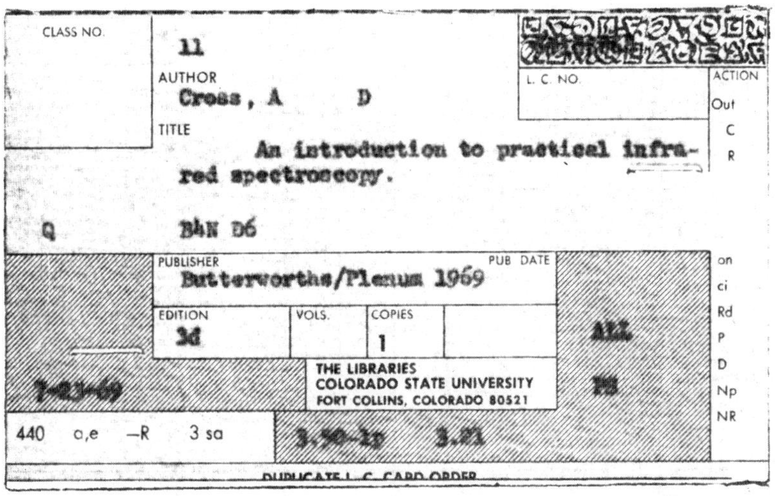

CLASS NO.
11
AUTHOR
Cross, A D
TITLE
An introduction to practical infra-red spectroscopy.
Q
B4N D6
L. C. NO.
ACTION
Out
C
R
PUBLISHER Butterworths/Plenum
PUB DATE 1969
EDITION 3d
VOLS.
COPIES 1
THE LIBRARIES
COLORADO STATE UNIVERSITY
FORT COLLINS, COLORADO 80521
7-23-69
ALL
PS
on
ci
Rd
P
D
Np
NR
440 o,e —R 3 sa
3.50-1p 3.21
DUPLICATE L. C. CARD ORDER

Library: CSU

*Type of Pub'n. 1 mono 2 serial
*Ordered 1 vendor 2 direct
3 Abel 4 gift
*Standing order 0 no 1 yes
*Handling 1 classed separate
2 classed together
Cycle time: (month-day-year)
date pub. ____________
date rec'd ____________
*date filed-SL ____________

*Call number ____________

L.C. Card # ____________
*Cataloging Modifications from L.C.
Main Entry ( ) yes ( ) no
Subject Headings:
Internal ( ) yes ( ) no
Deletions ( ) yes; # of____
( ) no
Additions ( ) yes; # of____
( ) no
Added Entries
Internal ( ) yes ( ) no
Deletions ( ) yes; # of____
( ) no
Additions ( ) yes; # of____
*Originally cataloged: ( ) yes
( ) no
*Still awaiting LC Copy:
( ) yes; as of ________(date)
( ) no

Library: CU

*Type of Pub'n. 1 mono 2 serial
*Ordered 1 vendor 2 direct
3 Abel 4 gift
*Standing order 0 no 1 yes
*Handling 1 classed separate
2 classed together
Cycle time: (month-day-year)
date pub. ____________
date rec'd ____________
*date filed-SL ____________

*Call number ____________

L.C. Card # ____________
*Cataloging Modifications from L.C.
Main Entry ( ) yes ( ) no
Subject Headings:
Internal ( ) yes ( ) no
Deletions ( ) yes; # of____
( ) no
Additions ( ) yes; # of____
( ) no
Added Entries
Internal ( ) yes ( ) no
Deletions ( ) yes; # of____
( ) no
Additions ( ) yes; # of____
( ) no
*Originally cataloged: ( ) yes
( ) no
*Still awaiting LC Copy:
( ) yes; as of ________(date)
( ) no

*Data collected in the field.

Figure A4.7

ABEL STUDY TABULATION SHEET: Part II

Cycle Time Correlation

Data Collector _____
Date _____

Item #	Date Received		If same, put X (if no more than 2 wks apart)	If not, record dates	Vendor Code	Date Filed in Shelf List		Total Lag Time for C.S.U.	Total Lag Time for C.U.	Difference (C.S.U. Total minus C.U. Total Use + and –)
	C.S.U.	C.U.				C.S.U.	C.U.			

APPENDIX FIGURES

A5.1 - A5.3

(Chapter V)

Figure A5.1

Recommended Procedure

Initial Order Procedure

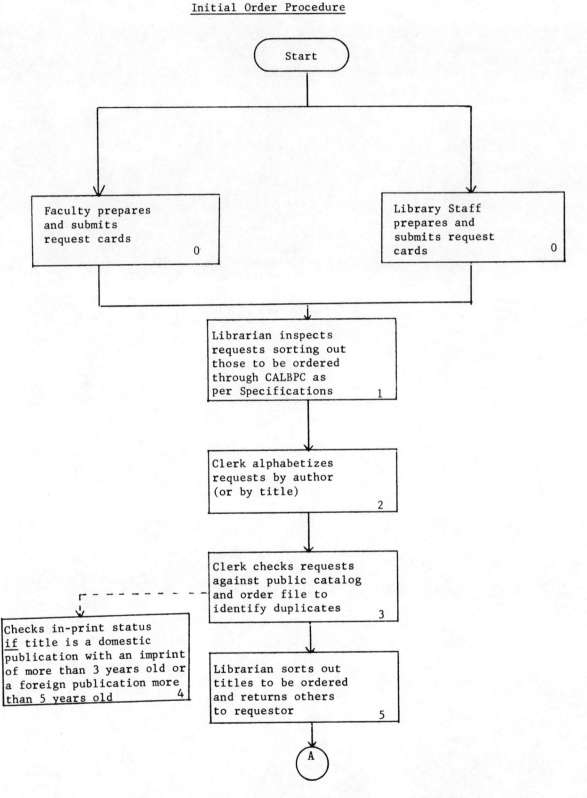

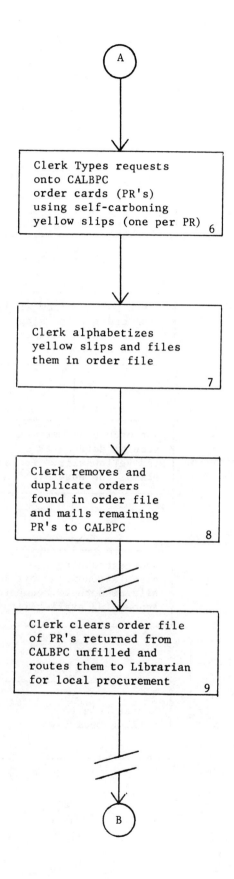

A

Clerk Types requests
onto CALBPC
order cards (PR's)
using self-carboning
yellow slips (one per PR)   6

Clerk alphabetizes
yellow slips and files
them in order file
                             7

Clerk removes and
duplicate orders
found in order file
and mails remaining
PR's to CALBPC   8

Clerk clears order file
of PR's returned from
CALBPC unfilled and
routes them to Librarian
for local procurement   9

B

Receiving and Integrating

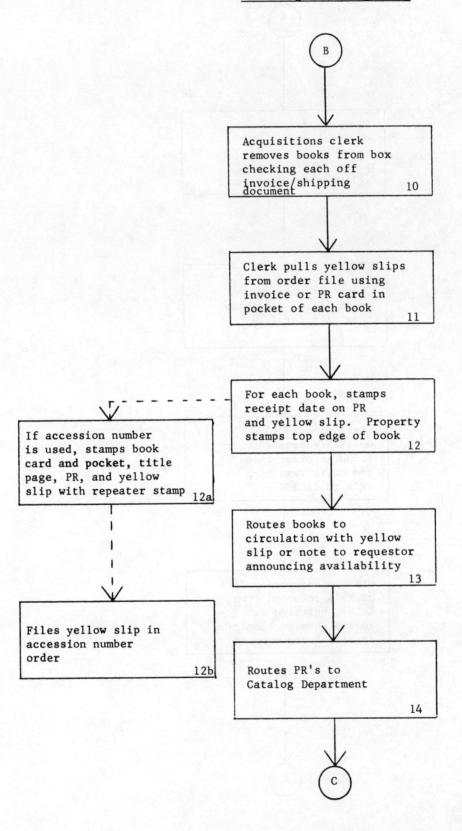

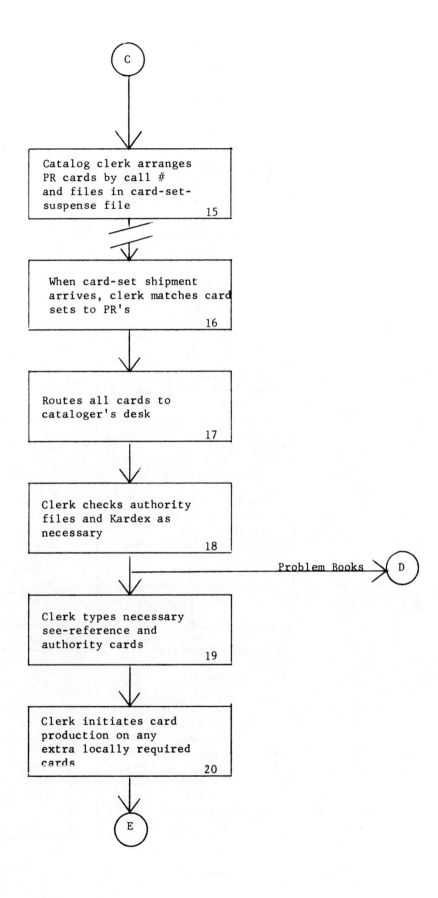

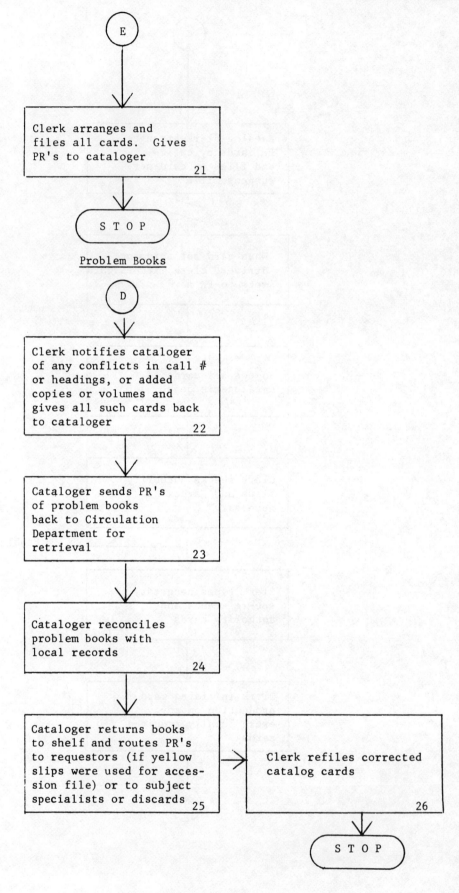

E

Clerk arranges and
files all cards. Gives
PR's to cataloger
                                21

S T O P

Problem Books

D

Clerk notifies cataloger
of any conflicts in call #
or headings, or added
copies or volumes and
gives all such cards back
to cataloger   22

Cataloger sends PR's
of problem books
back to Circulation
Department for
retrieval   23

Cataloger reconciles
problem books with
local records
                        24

Cataloger returns books
to shelf and routes PR's
to requestors (if yellow
slips were used for accession file) or to subject
specialists or discards 25

Clerk refiles corrected
catalog cards
                        26

S T O P

Figure A5.2

LIBRARY # 1

	A	B	C	TOTAL
Initial Order Procedure				
1. Faculty sends in local request cards.	0	1	0	1
2. Librarian revises requests and separates out those which are to be ordered through CALBPC.	0	1	1	2
3. Types request on the CALBPC PR card form.	0	1	1	2
4. Enters each PR in faculty ledger.	0	0	0	0
5. Mails PR cards to center.	0	1	1	2
6. Arranges original PR cards by title.	0	1	1	2
7. Files cards in outstanding order file.	0	1	1	2
Receiving and Integrating				
1. Unpacks books from cartons.	0	1	1	2
2. Arranges books alphabetically by title.	0	1	1	2
3. Checks books received against invoice.	0	1	1	2
4. Makes a Xerox copy of the invoice and sends it to the business office.	1	0	0	1
5. Corrects prices on CALBPC order cards from invoice information noting discounts.	1	0	1	2
6. Files invoice with bills in vendor file.	0	1	1	2
7. Checks CALBPC order card with book for absolute accuracy of title.	0	1	1	2
8. Checks call numbers on book spine, book card and pocket.	0	1	1	2
9. Checks all catalog cards to see that they agree exactly in every detail. Replaces cards in book pockets.	0	0	1	1
10. Indicates date received, discount, corrected price, etc., in faculty ledger.	0	0	0	0
11. Pulls yellow carbons for books received from "CALBPC OUT ORDER" file and discard.	0	1	1	2
12. Sends books on to processing.	0	1	1	2

LIBRARY # 1

	A	B	C	TOTAL
Processing				
1. Removes catalog cards from book pocket.	0	1	1	2
2. Puts shelf-list card aside for accessioning.	0	0	1	1
3. Enters titles in accession book showing net price, sources, etc.	0	0	0	0
4. Writes accession number of (1) shelf list card, (2) book pocket, (3) book card, and on the bottom of page 50 in the book.	0	0	0	0
5. Checks authority files and Kardex as necessary.	0	1	1	2
6. Alphabetizes catalog cards.	0	1	1	2
7. Files card catalog trays taking special care to replace each temporary catalog card with a permanent catalog card.	0	1	1	2
8. Arrange shelf list cards.	0	1	1	2
9. Files shelf list cards.	0	1	1	2
10. Adds call number to temporary catalog card to inform faculty member who requested the book that it has arrived, is cataloged, processed and is ready to circulate. (See # 7).	0	1	1	2
11. Stamps all three edges of the book with property stamp.	1	1	1	3
12. Clips blurb from dust jacket and pastes in book.	0	0	1	1
13. Sends books to be shelved.	0	1	1	2
14. Sends notices (See #6) to faculty.	1	1	1	3
Problem Books				
1. Cataloger corrects conflicts in subject headings or call numbers assigned on cards.	0	1	1	2
2. Corrects spine labels and cards and pockets.	0	1	1	2
Total Score	4	25	28	57
Total Steps	35	35	35	35

LIBRARY # 2

	A	B	C	TOTAL
Initial Order Procedure				
NOTE: Faculty use local order cards to submit requests. Most of them come in typed.				
1. Librarian inspects requests and assigns funds.	0	1	1	2
2. Routes order cards to Acquisitions Department.	0	1	1	2
3. Acquisitions Librarian inspects those orders with flyers attached for accuracy in typing.	0	1	1	2
4. Sets aside items over $15.00 to be handled later.	0	0	1	1
5. Sorts out remaining orders as to potential rushes, possible spending per publication and other criteria to determine what should be ordered through CALBPC.	0	1	1	2
Student checks:				
6. Public catalog by title.	0	1	1	2
7. House file by author.	0	0	0	0
8. CALBPC order file by title.	0	1	1	2
9. Supervisor inspects batch and weeds out dups.	0	1	1	2
10. Routes dups to the requestor.	0	1	1	2
11. When PR's accumulate at least 25 cards, student types these on CALBPC PR card stock.	0	1	1	2
12. Supervisor revises typing.	0	1	1	2
13. Separates yellow carbon from PR for each.	0	1	1	2
14. Files yellow slip by title.	0	1	1	2
15. Types envelope addressed to CALBPC.	0	1	1	2
16. Routes orders to Administration Office unsealed.	0	0	0	0
17. Files original request card by requestor and within requestor by author.	0	0	0	0
18. Secretary in administrative office Xeroxes PR cards, types cover sheet indicating source of order and total of order and date and records date of order and P.O. number on sheet.	0	0	0	0
19. Files in Purchase Order File (Notebook).	0	0	0	0

LIBRARY # 2

	A	B	C	TOTAL
Receiving and Integrating				
1. Library assistant removes books from shipping box, shelving the purchased books separately from the gift books.	0	1	1	2
2. Tags shipment with receipt date and checks invoice with books.	0	1	1	2
3. Checks invoice.	0	0	1	1
4. Adds Julian date to left column for secretary in Administrative office.	0	0	0	0
5. Revises card sets.	0	1	1	2
6. Dates book.	0	0	0	0
7. Adds date and cost to white slip. Refiles in book.	0	1	0	1

8. Pulls yellow slip
    adds date and price, and
    adds call number
	0	0	0	0

9. Refiles yellow slip in title file.	0	0	0	0
10. Puts requestor on order card if necessary.	0	1	0	1
11. Pulls request card and put with book.	0	0	1	1
12. Puts orange flag in professors' requests.	0	1	1	2
13. Receipts invoice and sends to main office.	0	1	1	2
14. Secretary posts amount paid, date received to card image in purchase order notebook.	0	0	0	0
15. Posts total amount and date received to cover sheet.	0	0	0	0
16. Files invoice in notebook by date of invoice.	0	1	1	2
17. Checks card set for: title card, incorrect pagination, holdings card, and makes holdings cards when needed.	0	1	1	2
18. Checks official catalog and official shelf list.	0	1	0	1
19. Makes extra Chemical Abstracts card when needed (classifications TP and QD).	0	0	0	0

LIBRARY # 2

		A	B	C	TOTAL
20.	Adds cost and source to shelf list card.	0	0	0	0
21.	Adds binding fee (if any).	0	0	0	0
22.	Checks subject authority and makes any cards needed.	0	1	1	2
23.	Checks series authority and makes any cards needed.	0	1	1	2
24.	Applies stamp in six places in book.	0	1	1	2
25.	Sends professors' request cards and envelopes.	0	1	1	2
26.	Writes in author on title page with pencil (to identify book).	0	0	0	0
27.	Label spine with any special location symbols.	0	1	1	2
28.	Files CALBPC card in "house file" drawer.	0	0	0	0
29.	Adds call number of "house card" when CALBPC does not.	0	1	0	1
30.	Correct title headings when CALBPC is in error.	0	1	1	2
31.	Correct subject and added entries when CALBPC is in error.	0	1	1	2
32.	Arranges and files shelf lists.	0	1	1	2
33.	Arranges and files catalog cards.	0	1	1	2
34.	Arranges and files official cards.	0	1	1	2
35.	Delivers books to Circulation Department.	0	1	1	2

Problem Books

		A	B	C	TOTAL
1.	Completes title for book card when CALBPC computer does not.	0	0	0	0
2.	Completes added entry cards when CALBPC does not.	0	0	0	0
3.	Enters request date on "house card."	0	0	0	0
4.	Completes author's full name on "house card," proof card and on title page.	0	0	0	0
5.	Corrects call number when incomplete on card set.	0	1	1	2
6.	Corrects call number for local Library when CALBPC number is not consistent with shelf list.	0	1	1	2

LIBRARY # 2

	A	B	C	TOTAL
7. Makes special statistics card for catalog Librarian in case of "dup.", etc.	0	0	0	0
8. Prepares card for Xeroxing (from proof sheet, or original cataloging) for card set when CALBPC does not meet local quality requirements for catalog cards.	0	1	0	1
9. Makes a record slip for reference Librarian on all computer books.	0	0	0	0
10. Makes new book card (blue) and stamps it as such when book is classified for "Closed Reserve."	0	0	0	0
11. Also makes a card for any translation from foreign language. (see reference)	0	0	0	0
Total Score	0	38	35	73
Total Steps	65	65	65	65

LIBRARY # 3

	A	B	C	TOTAL
Initial Order Procedure				
1. Receives faculty order requests (some on slips, some adv., some lists, etc.).	1	1	1	3
2. Sorts out requests to order through CALBPC.	0	1	1	2
3. Alphabetizes them by author.	0	0	0	0
4. Checks BIP and removes O.P. titles.	0	1	1	2
5. Checks card catalog by author and title in both Dewey and catalog for author, title and edition.	0	1	0	1
6. Sorts by title.	0	1	1	2
7. Checks order file.	0	1	1	2
8. Routes duplicates to requestor.	0	1	1	2
9. If not in BIP (possibly too new) checks BPR published weekly, CBI, and maybe NUC proof slips.	0	1	1	2
10. Assigns fund numbers.	0	1	1	2
11. Types on CALBPC PR form using two self-carboning slips.	0	1	1	2
12. Staples through two yellow slips to back of original request slip.	0	0	1	1
13. Arranges packs by title	0	1	1	2
14. Files in order file.	0	1	1	2
15. Arranges CALBPC orders by title.	0	0	0	0
16. Runs tape on list price of CALBPC PR's.	0	1	1	2
17. Enters total for sheet to obtain running total.	0	1	1	2
18. Inserts PR's in jiffy bag.	0	1	1	2
19. Addresses bag to CALBPC.	0	1	1	2
20. Delivers bag to courier, pick up box.	0	1	1	2
Receiving and Integrating				
1. Courier delivers boxes.	0	1	1	2
2. Order clerk checks invoice against shipment.	0	1	1	2
3. If any discrepancy, phones or sends note to CALBPC.	0	1	1	2

LIBRARY # 3

	A	B	C	TOTAL
4. Pulls order request slip from Order File, and inserts one NRC slip in its place.	0	1	0	1
5. Moves book(s) to Check-in clerk's desk.	0	1	1	2
6. Matches book(s) with order request slip.	0	1	1	2
7. Dates order request slips "received" line.	0	0	0	0
8. Inscribes second yellow NCR slip with "Author-Title-Edition" information. (Transcribed from Order Request Slip), unless Author entry changed on PR card.	0	0	0	0
9. Rechecks card catalog before inscribing "A-T-E" information if author entry changed on PR card.	0	0	0	0
10. Inserts NCR slip in book, along with a "P" slip giving name of requesting faculty member. (Circulation Department keeps this slip in book until faculty member comes to inspect book, or until he has been given sufficient time to do so).	1	0	0	1
11. Inserts colored slip in books which have special destinations: blue for Music Library, etc.	0	1	1	2
12. Places book on truck.	0	1	1	2
13. Places order request slip in temporary "psychedelic" file until Cataloger brings back PR card to signify that cards have been filed in Card Catalog.	0	0	0	0
14. Removes both order request slips and yellow NCR slips from their respective files.	0	0	0	0
15. Files order request slips being in "Finished File."	0	0	0	0
16. Files NCR slip in subject-arranged file for keeping tally. (Beginning with new orders for '69-'70 fiscal year, this NCR slip will be discarded at this point, instead of keeping tally.)	0	0	0	0

LIBRARY # 3

	A	B	C	TOTAL
17. Notifies Reference Department when truck is full, so that a member of the Ref. staff can inspect, and indicate by a colored slip any title that in her opinion should go to the Ref. Dept., regardless of requesting faculty member.	0	0	1	1
18. Pushes truck to Catalog Dept.	0	0	1	1
19. Counts books by gift and purchase.	0	0	1	1
20. Cataloger separates books from cards.	0	1	1	2
21. Types additional shelf list such as for Reference Department.	0	1	1	2
22. Stamps shelf list and PR card with date received.	0	1	1	2
23. Clips PR card to main entry card (PR is later routed to Acquisitions).	0	0	0	0
24. Cataloger checks series authority file.	0	1	1	2
25. Notes series authority needs on special form for this purpose.	0	1	1	2
26. Delivers slips to typist.	0	1	1	2
27. Typist prepares series authority cards and holding cards (as needed).	0	1	1	2
28. Gives them back to cataloger.	0	1	1	2
29. Cataloger revises them.	0	1	1	2
30. Stamps cards for content, see main entry.	0	1	1	2
31. Cataloger sorts out extension card of main entry and has these Xeroxed.	0	0	0	0
32. Makes separate card set for Music Library using main entry card as master.	0	1	0	1
33. Types new pockets for Music Library books.	0	0	0	0
34. Types any card in set which is not acceptable or uses proof slip to Xerox one.	0	0	1	1
35. Makes two book cards and pockets for Music Library for Educational Media Program, and for Educational Resource Center (uses call number and title).	1	0	1	2

LIBRARY # 3

	A	B	C	TOTAL
36. Sleeves all reference cards.	0	0	0	0
37. Stamps Music Cards with "In Music Library."	0	1	1	2
38. Places card sets for Music Library in new pocket of each book.	0	1	1	2
39. Cataloger gives all subject cards to clerk.	0	1	1	2
40. Clerk types salmon card for each subject.	0	1	1	2
41. Typist eliminates salmon cards for geographic project items.	0	0	0	0
42. Cataloger revises remaining cards.	0	1	1	2
43. Clerk sorts salmon cards into alphabetical order.	0	1	1	2
44. Clerk checks cards against LC Subject Heading List and notes X and see references on cards.	0	1	1	2
45. Cataloger checks these cards.	0	1	1	2
46. Typist prepares cross-references.	0	1	1	2
47. Delivers books to Circulation, Reference, Reserve, Faculty Member, or Stacks.	0	1	1	2
48. Sorts catalog cards into alphabetical order.	0	1	1	2
49. Files cards in public catalog.	0	1	1	2
50. Pulls old edition relating to any new edition and reclassifies the old edition into LC.	0	0	0	0
51. Sorts shelf list by call number.	0	1	1	2
52. Files shelf list.	0	1	1	2
53. Catalogers revise filing.	0	1	1	2
54. Sends the PR card to the Order Department.	0	0	0	0
55. Uses PR card to purge order file of yellow slip.	0	0	0	0
56. Discards yellow slip.	0	1	1	2
Total Score	3	52	55	110
Total Steps	76	76	76	76

LIBRARY # 4

	A	B	C	TOTAL

Initial Order Procedures

		A	B	C	TOTAL
1.	Search clerk checks for in-print status.	0	1	1	2
2.	CALBPC Project assistant assigns vendor.	0	1	1	2
3.	Clerk types order onto CALBPC PR using self carboning yellow slip.	0	1	1	2
4.	Sorts yellow slips by title.	0	1	1	2
5.	Files slips in order file.	0	1	1	2
6.	Returns duplicate orders to requestors.	0	1	1	2
7.	Sends out CALBPC PR's by mail to Center.	0	1	1	2

Receiving and Integrating

		A	B	C	TOTAL
1.	Shipping room clerk compares books with invoice.	0	1	1	2
2.	Checks in book order file and clears CALBPC dealer file.	0	1	1	2
3.	Delivers books of Head of Catalog Department.	0	1	1	2
4.	Files invoice in folder in Office of Acquisitions Librarian.	0	1	1	2
	NOTE: The books are received in batches from the Acquisitions Department, with catalog cards and other records inserted in the book pockets.				
5.	Principal cataloging assistant removes the packet of cards and other records from the book pocket.	0	1	1	2
6.	Verifies that the call-numbers shown on inscription, book pocket, book card and spine label agree with the call-number on the catalog cards, and that the title on book pocket and book card are accurate.	0	1	1	2
7.	Pulls out the book card.	0	0	0	0
8.	Verifies that the cards match the book by quickly comparing the descriptive cataloging with the title-page.	0	0	1	1

LIBRARY # 4

	A	B	C	TOTAL
9. Sets aside the book.	0	1	1	2
10. Writes the call-number on the process slip and order card, using carbon for the latter.	0	1	1	2
11. Sets aside the process slip for return to Acquisitions.	0	1	0	1
12. Sets aside the order card for the notification routine.	0	1	1	2
13. Tallies the title on the "Catalog Department Statistics--CALBPC Books" form, and tallies any discrepancies that have appeared up to this point. NOTE: The principal library assistant revises the cataloging, making appropriate tallies on the statistics form, and taking action to accomplish changes.	0	1	1	2
14. Determines if more secondary cards are required according to local rules, such as security card, or title card, science-technology card.	0	1	0	1
15. Determines if any entries (other than subjects) require cross-references.	0	1	1	2
16. Checks series notes to see if they require added entries and have been established in local authority file.	0	1	1	2
17. Stamps the shelf list cards with the current date in lower left.	0	1	1	2
18. Arranges cards in shelf list order.	0	1	1	2
19. Counts the shelf list cards and records on the statistics sheet.	0	0	0	0
20. Files the shelf list cards, watching for discrepancies, particularly in the use of Cutter numbers.	0	1	1	2

LIBRARY # 4

	A	B	C	TOTAL
21. Counts the cards for public catalog and records in the respective slots on the statistics sheet.	0	1	1	2
22. Distributes the cards for filing (behind the guide cards indicating that cards have already been counted).	0	1	1	2
23. Forwards the process slips to the Acquisitions librarian for use in clearing the process file.	0	0	0	0
24. Forwards the order cards to the Catalog Department assistant for use in the requestor notification routine.	0	1	1	2
25. Forwards the book cards to the Research and Development Librarian.	0	1	1	2
26. Forwards books to the Assistant for stamping with marks of ownership and other physical processing.	0	1	1	2
27. Stamps ownership on top edge of book.	0	1	1	2
28. Removes original PR cards from Catalog Department.	0	0	0	0
29. Purges order file of yellow slips and discards them.	0	0	0	0
30. Files original PR in order complete file by title.	0	0	0	0
31. Sends completed books to Circulation Department.	0	1	1	2
32. Routes order cards to requestor.	0	1	1	2

Problem Books

	A	B	C	TOTAL
1. If it is necessary to change a call-number, makes sure that all records and book lettering are corrected.	0	1	1	2
2. If shelf listing reveals that the CALBPC book is a duplicate, retrieves all cards and records, deletes tallies previously made for the title on the statistics sheet, tallies now as a duplicate, and returns book and records to the Acquisitions librarian.	0	1	1	2

LIBRARY # 4

	A	B	C	TOTAL
3. Places requests for extra cards and correction in the correction box.	0	1	1	2

NOTE: Any <u>cards</u> involved are counted later when the corrected cards are revised and distributed; the <u>discrepancy</u> involved is counted when first noticed.

	A	B	C	TOTAL
Total Score	0	35	34	69
Total Steps	42	42	42	42

LIBRARY # 5

	A	B	C	TOTAL
Initial Order Procedure				
NOTE: Request slips come from faculty or from typed list.				
1. Librarian inspects slips and assigns vendors.	0	1	1	2
2. Searches for in-print status and main entry, and public catalog.	0	1	1	2
3. Typist types PR cards from work slips.	0	1	1	2
4. Librarian inspects for multiple copy needs and to exclude reference or rush review title.	0	1	1	2
5. Alphabetizes by main entry.	0	1	0	1
6. Files yellow slip weeding out any duplicates found in on-order file.	0	1	1	2
7. Purges PR card stack of duplicate orders.	0	1	1	2
8. Mails remaining orders to CALBPC.	0	1	1	2
Receiving and Integrating				
1. Truck driver delivers boxes to office of Head of Technical Services.	0	1	1	2
2. Clerk removes books and places them on truck placing them in packing list order.	0	1	1	**2**
3. Removes flags and puts all flags back in shipping box.	0	1	1	2
4. Cataloger inspects each book.	0	1	1	2
5. Inspects its card packet.	0	1	1	2
6. Indicates correction to be made either on catalog card or on p-slip.	0	1	1	2
7. Sets packet aside and book back on truck.	0	1	1	2
8. Stores book truck in office to await corrected card packets.	0	0	0	0
9. Clerk delivers packets to Cataloging.	0	1	1	2
10. Typist makes correction as indicated.	0	1	1	2

LIBRARY # 5

		A	B	C	TOTAL
11.	Clerk obtains packets and matches them back to books.	0	0	0	0
12.	Clerk delivers truck to Processing Room.	0	0	0	0
13.	Stores books in area designated CALBPC.	0	1	0	1
14.	Processing clerk pulls PR cards from pockets in packing list order.	0	1	1	2
15.	Delivers PR cards to Order Department.	0	1	1	2
16.	Order clerk purges order file of yellow order slip (still in packing slip order).	0	1	1	2
17.	Clerk returns to Processing Department and matches order slip and PR combinations to books.	0	0	0	0
18.	Removes each book, opens to expose packet, removes cards, obtains shelf list, stamps accession number on packet verso of title page, on shelf list, on PR card.	1	0	0	1
19.	Files PR card in accession record drawer.	0	0	0	0
20.	Delivers invoice record to administration clerk.	0	1	1	2
21.	Files in a notebook.	0	1	1	2
22.	Separates shelf list from rest of card set.	0	1	1	2
23.	Stamps receipt date on yellow slip and sets aside in one stack.	0	1	1	2
24.	Replaces book on truck.	0	0	1	1
25.	Takes yellow slips to in-process file.	0	0	0	0
26.	Alphabetizes them by main entry.	0	0	0	0
27.	Files them in Process File.	0	0	0	0
28.	Delivers shelf list cards to cataloging and cards from main catalog to filing clerk adjacent to Circulation Desk	0	1	1	2
29.	Delivers truck to hallway where page can pick it up.	0	1	1	2
30.	Filing clerk arranges and files shelf list.	0	1	1	2
31.	Arranges and files catalog cards.	0	1	1	2

LIBRARY # 5

	A	B	C	TOTAL
32. Processing clerk purges processing file one per month of any slips at least a month old.	0	1	0	1
33. Librarian notifies requestors.	0	1	1	2
Total Score	1	31	29	61
Total Steps	41	41	41	41

Figure A5.3

LAG TIME STUDY
TIME PERIODS COVERED BY SAMPLE I AND SAMPLE II
Complete Size of Samples
Sample I 1999 items
Sample II 1812 items

Month	Number of Items Received at the Center				Number of Items Cataloged			
	Sample I 1303 Items	%	Sample II 1121 Items	%	Sample I 1408 Items	%	Sample II 936 Items	%
1968 Before Sept.	14	1.08						
September	13	1.00						
October	8	0.61	2	.18				
November	141	10.82	17	1.52	3	.21		
December	169	12.97	69	6.15				
1969								
January	183	14.04	115	10.26	41	2.91	1	0.11
February	250	19.19	229	20.43	101	7.17	5	0.53
March	210	16.12	208	18.55	197	13.99	3	0.32
April	154	11.82	154	13.74	269	19.11	6	0.64
May	74	5.68	116	10.35	249	17.69	33	3.53
June	24	1.84	112	9.99	336	23.86	30	3.20
July	29	2.23	58	5.17	178	12.64	219	23.40
August	2	.15	16	1.43	28	1.99	351	37.50
September	0	0	7	.62	5	.36	229	24.47
October	1	.07	1	.09	0	0	57	6.09
November	16	1.23	2	.18	0	0	2	.21
December	15	1.15	15	1.34	1	.07	0	0
Total Sample	1303*	100.00	1121	100.00	1408*	100.00	936	100.00

* Not all items had these two dates recorded

INDEX

* - Figures
A - Appendix

Due